COME HOLY SPIRIT

Learning to Minister in Power

COME HOLY SPIRIT
Learning to Minister in Power

David Pytches

HODDER AND STOUGHTON
LONDON SYDNEY AUCKLAND TORONTO

To my wife
MARY
whose questing spirit
for the things of God
has continually challenged
and inspired me since we
first met thirty years ago

British Library Cataloguing in Publication Data

Pytches, David
   Come Holy Spirit: learning to minister in power.
   ——(Hodder Christian paperbacks)
   1. Gifts, Spiritual
   I. Title
   234'.12   BT767.3

   ISBN 0 340 38513 6

Hodder and Stoughton Editorial Office: 47 Bedford Square, London, WC1B 3DP.

CONTENTS

FOREWORD

I am delighted to commend this useful manual produced by my dear friend and co-labourer David Pytches who is the Vicar of St Andrew's Church, Chorleywood in England.

As I mentioned in my first book 'Power Evangelism', I visited St Andrew's originally on Pentecost Sunday 1981 and on my subsequent visits have been encouraged to see how the church has continued to develop its own ministry in the power of the Holy Spirit. Today they are sharing this on a wide front with Christian Churches of all denominations, be they Anglicans, Roman Catholics, Pentecostalists or 'House' churches. Bishop David Pytches has also been involved in the organisation of my teaching conferences in the United Kingdom since and has led several of our seminar workshops.

I hope this book will be greatly used as a practical handbook to help many other English-speaking churches around the world wanting to learn how to do what we believe the Holy Spirit is telling the churches to do today.

John Wimber

ACKNOWLEDGMENTS

Any reader who knows of the pioneer work of John Wimber in Los Angeles will recognise within these pages how great is our debt to him and to those who have worked with him in producing material on this subject. I am grateful to John too for his encouragement to me to write this book.

I am most grateful to Mr Geoffrey Hodgkins B.A., Mr Richard Bedwell M.A. and the Rev. Iain Roberts F.R.C.S. for reading this manuscript. They do not necessarily agree with all that I have said, but their positive criticism and suggestions have been most helpful.

Thanks are also due to a number of people for permission to quote from their works. They are listed fully on page 287.

Finally, I must thank Mrs. Shirley Bloomfield for so much assistance in typing and retyping this manuscript, which she has done so willingly and well.

INTRODUCTION

Many churches today have experienced a degree of spiritual renewal. Unlike the situation twenty-five years ago, there is no dearth of suitable literature to demonstrate that anointings from the Holy Spirit and manifestations of spiritual gifts are biblically authentic. All this is widely acceptable now.

The urgent need today is to help churches that want to move forward in their renewal by demonstrating how the gifts can be integrated into the ministry of the Church.

In the New Testament the proclamation of the Gospel of Jesus Christ was confirmed by signs and wonders. We are learning, through the use of the gifts of the Spirit, that the gospel is still confirmed in this way today as the Body of Christ discovers how to minister in power. And we believe that such confirmation is more relevant than ever in the 1980s.

Though one man's miracle is another man's coincidence, I believe I have witnessed many miraculous healings – especially through the ministry of Gigi Avila, a Puerto Rican evangelist visiting Chile in 1974. But I had always imagined that 'healers' were exceptional people. Since then I have become convinced that signs and wonders are a proper element in the ministry of all the people of God. Experience has shown us that this can become an integral part of regular worship and of the ministry of Christian people out in the world, complementing the proclamation of the kingdom of God.

Though it is our conviction that all are in fact spiritually blessed who receive ministry of this kind, we have not seen nearly as many obvious physical healings as we would expect, but the more healing we engage in, the more we see. To God be the glory!

We do not pretend that we have arrived. We try to share simply, and I hope humbly, out of what we are learning slowly and often painfully. This book is no missive from Cloud Nine! During the preparation of material for it, I have been hospitalised for the second time in two years. I thank God for the help I have had from our National Health Service personnel. But all this has in no way undermined my conviction that the commission to be involved in divine healing is still God's will for the whole Christian Church.

From the beginning this ministry has proved a very positive blessing to our local church, though it has not been without its problems. Part of the answer has been monthly talk-backs and teach-ins as we have been learning how to minister in power. With ample help from material produced by our American friend John Wimbler we cobbled together some studies which have been used as the basis of our training. In this sort of thing there is bound to be a degree of repetition, but we make no apology for that. We have not relied on the original material only; we have discussed it, shared individual insights and in the light of Bible study, prayer, wider reading and increasing experience, we have revised it.

If this seems to be a kind of manual, it is a manual with a difference. It is not a rule book – more a set of guidelines offered to any who want basic material to adopt or adapt for teaching the local church to minister in power. Such a ministry is, of course, an affair of the Spirit, who will never be 'cabin'd, cribbed or confin'd' to natty formulas or fancy methods. Others have been led to develop along lines of ministry in the Spirit which may differ radically. Our method is simply that there is no method. We share ways we have been led to minister, and what we have seen the Spirit do, to encourage others to begin.

For those who have been involved in renewal, yet have never witnessed any ministry in signs and wonders, these teach-ins will probably leave the reader initially mystified, but for those who have witnessed such signs and who are convinced that such a ministry is biblically wholesome, it is hoped that these pages will provide some enlightenment.

The Church has a tradition of accumulated wisdom in many areas to provide wholesome pointers for its leaders, but in this vital area there is little to help and much to hinder, with a tradition of accumulated prejudices surrounding us. This book is a small contribution which may go a little way towards filling the gap.

1
SIGNS AND WONDERS

As a one-time missionary I often preached on the 'Great Commission' found in Matthew 28: 18-20. I thought I had squeezed every drop of teaching one could out of those tremendous verses. It is only during the last four years or so that I have begun to realise that in fact I had totally overlooked one of the major dimensions of that text. Jesus had told his disciples to make other disciples, baptise them and teach them 'to *obey everything I have commanded you*'. I see now that this *'everything'* included a ministry of 'signs and wonders'. Every time the kingdom was preached by the disciples they would minister in 'signs and wonders'. This was what Jesus had taught them to do.

A careful look at the gospels reveals that one fifth of the material is dedicated to reporting Christ's healing ministry and his teaching about it. He had shown the first disciples how to heal – then he chose the twelve and called them together, 'gave them power and authority to drive out all demons and to cure diseases, and he sent them out to preach the kingdom of God and to heal the sick' (Luke 9: 1,2). So they went, 'preaching the gospel and healing people everywhere' just as Jesus had done (verse 6). Then they reported back and told Jesus how their mission had gone (verse 10) before he once again, accompanied by his disciples, became involved in preaching about the kingdom of God, and healing the sick.

Then Jesus commissioned another seventy-two to go and do the same. They reported back with joy and amazement that 'even the demons submit to us in your name' (Luke 10: 17). So when Jesus told the disciples to make other disciples and teach them *'to obey everything I have commanded you'*, we cannot doubt that casting out demons and healing the sick was integral to that commission. Mark endorses with even more detail what will happen to those who go out preaching the Good News: 'these signs will accompany those who believe: In my name they will drive out demons... they will place their hands on sick people, and they will get well' (Mark 16: 17, 18). After the ascension the disciples 'went out and preached everywhere, and the Lord worked with them and confirmed his word by the signs that accompanied it' (Mark 16: 20).

The book of Acts is full of the 'signs and wonders' which accompanied the disciples' preaching. The Church continued to grow amazingly following such manifestations of God's power. Paul reminds the Corinthians 'My message and my preaching were not with wise and persuasive words, but with *a demonstration of the Spirit's power*' (1 Corinthians 2: 4). The writer to the Hebrews wrote that God testified to the salvation 'first announced by the Lord', *'by signs, wonders* and *various miracles*, and gifts of the Holy Spirit distributed according to his will' (Hebrews 2: 4).

Quite simply, the ministry in the early Church was full of 'signs and wonders'. The question is 'How did we ever lose sight of it?' We can suggest *four* possibilities:

1 *Our world view* blinds our understanding of the spirit world. Everyone has a world view, which is a set of assumptions about the world around us that affects, even controls, our thinking about any given situation or on any given subject. We are not taught it; we begin to imbibe it with our mother's milk. We pick it up from the society we live in. The Western world view is both materialist and rationalist. Our materialism blurs our perception of the spiritual. Our rationalism (which has helped the West to advance rapidly in the world of science) is incapable of understanding the spirit, which can never be reduced to rules of logic, or theories requiring proof.

What we should endeavour to do is to discover the world view of Jesus (this is not to be confused with the first-century world view, which also had its distortions). Christ has plainly revealed to us how he saw the world in the context of the kingdoms of light and darkness. We should be viewing our culture in that context. But, unwittingly, what most of us actually do is to don the spectacles of the Western world view when we read the Bible and thus we find 'good' cause for discounting the supernatural and the miraculous.

2 Another reason is that the very idea of *ministering in signs and wonders sounds presumptuous.*

Signs and wonders and miracles were clearly the marks of an apostle (2 Corinthians 12: 12) and the works of an apostle (Acts 5: 12). But signs and wonders were never understood as the sole prerogative of an apostle, as is plain from Mark 16: 17 (any believer), Acts 6: 8 (Stephen) and Acts 8: 6 (Philip). Though signs and wonders were never to be considered as the exclusive work of an apostle, no man would be regarded by the Church as a true apostle who did not work signs and wonders.

Many recall how Jesus discouraged demands for signs and wonders when he refused to perform any miracle, saying 'A wicked and adulterous generation asks for a miraculous sign' (Matthew 12: 39). We are reminded that Paul also seemed to write disparagingly of Jews demanding signs, (1 Corinthians 1: 22). Others also cite how Jesus rejected the temptation from Satan to throw himself from the pinnacle of the Temple, expecting God to protect him (Matthew 4: 5-7). All this is true.

Yet Jesus said that even the adulterous generation which asked for a sign would be given *one* – the sign of the prophet Jonah (Matthew 12: 39,40). And Jesus in fact continued to minister in 'signs and wonders'. He also commissioned his disciples to minister, and said that anyone who had faith would do what he had been doing – and even greater things (John 14: 12). And his disciples went out to do them (e.g. Acts 6: 8; 8: 6 and Galatians 3: 5).

Jesus once addressed a desperate man, saying 'Unless you people see miraculous signs and wonders you will never believe.' His purpose was not to denigrate signs and wonders, but to test the man's faith. The father of the sick child answered by begging him to intervene before his child died. And Jesus responded with a miraculous healing sign: 'You may go. Your son will live' (John 4: 46–53). On another occasion Jesus stopped working miraculous signs because there was a danger the crowd would make him a king by force and the whole purpose of his mission would be threatened (John 6: 14,15).

The plain fact is that the Church is never to supply signs and wonders on demand, but neither must it deny signs and wonders, which are part of the Church's commission.

3 Yet another reason has been our own *sense of powerlessness*. No one likes to undertake something for which he does not feel he has the resources. Better to forget it! Where did Jesus (divested of his omnipotence) get his power? At no time did Jesus ever cease to be God (Colossians 2: 9) but the 'power' ministry of Jesus followed his baptism. Jesus (being sinless) did not need a baptism for remission of sins, but he did need a baptism of 'Holy Spirit' power. Omnipotence (like his omnipresence and omniscience) was one of the major attributes of his divinity which he willingly laid aside when he became man. Soon after his baptism Jesus testified publicly *'The Spirit of the Lord is on me, because he has anointed me to preach good news to the poor. He has sent me to proclaim freedom for the prisoners and recovery of sight for the blind, to release the oppressed, to proclaim the year of the Lord's favour'* (Luke 4: 18,19). The way Jesus *ministered in power* was through the Holy Spirit. That same power, through the Holy Spirit, is available to us today.

4 Finally, we simply have *no idea how to minister in power*. Our clergy are not trained to do it. We have rarely (many never) seen it as it was clearly practised in New Testament times. So we do not do it.

Recently some churches in Britain of all denominations have become increasingly indebted to a leader from California who is teaching how to minister in 'signs and wonders' in the Church today. This is John Wimber, who heads up the Vineyard Christian Fellowships which are spreading across America and beyond. He was formerly an assistant pastor of a Quaker church in Yorba Linda, Los Angeles. This church saw rapid growth during his time on the staff, growing from some 200 to 900 members in three or four years. Because of this John was frequently called upon to lecture on the subject of 'Church Growth'. Professor Peter Wagner 'spotted' him and invited him to take over the leadership of the Department of Church Growth in the School of World Mission at the Fuller Theological Seminary.

A vital insight came through the growing number of third world church leaders attending Fuller. They congratulated John Wimber for identifying the major factors in church growth, but isolated one which had apparently eluded him – 'signs and wonders'. Wherever there were signs and wonders in the third world, there was rapid church growth. Our own limited experience confirmed this, remembering a big step forward in church growth in southern Chile following the dramatic exorcism of a woman who was dangerously mad. People began to flock to the church at Petraco and a number of new churches soon sprang up round about.

Eventually, John Wimber believed he was called by God to leave his travelling consultancy work and pioneer a new style of church planting whilst maintaining his teaching links with Fuller. A small group had come into renewal at the Quaker church that John had formerly helped to pastor. A traditionalist majority, acting before renewal could spread any further, ejected the group of some forty-five affected members, which included John's wife Carol.

John was now asked to lead this group. Within four years it had outgrown its premises several times. From this beginning, many new fellowships have appeared up and down California, across the USA and spreading out worldwide. There are about eighty fellowships today – some with membership well over 1000 and one at least equals the size of the Vineyard Fellowship John himself leads of some 6000 members. There are another seventy affiliated churches.

These fellowships are orthodox in the Christian faith and there is a great openness among them. Whilst there is some variety between each congregation, in general the gatherings follow a similar pattern – they minister worship to God over a prolonged period (some forty-five minutes), then they allow God to minister to them through the exposition of the 'word' and prophecy. Finally they minister to each other. They are notably evangelical, but not narrow; they emphasise love and mercy, and the gifts of the Spirit are exercised by the whole body for the whole body, not excluding, of course, the needs of visitors. Perhaps the most remarkable aspect is the way God has led John into a very unemotional matter-of-fact ministry of 'signs and wonders'. And he has consistently trained others to be naturally supernatural in this ministry not only in his own church, but across all denominational barriers, working on the basis of 'Freely you have received – freely give.' A powerful ministry is being developed without powerful personalities.

In 1980 John initiated a special 'Signs and Wonders' course at Fuller, where he had kept on his teaching links. This attracted large numbers of students, becoming the most popular course in the seminary. *Christian Life* magazine in the USA dedicated the whole October 1982 edition to this explaining how the course was organised, the biblical and historical basis for it, along with comments and some criticism by the staff and students. 'Ministry' is actually exercised in the classroom following teaching. Some seven or eight other seminaries in the United States have since developed similar courses.

When Dr Eddie Gibbs was attending a 'Church Growth' course at Fuller he went to see the Vineyard Christian Fellowship (now at Anaheim) and was so impressed by what he saw that he persuaded the late Canon David Watson, on his way to Fuller to lecture, to visit the Fellowship. David's reported comment after his visit was that his own ministry would never be the same again. Hearing this, we wrote to John Wimber to invite him to St Andrew's, Chorleywood. He came with a team of some twenty-five.

That visit over the weekend of Pentecost six years ago, 1981, was most eventful for us and has been followed by others since. Some vital aspects of our own church life have been revolutionised. Many of us have since been to California to learn more for ourselves.

Recommended reading:
John Wimber *Power Evangelism* Hodder & Stoughton 1985
Donald Bridge *Signs and Wonders Today* I.V.P. 1985

2

TWO SPIRITUAL KINGDOMS

What we know about the kingdom of God

1 In the New Testament, God's kingdom is the central theme for Matthew, Mark and Luke's gospels. It is also mentioned in John 3, which affirms its spiritual nature.

2 The phrase 'kingdom of God' (or 'the kingdom of heaven', which is used by Matthew) does not actually occur in the Old Testament, though many verses (such as Daniel 4: 3, 3: 4b and 6: 26b) clearly refer to it.

3 The political kingdom under David over a united Israel was idealised by the Jews. They dreamed of God setting up a new kingdom over a geographical area (Isaiah 9: 6,7).

4 The Old Testament promises refer to a coming king who would reign: 'See, your king comes to you, righteous and having salvation, gentle and riding on a donkey, on a colt, the foal of a donkey' (Zechariah 9: 9).

5 The Old Testament prophets indicated that this kingdom would break into the present world order to establish the new order, of eternal character (Daniel 7: 13,14).

6 Four hundred years after the appearance of the Old Testament prophet Malachi, the kingdom (*basileia*) of God was at last heralded by John the Baptist – 'Repent, for the kingdom of heaven is near' (Matthew 3: 2).

7 Following his baptism, Jesus preached the same: 'From that time on Jesus began to preach, "Repent, for the kingdom of heaven is near"' (Matthew 4: 17).

8 The concept in the New Testament is more of a *reign* than a realm. Not a geographical area (territory to be found

in purple on a map of the world!), but a sphere under God's
rule.

9 The kingdom Christ speaks about *had clearly already come*:
'From the days of John the Baptist until now, the kingdom
of heaven has been forcefully advancing, and forceful men
lay hold of it' (Matthew 11: 12); 'if I drive out demons by the
Spirit of God, then the kingdom of God has come upon you'
(Matthew 12: 28).

10 BUT Jesus also taught that the kingdom was *still to
come*:

a) He taught his disciples to pray 'your kingdom come,
your will be done on earth as it is in heaven' (Matthew 6: 9).

b) He spoke about the (coming) kingdom and was
asked when he would establish it (Acts 1: 3,6).

c) He illustrated this from a parable: '*Then* the King will
say to those on his right, "Come, you who are blessed by my
Father; take your inheritance, the kingdom prepared for
you since the creation of the world"' (Matthew 25: 34).

d) Again obviously with the future in mind, he said to
the apostles: 'And I confer on you a kingdom, just as my
Father conferred one on me, so that you may eat and drink
at my table in my kingdom and sit on thrones, judging the
twelve tribes of Israel.' (Luke 22: 29,30).

Summary

The kingdom of God has already come as a *reign* on earth,
but the kingdom will come ultimately when Christ returns
and the whole earth will then become his *realm*, one where
every knee shall bow 'in heaven and on earth . . . and every
tongue confess that Jesus Christ is Lord' (Philippians 2: 10):
'Then the end will come, when he (Christ) hands over the
kingdom to God the Father after he has destroyed all
dominion, authority and power' (1 Corinthians 15: 24). The
kingdom of God is '*here now*' and '*not yet*'!

What we know about the kingdom of evil

1 Man (Adam) was given dominion over the earth
(Genesis 1: 26). Satan usurped this through the fall and

offered it back to Christ (the second Adam) in the wilderness temptation (Matthew 4: 8,9).

2 It is a kingdom of darkness – 'this dark world' (Ephesians 6: 11,12). It is the spiritual domain of Satan: 'The whole world is under the control of the evil one' (1 John 5: 19). It spans the earth: 'The whole world is a prisoner of sin' (Galatians 3: 22).

3 Jesus makes it clear in Matthew 12: 22–30 that the struggle in which he is engaged is not a *civil war* within a kingdom, but a *battle* between the kingdom of God and the kingdom of Satan. The strong man (Satan) is bound (the Greek word *deo*, 'to bind', indicates a curbing of power) so that his house (Satan's kingdom) may be plundered. Paul states where and how the battle was won; 'having disarmed the powers and authorities, he (God) made a public spectacle of them, triumphing over them by the cross' (Colossians 2: 15). John too emphasises the work of Jesus in his victory over Satan's kingdom, for 'The reason the Son of God appeared was to destroy the devil's work' (1 John 3: 8b).

4 Satan's power is curbed. His doom is sealed, *but* he is not totally impotent, as the following warnings indicate:

a) 'Your enemy the devil prowls around like a roaring lion looking for someone to devour. Resist him, standing firm in the faith' (1 Peter 5: 8–9a).

b) 'Put on the full armour of God so that you can take your stand against the devil's schemes' (Ephesians 6: 11).

c) 'This is the spirit of the antichrist, which you have heard is coming and even now is already in the world' (1 John 4: 3b).

Summary

Satan's defeat was determined by the death and resurrection of Jesus, but he himself is not yet destroyed. Such a state is well illustrated from the history of the second world war. There were two major victories in Europe – D Day and VE Day. D Day was June 6th, 1944, when to all intents and purposes the result of the war was decided by the victorious landing of the Allies on the coast of France. In fact the war in Europe was not finally over till VE Day, nearly a year

later on May 8th, 1945. There were still months of battles
to go and many lives to be lost – more than in any other
period of the war – but no one doubted the final outcome.
Jesus Christ won the 'D Day' victory at Calvary (Colossians
2: 15) which determined the outcome, but the church is
called to be God's army, continually assaulting the citadels
of Satan and extending the rule of God till 'VE Day' when
Christ will come again and all evil will be finally put down.

The kingdom of God is a reign of spiritual power

Jesus' ministry of signs and wonders is fundamental to the
preaching of the kingdom of God. Jesus *taught* what the
kingdom was like through his *parables* (Mark 4: 11,12,26,30
etc.). Jesus *showed* what the kingdom was like through his
miracles (Luke 11: 20). The parables were *verbal proclamations*
about the kingdom of God. The miracles were *visible
manifestations* of the kingdom of God.

Some ways in which the kingdom of evil manifests its power and the power of Jesus is shown to be greater

1 Satan manifests his power through *sin*
   a) Sin separates us from God (Isaiah 59: 2) – Jesus
reconciles us to God (1 Peter 3: 18).
   b) Worldlings are controlled by their sinful nature –
Jesus sets man free (John 8: 38).
2 Satan manifests power through *disease*
   a) The woman with a haemorrhage – Jesus set her free
(Mark 5: 25–34).
   b) The crippled woman – Jesus set her free (Luke 13:
10–17).
3 Satan manifests power through *demonisation*
   a) Legion was possessed by demons – Jesus set him
free (Mark 5: 1–20).
   b) The epileptic boy was afflicted by a demon – Jesus
set him free (Mark 9: 14–29).
4 Satan manifests power through *destruction*

a) The thief comes to steal and kill and destroy – Jesus the good shepherd came to give life to the full (John 10: 10).

b) The boat in which Jesus and his disciples were crossing the lake was nearly sunk – Jesus rebuked the storm (Matthew 8: 23–27).

5 Satan manifests power through *death*

a) The little girl was dead – Jesus raised her up (Matthew 9: 18–26).

b) Lazarus was dead – Jesus raised him up (John 11: 38–44).

c) The widow of Nain's son was dead – Jesus raised him up (Luke 7: 11–17).

d) Christ was crucified, dead and buried, but was raised from the dead by the power of God (John 10: 18; Acts 3: 15; Romans 1:4).

Summary

Every time someone turns to Christ in repentance, finding forgiveness and eternal life, the kingdom of God is *extended*. Each time Jesus heals, casts out demons, prevents destruction or raises the dead the kingdom of God is *advanced*. Every healing or deliverance in the name of Jesus is a curbing of the enemy's powers and the frontiers of darkness are pushed back. Speaking of his approaching death and triumph through the cross, Jesus said, 'now the prince of this world will be *driven out*' (John 12: 31). The process of 'driving out' still continues today. We are all meant to be actively involved in it.

The loosening of Satan's grip was proof that the kingdom of God had come

'If I drive out demons by the Spirit of God, then the kingdom of God has come upon you' (Matthew 12: 28). The coming of the kingdom of God finds its verification in conversions to God's side, in *the driving out of demons* and in *the healing of diseases*, etc. As diseases are healed and demons driven out, the message of Jesus and his disciples is vindicated. The healings and deliverances are signs of the power and confirmations of the truth of their ministry. 'This salvation ... was confirmed to us by those who heard him. God also testified to it by signs, wonders and various miracles ...' (Hebrews 2: 3,4; see also Mark 16: 20).

Summary

All Christ's disciples are given both the authority and power to preach, heal and cast out demons. As this is done the domain of the evil one is driven back; the kingdom of God is advanced.

Recommended reading:
George Eldon Ladd *Crucial Questions about the Kingdom of God* Eerdmans 1952
George Eldon Ladd *The Presence of the Future* S.P.C.K. 1974
George Eldon Ladd *The Gospel of the Kingdom* Eerdmans 1983

3
WHOLENESS

Introduction

1 Christian teachers rightly proclaim with great conviction that it is Christ's desire to save us (2 Peter 3: 9b) and to cleanse from sin (1 John 1: 9), which is the sickness of the soul. This message effects the greatest miracle – the new birth (1 Peter 1: 23).

2 Christian teachers have too often failed to emphasise that it is also the will of God that such proclamations would normally be accompanied by signs and wonders (Mark 16: 17; Acts 14:3; Hebrews 2:4). These signs confirm the truth of the message proclaimed. Judging by the model we have from Christ's own ministry (in the gospels), the commonest signs are healing and deliverance from demons. One fifth of the gospel material is dedicated to Christ's healing ministry and his teaching about it. As noted earlier, we see the same signs in the ministries of the first Christians in Acts.

Popular attitudes to sickness

The attitude of most people today regarding sickness is coloured by pagan rather than Christian thinking. Sermons on sickness and suffering generally reflect the influence of Stoicism rather than the insights of Jesus. In the Church of England Prayer Book (1662) 'Service for the Visitation of the Sick' this approach is crystallised:

Sanctify, we beseech thee, this thy fatherly correction to

him that the sense of his weakness may add strength to
his faith and seriousness to his repentance, that if it shall
be thy good pleasure to restore him to his former health
he may lead the residue of his life in thy fear, and to thy
glory, or else give him grace so to take thy visitation, that
after this painful life is ended he may dwell with thee in
the life everlasting: through Jesus Christ our Lord.
Amen.

There was much more in this vein in that service.

The curse of sickness

In the beginning God made everything 'very good' (Genesis
1:31). Sickness and pain came in with the fall (Genesis 3:
16,17). All too often sickness has mistakenly been
presented as a blessing in disguise because of the good
which may come to the sick man's soul through suffering.
(The passage generally cited to support such a view comes
from Paul's second letter to the Corinthians, chapter 12:
9,10, though the context seems to indicate that Paul's
'thorn in the flesh' was more likely to have been the
opposition of those who were against him – a messenger of
Satan, as Paul himself said. Relevant cross references to
confirm this view are found in Numbers 33: 55; Joshua 23:
13 (KJV) and 2 Samuel 23: 6.)

Christ's view of man

Jesus did not divide man into two – a soul to be saved and a
body to be left sick and unhealed. He ministered to those
whose spirits were sick and those who needed deliverance
or forgiveness. He also healed those whose bodies were
lame, blind or leprous.

   The New Testament reveals that Jesus endorsed the
Hebrew view of man. He treated man as a *whole* person as
the following three examples illustrate.

Case 1

A paralytic was brought by friends to Jesus. Jesus said,

'Take heart, son; your sins are forgiven.' The unbelieving scribes considered this blasphemy. Knowing their thoughts, Jesus replied, 'Which is easier: to say, "Your sins are forgiven", or to say "Get up and walk"?' But to prove to you that the Son of Man has authority on earth to forgive sins, he said to the paralytic, 'Get up, take your mat and go home.' Jesus demonstrated the same authority over both these forms of evil (Matthew 9: 1–8).

Case 2

Jesus found another paralytic by the Pool of Bethesda and healed him on the sabbath day (John 5: 8, 9). The next time Jesus met him he said, 'See, you are well (whole) again. Stop sinning or something worse may happen to you' (John 5: 14). Later, in reference to this healing, Jesus asked the Jews, 'Why are you angry with me for *healing* the *whole* man on the Sabbath?' (John 7: 23).

Case 3

Ten lepers approached Jesus and asked for pity. He told them to go and show themselves to the priests (the health officials of the day) and 'as they went, they were cleansed' (Luke 17: 14). One of them returned to give thanks, praising God. Jesus said, 'your faith has made you well (*whole*)' (Luke 17: 19).

Modern psychology

Where the Church has strayed from a biblical approach, modern psychology has helped some to rediscover the Hebrew view of man – a person cannot be separated into body and soul, but is a psychosomatic individual, whose emotions and body affect the state of his mind, will, and soul; and vice versa.

Misconceptions about man's body

Some of us have neglected to minister wholeness in the

past, not solely through lack of faith or power, but because we had been taught to view the flesh as an enemy – confusing the two meanings of the Greek word *sarx*.

1 One meaning is the 'flesh', to be understood as the body, which is *wholesome*. Christ took this *our flesh* when he became incarnate (Romans 1: 3).

2 The other meaning is our fallen nature with its lusts and desires (Ephesians 2: 3), which is at enmity with God (Romans 7: 5) and lusts against the Spirit (Galatians 5: 17). An appalling list of 'the works of the flesh' appears in Galatians 5: 19–21. This is the side of us which is plainly *unwholesome*. We should not minister life to this – no healing of any kind; not helping it in any way. This 'fleshly nature' should be denied and put to death every time it raises its ugly head. Jesus said, 'If anyone would come after me, he must deny himself and take up his cross daily and follow me' (Luke 9: 23) Paul said: 'I die every day' (1 Corinthians 15: 31). So must we.

But we must not neglect the work of ministering wholeness to the human body – the flesh used in the former sense – as well as the mind and the spirit.

The biblical view of man is wholeness

In rediscovering the biblical view of man we see that salvation (wholeness) is for the whole person. Jesus came to bring man to fullness of life in every possible dimension: 'I have come that they may have *life*, and have it *to the full*' (John 10: 10).

Paul expresses this clearly: 'May the God of peace himself sanctify you *wholly*; and may your *spirit* and *soul* and *body* be kept *sound* and *blameless* at the coming of the Lord Jesus Christ. He who calls you is faithful, and he will do it' (1 Thessalonians 5: 23,24 RSV). The purpose and the aim of the God of peace is to bring his creation to the fullness of life he intended for it. He desires that our spirit, soul and body be *sound* (literally, 'undamaged') through and through at the coming of our Lord Jesus Christ.

Salvation means wholeness

The Greek word *sozo*, found in the New Testament, is used for 'saving', 'healing', 'preserving' and 'making whole', from which the theological word 'soteriology', or the study of salvation, is derived. Wholeness is much broader than (though it implicitly includes) the healing of the body, etc. This is in line with the prophet Isaiah's message 'to those with fearful hearts', whose God 'will come with vengeance ... to save'; for 'Then will the eyes of the blind be opened and the ears of the deaf unstopped ... the lame leap like a deer, and the tongue of the dumb shout for joy' (Isaiah: 4–6a).

The atonement and wholeness

I am indebted to Christiaan De Wet for much of the following:

1 The particular verse that highlights the belief that there is healing in the atonement is Matthew 8:17, which is of course based on Isaiah 53: 4: 'He took up our infirmities and carried our diseases.'

2 In Isaiah 53: 4ff. the Hebrew words *choli* and *makob* are translated 'griefs' and 'sorrows'. Matthew's interpretation of these as 'infirmities' and 'diseases' is simply respect for the actual meaning of the original words. *Choli* is properly translated 'disease' or 'sickness' in the majority of instances in the Old Testament. *Makob* can be translated either 'sorrow' or 'pain'.

We may not dismiss lightly the question of whether Christ was bearing our *sicknesses* and *sorrows* along with all the other effects and judgments of *sin* on the cross.

The words *nasa* ('to bear') and *sabal* ('to carry') are used both for iniquities and for sorrows and disease. The representative and substitutionary trend of the passage seems clear. This latter emphasis appears to be related specifically to healing and wholeness in verses 5 and 10, where we read 'upon him was the chastisement that made us *whole*, and with his stripes we are *healed*' and '... it was the will of the Lord to bruise him; he has made him sick' (RSV, alternative reading).

3 Certain Old Testament sacrifices (which were all types of the sacrifice of Christ on the cross) focus on the link between the atonement and healing, e.g. the sacrifices for the cleansing of infectious skin diseases in Leviticus 14,15.

4 The bronze serpent in Numbers 21: 4–9 is another example. This is taken up by Christ as a type of his atonement on the cross, 'Just as Moses lifted up the snake in the desert, so the Son of Man must be lifted up, that everyone who believes may have eternal life in him' (John 3: 14,15). The people were commanded to look to the serpent on the pole, *not only for forgiveness*, but also for *the healing of their plague.*

5 The *forgiveness* of 'all my sins' and *healing* of 'all my diseases' are also plainly linked by David in Psalm 103: 3.

6 Finally the name of God Yahweh-Rapha, 'the Lord (who) heals', is one of seven titles which are compounded with God's covenant name 'Yahweh' in the Old Testament. All seven serve as promises to God's people as a whole and without discrimination. We cannot limit the extent or validity of one without doing the same for all the others. (cf. Christiaan De Wet, *Signs and Wonders Today* Christian Life Missions 1983 p. 27).

7 There would appear to be enough clear evidence in the Bible for believing that there is healing in the atonement. We worship Jesus Christ not only because he paid the price on Calvary for our sins, but also because he carried our sicknesses and our sorrows. We can be physically and spiritually whole.

The epistles and wholeness

There are a number of statements in the epistles expressing the conviction that mankind had been under the influence of evil forces. Paul spoke of these as dominions, sovereignties, powers, elements, demons, idols, the law, the flesh, sin and death. One of the primary effects of their domination over human beings was sickness. And one of the reasons for the coming of Christ, as Paul clearly revealed, was to rescue men from this domination; to set us free both from evil forces and from the sickness – moral, mental and physical – that follows in their wake (cf. 1 Corinthians 15: 24; Romans 6: 11; 8: 38; Galatians 4: 8,9; Ephesians 6: 12; Colossians 2: 14,15; Hebrews 2: 14,15).

Wholeness of the future age

This is beautifully envisaged in Revelation 21: 1–4 and Revelation 22: 1–5. This wholeness of the future age came into the present with Jesus healing *every* type of disease, affliction or weakness. He healed *all* those who came to him. He offered healing (body, spirit, mind and emotions) to those who would receive it. Each miracle or healing was a sign of the presence of the Kingdom which is yet to come in its fullness.

Where does this leave the Church today?

If God's kingdom in its complete form is a future event and if the imperfection of our present age is in some way permitted by God, what should the Church be doing in its ministry to bodies, minds, emotions, spirits and social structures?

There seem to be a number of possible responses:

a) Sit back and do nothing. We should just wait for the kingdom to come.

b) Go out and try to heal all we can, etc., and show people some of the reality of the kingdom as it has already come.

c) Seek to do what Jesus did! Try to know God's will in each situation. Jesus said, 'the Son . . . can do only what he sees his Father doing' (John 5: 19).

This last is the vital clue (Matthew 15: 13).

Problems with wholeness

1 It has been suggested that such teaching on wholeness implies *ipso facto* that if a born-again Christian is physically sick then it is either his fault or the fault of those ministering that he is not healed. It would be quite wrong to apportion blame in any case. We can only say that the key to

our healing is often hidden from us (and from those ministering) due to human frailty. We all, both those sick and those ministering healing, have damaged areas in our lives, often way back in the past, of which we may as yet be unaware, even though it hinders the healing process in us.

2 It has been suggested that to offer healing on the same basis as forgiveness is misleading. Any who come to Christ will be forgiven, but will everyone who comes to Christ be healed? The problem is not really ours, but the gospel's (Mark 2: 1–12). The fact is there are many who come to Christ who, for one reason or another, do not find forgiveness – through some hardness of heart, or wanting Christ's forgiveness but being themselves unwilling to forgive, etc. Some are forgiven, but are not physically healed. Some are physically healed, but not forgiven. Some experience both spiritual healing (forgiveness) and physical healing (cure). Some experience neither. 'Many are called. Few are chosen.'

Conclusion

It is not God's creative will for anyone to be sick, but as Christians we must face the facts. All of us get sick – not everyone gets healed. We are still part of a fallen and groaning creation. Healings are a sign that the kingdom has come, but the limited number only goes to show that the kingdom of God has not yet fully come.

The following extract from a letter by Christopher Cocksworth (February, 1985) is most helpful:

1 Our concept of healing is big enough to accept the apparent failure of a lack in physical healing. If healing is for wholeness, then healing may be present even when eyes remain blind and ears remain deaf. The spirit, the mind, the emotions, may be the object of God's healing in these situations...

2 We will see signs of the victory God has already won in Christ. We will see eyes and ears opened, but we will not see every eye nor every ear opened. To expect to do so is to miss the tension between the 'now' and the 'not yet' of

God's kingdom and to attempt to by-pass the mystery between God's creative and his permissive will.

This tension is the 'x factor' in healing, the unknown quantity which God in his sovereignty does not choose to reveal. Humility will always be the right approach. But failure to continue ministering wholeness because we cannot see all being healed is plain disobedience to the Great Commission.

Recommended reading:
Selwyn Hughes, *God Wants You Whole*, Kingsway Publications, 1984.

APPENDIX A

The same Greek word *sozo* is used in the New Testament
with various senses: to save, to heal, to make whole, to
preserve or to rescue. These are enumerated below,
according to the following scheme H = healed; W = whole or
well; R = rescued; P = preserved.

Matthew

	1:21	You are to give him the name Jesus, because he will *save* his people from their sins.
R	8: 25	Lord, *save* us! We're going to drown! (Disciples in a storm.)
H	9: 22	'Your faith has *healed* you.' And the woman was *healed* from that moment. (Woman with haemorrhage.)
	10: 22	He who stands firm to the end will be *saved*.
R	14: 30	Lord *save* me (Peter sinking).
	16: 25	Whoever wants to *save* his life will lose it.
	18: 11	The Son of Man came to *save* what was lost.
	19: 25	Who then can be *saved*?
	24: 13	He who stands firm to the end will be *saved*.
	24: 22	If those days had not been cut short, no-one would *survive*.
	27: 40	*Save* yourself. (People to Jesus on the cross.)
	27: 42	He *saved* others but he can't save himself!
	27: 49	Let's see if Elijah comes to *save* him.

Mark

	3: 4	Which is lawful on the Sabbath ... to *save* life or to kill?

H 5: 23	So that she will be *healed*. (Jairus' daughter.)
H 5: 28	If I just touch his clothes, I will be *healed*.
H 5: 34	Your faith has *healed* you. (See also Matthew 9: 22.)
H 6: 56	All who touched him were *healed*.
8: 35	Whoever wants to *save* his life will lose it. (See also Matthew 16: 25.)
10: 26	Who then can be *saved*. (See also Matthew 19: 25.)
H 10: 52	Your faith has *healed* you. (Blind Bartimaeus.)
13: 13	He who stands firm to the end will be *saved*. (See also Matthew 27: 13.)
13: 20	No-one would *survive* (See also Matthew 24: 13.)
15: 30,31	*Save* yourself! He *saved* others, but can't *save* himself! (See also Matthew 24: 40.)
16: 16	Whoever believes… will be *saved*.
H 16: 18	They will *get well*.

Luke

6: 9	Which is lawful… To *save* life or to destroy it? (See also Mark 3: 4.)
7: 50	Your faith has *saved* you. (Woman who washed his feet.)
8: 12	… so that they cannot believe and be *saved*. (Parable of Sower.)
H 8: 36	(They) told the people how the demon-possessed man had been *cured*.
H 8: 48	Daughter, your faith has *healed* you. (See also Matthew 9: 22; Mark 5: 28.)
H 8: 50	Just believe, and she will be *healed*. (Jairus' daughter.)
9: 24	Whoever wants to *save* his life will lose it. (See also Matthew 16: 25; Mark 8: 35.)
9: 56 (AV)	The Son of Man is not come to destroy men's lives, but to *save* them. (See also Matthew 18: 11.) (A.V.)
13: 23	Lord, are only a few people going to be *saved*?

W 17: 19	Your faith has made you *well*. (Leper who returned to give thanks.)
18: 26	Who then can be *saved*? (See also Matthew 19: 25; Mark 10: 26.)
H 18: 42	Your faith has *healed* you. (Blind man, see also Mark 10: 52.)
19: 10	The Son of Man came to seek and to *save* what was lost. (See also Matthew 18: 11.)
23: 35	He *saved* others; let him *save* himself.
23: 37	If you are the king of the Jews, *save* yourself. (Christ on the Cross, see also Matthew 27: 40; Mark 15: 30.)
23: 39	*Save* yourself and us! (Dying thief.)

John

3: 17	But to *save* the world through Him.
5: 34	I mention it that you might be *saved*.
10: 9	I am the gate; whoever enters through me will be *saved*.
H 11: 12	If he sleeps, he will *get better*. (Lazarus.)
12: 27	Father, *save* me from this hour.
12: 47	I did not come to judge the world, but to *save* it.

Acts

2: 21	Everyone who calls on the name of the Lord will be *saved*. (Quoting Joel 2: 32.)
2: 40	*Save* yourselves from this corrupt generation.
2: 47	The Lord added to their number daily those who were being *saved*.
H 4: 9,10	If we ... are asked how he was *healed* ... By the name of Jesus ... this man stands before you completely *healed*.
11: 14	He will bring you a message through which you ... will be *saved*. (Cornelius.)
H 14: 9	Paul ... saw that he had faith to be *healed*. (Lame man.)

15: 1	Unless you are circumcised... you cannot be *saved*.
15: 11	We believe... that we are *saved*.
16: 30	Men, what must I do to be *saved*?
16: 31	Believe in the Lord Jesus, and you will be *saved*.
R 27: 20	We finally gave up all hope of being *saved* (from shipwreck)
R 27: 31	Unless these men stay with the ship, you cannot be *saved*.

Romans

5: 9	How much more shall we be *saved*... through him!
5: 10	*Saved* through his life.
8: 24	For in this hope we were *saved*.
9: 27	Only the remnant will be *saved*. (See also Isaiah 10: 22,23.)
10: 9	If you... believe... that God has raised him... you will be *saved*.
10: 13	Everyone who calls on the name of the Lord will be *saved*.
11: 14	...and *save* some of them.
11: 26	So all Israel will be *saved*.

1 Corinthians

1: 18	To us who are being *saved* it (the message of the cross) is the power of God.
1: 21	God was pleased... to *save* those who believe.
3: 15	He himself will be *saved*, but only as one escaping through the flames.
5: 5	...so that his spirit (may be) *saved* on the day of the Lord.
7: 16	How do you know, wife, whether you will *save* your husband?
7: 16	How do you know, husband, whether you will *save* your wife?

9: 22	So that ... I might *save* some.
10: 33	So that they may be *saved*.
15: 2	By this gospel you are *saved*, if you hold firmly to the word ...

2 Corinthians

| 2: 15 | ... those who are being *saved* and those who are perishing. |

Ephesians

| 2: 5 | It is by grace you have been *saved*. |
| 2: 8 | For it is by grace you have been *saved*, through faith. |

1 Thessalonians

| 2: 15,16 | They displease God ... in their effort to keep us from speaking to the Gentiles so that they may be *saved*. |

2 Thessalonians

| 2: 10 | They perish because they refused to love the truth and so be *saved*. |

1 Timothy

1: 15	Christ Jesus came into the world to *save* sinners.
2: 4	God our Saviour ... wants all men to be *saved*.
P 2: 15	But women will be *kept safe* through childbirth.
4: 16	You will *save* both yourself and your hearers.

2 Timothy

1: 9 God who has *saved* us and called us to a holy life ...

4: 18 The Lord will *rescue* me ... and will bring me safely to his heavenly kingdom.

Titus

3: 5 He *saved* us, not because of righteous things we had done.

Hebrews

5: 7 To the one who could *save* him from death.

7: 25 He is able to *save* completely those who come to God through him.

James

1: 21 The word ... which can *save* you.

2: 14 Can such faith *save* him?

4: 12 There is only one Lawgiver and Judge, the one who is able to *save* and destroy.

H 5: 15 The prayer offered in faith will make the sick person *well*.

5: 20 ... will *save* him from death and cover over a multitude of sins.

1 Peter

3: 21 This water symbolises baptism that now *saves* you also.

4: 18 If it is hard for the righteous to be *saved*, what will become of the ungodly and the sinner?

4
AUTHORITY AND POWER

Introduction

There are times when we feel great authority and power in our ministries and other times when we feel nothing. Sometimes disease and demons respond immediately and sometimes they do not. The question arises: 'What is spiritual authority and/or power and how do they relate to each other?' Once we know God's authority and can exercise his power, we will be like Jesus to those in need. In this section we examine the background and nature of authority and power, how they have been given to us to heal and how they may be abused.

Defining authority and power

Authority and power are often confused:

1 Authority (*exousia*) is the right and liberty to exercise power.

2 Power (*dunamis*) is the might or ability inherent in the word often used for 'miracle' (a work of power – Mark 6: 5).

A *policeman* may stand out on the road in the path of a speeding vehicle and have all the *authority* (demonstrated by his uniform) to stop the driver. But he may not have the *power* to do so and will have to jump aside to avoid being killed.

A *jailor* may have the *power* (demonstrated by the keys) to open a prison cell and release a prisoner, but he may lack the *authority* to do it.

3 Sometimes, however, the word 'authority' seems also to include the idea of power and vice-versa (e.g. Luke 10: 19).

The origin of authority and power

God has absolute authority and power.

1 He is omnipotent.

His name, *El Shaddai* has been traditionally understood to mean 'God Almighty' (Genesis 17: 1).

The Creed of St Athanasius states: 'The Father is Almighty; the Son is Almighty; the Holy Ghost is Almighty. And yet there are not three Almighties but one Almighty.' (*Book of Common Prayer*, 1662.)

  a) He has creation power. He made us (Genesis 1: 27).

  b) He has damnation power. He can destroy us (Luke 12: 5).

  c) He has salvation power. He can save us (1 Corinthians 1: 18).

  d) He has eternal and elective power (Daniel 4: 34,35; Isaiah 46: 10).

Paul says that since the creation of the world God's invisible qualities – his eternal *power* (*dunamis*) and divine nature – have been clearly seen, being understood from what has been made, so that men are without excuse (Romans 1: 20).

Paul compares God's *authority* (*exousia*) to that of the potter over the clay (Romans 9: 21; Jeremiah 18: 6).

God has delegated authority and power

1 All authority and power is derived from God (Romans 13: 1b).

2 Man was given authority and power.

  a) To be and to reveal God's image and glory (Genesis 1: 26, cf. Psalm 8: 3,4)

  b) To rule over the earth (Genesis 1: 26).

  c) To have all things under his feet (Psalm 8: 6–8).

Satan has temporarily contrived to acquire this authority and power, which God originally intended for man (Luke 4: 6).

1 Adam, through being deceived and through his own deliberate disobedience, lost his privileges of authority and power (Genesis 3: 23).

2 Satan became the prince, ruler and god of this world (2 Corinthians 4: 4).

3 Everything under Satan's rule has been enslaved and has suffered through his policy of sin, sickness, destruction and death (John 8: 34–44).

Christ came as man (the second Adam) to re- establish God's authority and power over the earth.

Satan appeared to tempt Jesus and sought to bargain, offering his dominion over all the earthly kingdoms back to Christ (Luke 4: 6) who, though conscious of his right to them, refused, awaiting the divinely appointed means and moment (John 8: 14; John 10: 14–18).

Christ's authority and power

Christ's authority

1 Jesus received authority (*exousia*) through his filial relationship with the Father. He knew his identity and commission as the Son, sent from the Father (John 17: 2; cf. John 3: 35).

2 Jesus was under authority (in a right relationship with the Father) and so could exercise authority which others recognised (Matthew 8: 5–9).

3 Jesus's teaching was recognised to be authoritative (Matthew 7: 29) because he spoke only what he heard from the Father (John 7: 17,18; John 8: 38).

4 Jesus received all authority in heaven on earth with his exaltation to glory (Matthew 28: 18; cf. Philippians 2: 6–11 Ephesians 1: 20–23).

5 Jesus will eventually hand back his authority and power to God (1 Corinthians 15: 24–28).

Christ's power

1 Jesus received power through the anointing of the Holy Spirit at His baptism (Luke 3: 22; cf. Luke 4: 1,14,18).

2 Jesus had power from this time forward over the forces of nature, sin, sickness, demons and death – all these obeyed his orders (see Mark 1: 22,27; Matthew 9: 6,8; Mark 4: 39–41; Luke 7: 1–17).

3 Jesus, through his life, death and resurrection, disarmed and despoiled the spiritual powers of the adversary (John 12: 31; Colossians 2: 15; Hebrews 2: 14).

Authority and power for the people of God

Authority and power received

1 Jesus dispensed spiritual power to his *apostles* (Luke 9: 1) and the *disciples* (Luke 10: 18,19) who had been with him physically.

2 Jesus promised power to *all believers* through the Holy Spirit after he had ascended (Acts 1: 8).

3 a) We exercise this power out of our *position* – being adopted into God's family, with all the rights of a child of God (John 1: 12).

b) We exercise this power out of our *submission* – being subjects of God's kingdom. Being under authority, we have authority (Matthew 8: 8,9).

c) We exercise this power out of our *relationship* – being branches of the vine. Jesus said, 'I am the vine; you are the branches ... apart from me you can do nothing' (John 15: 5).

d) We exercise this power out of *anointing*. When the Holy Spirit comes, we may either be open to welcome him or closed to deny him place to empower us. The promise stands: 'You will receive power when the Holy Spirit comes on you' (Acts 1: 8).

Authority and power for service

The believing Christian has a commission to minister in power under Jesus's authority (see Matthew 10: 8; Matthew 28: 18–20; Mark 16: 15–20; John 20: 21).

a) To proclaim the good news of the kingdom, b) to baptise and teach, c) to drive out demons, d) to heal the sick, e) to speak in new tongues, f) to raise the dead, g) to make disciples, h) to act as Jesus would in this world (forgiving sins, etc. – John 20: 21–23).

Jesus has given us authority (*exousia*) over all the power (*dunamis*) of the enemy, and nothing will harm us (Mark 16: 18b; Luke 10: 19).

Power must never be used without authority. The soldier must not fire his rifle (though the authorities may have supplied both the rifle and the bullets) until he receives the order to fire.

There were times when Old Testament prophets were restrained from action because the Lord had not revealed what caused the problem (2 Kings 4: 27).

There were also times when the Lord held back because presumably it had not been revealed to him what he should do. To the plea of the Canaanite woman, 'Jesus did not answer a word' (Matthew 15: 23). In response to the pleas of the two sisters, Mary and Martha, for their brother Lazarus, we are told Jesus 'stayed where he was two more days' (John 11: 6). In the end he ministered to both after he had ascertained the Father's will and knew that he had the authority to act. *Without the revelation* from God the Father, there was *no authority* to use the power given to him through the Holy Spirit (Luke: 5: 17).

The early disciples also had power to go and work signs and wonders, but they did not heal everyone every time they saw a sick person either. They needed a specific revelation to assure them of their authority regarding a particular person or situation. This is equally true for us today. But how will we know when we have the right (authority) to use the power of God? We will need the gifts of the Holy Spirit, such as those listed in 1 Corinthians 12 – the gifts of knowledge, wisdom, discernment, etc., to show us (cf. the following chapters).

Authority and power questioned

1 His enemies asked *Christ* by what authority he was doing what he did, 'Who gave you this authority?'

(Matthew 21: 23). He would not tell them, but he did tell his own disciples (John 5: 26–30).

2 Immediately after Pentecost, when *Peter* had healed the lame man, he likewise was questioned about his power and authority. How did you heal the man? Who said you could do it? Who told you to do it? Such questions naturally follow any manifestation of power wrought through man. Peter readily explained it. 'Men of Israel, why does this surprise you? Why do you stare at us as if by our own power or godliness we made this man walk?' (Acts 3: 12). 'By faith in the name of Jesus, this man . . . was made strong' (Acts 3: 16).

Soon after, the authorities repeated the question, 'By what power or what name did you do this?' (Acts 4: 7). Peter replied, 'It is by the name of Jesus Christ of Nazareth' (verse 10). Their power was *in the name of Jesus*.

Pre-Pentecost power: In general it appears that before the outpouring of the Holy Spirit Jesus *'backed-up'* the work of healing or deliverance in his name performed by his disciples.

Post-Pentecost power: After *Pentecost* the Holy Spirit would *'back-up'* the disciples' ministry of healing and deliverance in Jesus's name. Christ's disciples still have this *'back-up'* through the Holy Spirit.

Misusing authority and power

1 The details of the temptation of Jesus were without human witness. He himself revealed what took place for *our* benefit.

2 The passages regarding the temptations of Jesus in the wilderness (Matthew 4 and Luke 4) are normally considered in the light of their unique application to the Son of God and their general application for the Christian life.

3 In their context, following, as they do, immediately after the baptism of Jesus and his anointing by the Holy Spirit, there must also be a *specific application* from the temptations of Jesus *to the ministry of 'power'.*

4 Jesus is not recorded as having worked any miracle, healed any sick, cleansed any leper nor raised any dead until *after* this anointing, which was straightaway followed by the temptations.

5 The order of the temptations is different in the two accounts, but the details are the same. We take them in the order found in Luke. Anyone aware of an anointing of 'power' to work signs and wonders will soon become aware of the relevance of these temptations.

Temptation 1: 'Tell this stone to become bread.'

1 Jesus was hungry after forty days of fasting.

2 The temptation was to use his spiritual power to satisfy the physical needs of his body. He certainly had a physical need – hunger.

3 But Jesus was aware of a greater need. To be engaged in a ministry of 'signs and wonders' he needed to give priority to the development of his own spiritual life. 'Man does not live on bread alone.'

4 Jesus used the sword of the Spirit (which is the word of God, Ephesians 6: 17) to overcome Satan in this temptation.

There are several lessons here for those ministering in the power of the Holy Spirit:

1 We need to maintain the priority of a close relationship with the Lord. We can so easily be deflected as we discover how powerfully God can work through us.

2 We need to beware, as we are confronted by pressing physical needs, that the spiritual needs of the afflicted person are paramount and not be distracted by distressing physical symptoms. So often the presenting problem is not the problem God wants us to deal with.

3 We will often be emotionally pressurised to act. We must only do what we sense to be God's specific will in any particular situation.

4 We will need the sword of the Spirit – God's word – to help us in this conflict. At times we may have to do as Elisha did and say, 'The Lord has hidden it from me and has not told me why' (2 Kings 4: 27).

Temptation 2: 'Worship me and the world is yours.'

1 Jesus had come to win back the world. This dominion had been usurped by the devil, who now offered back to Jesus 'all their authority and splendour'.

2 The temptation for Jesus was to by-pass the will of the Father. It is clear that everything was eventually to be

brought under the authority of Christ (1 Corinthians 15: 27), but Jesus rejected the temptation to win it back the devil's way.

3 Jesus knew too well that there could be no way round suffering, persecution and the cross (Mark 8: 31; 9: 12,31; 10: 33–34,45).

4 Jesus used the sword of the Spirit to overcome evil: 'It is written: "Worship the Lord your God and serve him only"' (Luke 4: 8).

We can learn a number of lessons from this temptation as we seek to minister in the power of the Holy Spirit:

1 There is no way to heaven except through the cross (1 Corinthians 1: 18).

2 The cross of Christ must be preached. The disciples preached this into the healing miracles (Acts 3: 12–16).

3 The disciple also has to take up the cross daily. Nearly every healing miracle was followed by some kind of counterattack, whether it was false accusation, threats (Acts 4: 21), imprisonment (Acts 4: 3), beating (Acts 5: 40), stoning (Acts 7: 58) or whatever. The servants were not above their master. Paul certainly was not – see the list of his sufferings (2 Corinthians 7: 4b and 11: 23–27).

4 We will need the word of God to overcome this second temptation: 'Worship the Lord your God and serve him only' (Luke 4: 8). 'Signs and wonders' are only a means to an end, not the major focus of the Christian life.

Temptation 3: 'Throw yourself down from the top of the Temple.'

1 The devil quotes a promise of scripture.

2 The devil tempts Jesus to gain instant recognition.

3 But Jesus 'only did what he saw the Father doing'. Through his relationship with the Father and through his understanding of scripture he knew what the Father wanted.

4 Jesus used the word of God to overcome this temptation too: 'Do not put the Lord your God to the test' (Luke 4: 12).

There are several points to note here:

1 We shall need to discern carefully the 'words' given to

us – even scripture. 'A text out of context becomes a pretext.'

2 Everyone wishes for some kind of recognition and we can all too easily fall into the sin of presumption, using God's power for things God is not telling us to do, so we need to pray in the spirit of Psalm 19: 12–14.

When the disciples felt rejected by the Samaritans they were tempted to use God's power to call down fire on their village to destroy them and earned Jesus's rebuke (Luke 9: 54,55).

When Simon (Magus) saw that the Spirit was given at the laying on of hands, he offered Peter money, saying 'Give me also this ability' (Acts 8: 19). Peter resisted the temptation, saying 'May your money perish with you, because you thought you could buy the gift of God with money!' (verse 20). Note also the tragic cases of Balaam and Gehazi (Jude verse 11 and 2 Kings 5: 20–27).

3 We too will need 'the sword of the Spirit' – which is the word of God – to overcome any temptation to abuse God's power.

5

HOW DID JESUS MINISTER?

Jesus was God and by his incarnation, when 'the Word became flesh and lived for a while among us' (John 1: 14), he became man. He was 'made like his brothers in every way ... that he might make atonement for the sins of the people' (Hebrews 2: 17). He was not then half divine and half human. He was, is and always will be, 100% divine and he became 100% man. When Jesus became man and had a truly human body he laid aside some divine attributes of his glory, though he always remained fully and essentially God (Colossians 2: 9).

He became man to communicate God's word of life and love to us, to represent our humanity on the cross, and to model our ministry in the world.

The attributes of his divine glory which he voluntarily and deliberately laid aside were notably three: his omnipresence – being everywhere, his omniscience – knowing everything, his omnipotence – having all power.

Omnipresence – laid aside

Once Jesus had deliberately limited himself to partaking of our flesh and blood he could only be in one place at one time; he could not be everywhere.

Omniscience – laid aside

1 There are a number of instances in the life of Jesus which reveal there were things he did not know.

2 As a twelve-year-old boy in the Temple he was unaware of his parents' concern that he was not among the

crowd returning from the feast of the Passover (Luke 2: 41–49).

3 The phrase 'Jesus grew in wisdom' (Luke 2: 52) implies that his wisdom had been limited.

4 When the woman with the haemorrhage was healed, he asked the crowd who had touched him (Mark 5: 30), and he 'kept looking around to see who had done it' (Mark 5: 32).

5 He asked the disciples how many loaves they had before he fed the 4000 (Mark 8: 5).

6 He asked the father of the epileptic boy:

a) 'What are you arguing with them (the disciples) about?' (Mark 9: 16).

b) 'How long has he been like this?' (Mark 9: 21).

7 Jesus set out with his disciples by boat to escape the crowds and go by themselves to a quiet place and get some rest. When they reached the place he 'saw a large crowd' (Mark 6: 34). He was obviously taken by *surprise*.

8 When asked about his own return to establish his kingdom on earth, Jesus replied, 'No one knows about that day or hour, not even the angels in heaven, nor the Son, but only the Father' (Mark 13: 32).

All such references illustrate that Jesus had really divested himself of his omniscience during his time on earth.

Omnipotence – laid aside

Prior to his baptism. Jesus apparently had no ministry of power until after his anointing by the Holy Spirit. He cast out no demon, he healed no sick person, he raised no dead, he calmed no storm nor fed the multitude miraculously until after his baptism in power by the Holy Spirit. Immediately following this anointing Jesus began a ministry which was accompanied by extraordinary manifestations of power.

Following his baptism.

1 'Jesus returned to Galilee in the *power* of the Spirit' (Luke 4: 14).

2 He went to the synagogue and read from Isaiah 61 '*The Spirit of the Lord is on me*, because he has anointed me to preach good news to the poor. He has sent me to proclaim freedom for the prisoners and recovery of sight for the blind, to release the oppressed, to proclaim the year of the Lord's

favour... *Today* this scripture is fulfilled in your hearing'
(Luke 4: 18–21).

3 'With authority and *power* he gives orders to evil spirits
and they come out!' (Luke 4: 36).

4 'The *power* of the Lord was present for him to heal the
sick' (Luke 5: 17b).

5 'The people all tried to touch him, because *power* was
coming from him and healing them all' (Luke 6: 19).

Divine power came to Jesus through his baptism. Peter said 'You
know what has happened throughout Judea beginning in
Galilee after the baptism that John preached – how God
anointed Jesus of Nazareth with the Holy Spirit and *power*,
and how he went around doing good and healing all who
were under the power of the devil, because God was with
him' (Acts 10: 37–38).

As R A Torrey says, 'Jesus Christ obtained power for His
divine works not by His inherent divinity, but by His
anointing through the Holy Spirit. He was subject to the
same conditions of power as other men.' (R A Torrey *What
the Bible Teaches*, Fleming H Revell Company p. 94)

There were times when his power after his baptism was
clearly limited. In his home town of Nazareth he did not do
many miracles because of their lack of faith (Matthew 13:
58). There were other times when it seemed to 'flow' (Luke
5: 17 and 6: 19).

*Jesus worked by the power of God and encouraged his disciples to work in
the same way.* 'I tell you the truth, *anyone* who has faith in me
will do what I have been doing. He will do even greater
things than these, because I am going to the Father' (John
14: 12). (Here, 'greater things' must refer to *quantity* not
quality.)

*Jesus apparently operated through the gifts of the Holy Spirit, which
came to him following his anointing.* Some 'Reformed' theologians have suggested that the gifts of the Holy Spirit
provided a connecting link between Jesus's human and
divine nature (cf. T C Hammond *In Understanding be Men* IVF
1947 p. 129). We suggest some examples of the gifts of the
Spirit operating in the ministry of Jesus, taking in turn the

gifts of revelation, the gifts of power and the gifts of communication.

Gifts of revelation

Discerning of spirits

Jesus clearly exercised the gift of discernment. The classic example follows the confession of Peter at Caesarea Philippi. Peter recognised who he really was: 'You are the Christ, the Son of the living God.' Jesus discerned the spiritual source of such revelation, saying 'this was not revealed to you by man, but by my Father in heaven' (Matthew 16: 16,17).

Then when Jesus spoke of the nature of his mission, which entailed his being put to death Peter rebuked Jesus, '"Never, Lord! This shall never happen to you!" Jesus turned and said to Peter, "Out of my sight, *Satan!*"' Jesus discerned the spiritual source of Peter's rebuke (Matthew 16: 22,23).

Words of knowledge

1 In a conversation with the Samaritan woman, Jesus received a 'word' that she was an adulteress, 'The fact is, you have had five husbands, and the man you now have is not your husband. What you have said (i.e. that she had no husband) is quite true' (John 4: 18).

2 When asked about the cause of a man's blindness, Jesus was given a 'word of knowledge' that it was not due to the blind man's sin nor that of his father (John 9: 3).

3 Nathaniel was amazed that Jesus knew about him before they had met. 'Here is a true Israelite, in whom there is nothing false', said Jesus (John 1: 47). (This could be linked with the gift of discerning of spirits cf. 1 John 4: 1.)

4 In the case of the demon possessed boy, the father told Jesus he had a spirit which robbed him of his *speech* (Mark 9: 17). But Jesus knew it was a *deaf* and *dumb* spirit and cast it out (Mark 9: 25). (This too could be linked with the gift of discerning of spirits.)

5 When Jesus went to the home of Jairus he *knew* before

he went in to see her that the twelve-year-old girl was going to be raised up and told the scoffing mourners so (Mark 5: 36,39,40).

6 On the way there he was surrounded by crowds who pressed around him yet he *knew* that a woman amongst them had come up behind and touched his cloak, believing she could be healed. Jesus turned round in the crowd and asked 'Who touched my clothes?', which caused his disciples some amazement (Mark 5: 30,31).

7 Faced with the need to pay the temple tax, Jesus told Peter to fish in the lake for it. 'Take the first fish you catch: open its mouth and you will find a four-drachma coin. Take it and give it to them for my tax and yours' (Matthew 17: 27). He *knew* he would catch fish; he *knew* which fish's mouth to open and he *knew* that he would find a coin there and what it would be. This is not uncommon to those who are experienced in having 'words of knowledge'. I have a friend who has had up to thirty facts that exactly fitted the condition of a person totally unknown to him who was present. He spoke these out just as the Spirit of God gave them to him and the man responded.

8 In preparation for his triumphal entry, Jesus *knew* about the donkey tied up in the next village with her colt beside her, and he *knew* what the owner's response would be (Matthew 21: 2,3; cf, Luke 19: 33). It is, of course, possible (in this instance and the next) to believe that Jesus had arranged this previously, but there seems little point in mentioning it if he had.

9 In preparation for the Passover, Jesus *knew* that the disciples he sent would meet a man carrying a jar of water, whom they were to follow and ask the owner of the house he entered for the use of his guest room. They found things just as Jesus had told them (Luke 22: 10–12).

10 Jesus *knew* who would betray him (John 13: 26).

11 Jesus *knew* his disciples' thoughts (Luke 9: 47) and the Pharisees' thoughts too (Luke 5: 22; 6: 8).

12 The disciples had been fishing all night and had caught nothing. Without their knowing who he was, the resurrected Christ told them to cast their nets on the other side of the boat. When they did this, they landed a huge catch of fish which made Peter recognise who he was (John

21: 1–14). This 'word of knowledge' from Jesus went counter to their personal experience. They had toiled all night and caught nothing. It also went counter to their professionalism. As fishermen, they should know the best places to fish (cf. also Luke 5: 4–6 for a similar example).

Words of Wisdom

These were shown to Jesus by the Father in critical situations.

1 During his meeting with the woman of Samaria Jesus perceived through a 'word of knowledge' that she was an adulteress. When she expressed interest in the water of life Jesus told her gently to go and call her husband. By a word of wisdom we can believe that this was revealed to Jesus as the Father's dignified and gracious way of confronting her with a major problem in her life (John 14: 16–18).

2 When a young man came to Jesus asking how he could inherit eternal life it was revealed to Jesus that his obstacle was wealth. We believe Jesus was shown through a 'word of wisdom' how to approach the problem. Gently he listed the commandments and discreetly omitted the last and relevant one. The young man would of course have spotted the omission and the lesson went home without humiliation (Mark 10: 17–22).

3 In preparing to meet the crisis of feeding the 5,000 and 4,000, Jesus was shown how to prepare for the miracles by making the crowds sit down and told the disciples to go and see what minimal provisions were available (Mark 6: 30–43; Mark 8: 1–9).

4 When the wine ran out prematurely at the wedding, Jesus was shown how to prepare for the miracle. He told the servants to fill up the water pots with water (John 2: 7).

5 Jesus was 'shown' how to minister to Peter after his three-fold denial. He did not humiliate him further by a rebuke which was well-merited but asked him simply if he still loved him. He then trusted him with a fresh commission.

6 In many situations when his enemies were trying to trap him or criticise his ministry Jesus responded with a 'word of wisdom' over, for example, a political issue (Matthew 22: 21), a legal issue (Mark 2: 27), a moral issue

(John 8: 7), a question of his authority (Matthew 21: 24,25) and the accepted priority of charity to the poor (John 12: 8).

Gifts of power

The three 'power' gifts of faith, healing and miracles were very evident in the ministry of Jesus.

Gift of Faith

1 In healing the epileptic boy Jesus explained to the disciples afterwards why they could not cast out the demon. It was their lack of *faith*. Faith moves mountains. With this gift nothing is impossible. (Matthew 17: 21).

2 The disciples panicked in a storm on the lake. Jesus rebuked the wind and the waves. The disciples *had enough faith* to give up all and follow him, but they *did not have the 'gift of faith'* to do what Jesus did. 'You of *little faith*, why are you so afraid?' said Jesus. He rebuked the winds and the waves and calmed them (Matthew 8: 26).

3 Jesus walked on water. Peter did the same at Jesus's bidding, but soon began to sink. Jesus rescued him and chided him for his *lack of faith*, which implies that it was his faith which enabled Jesus himself to walk on water (Matthew 14: 31).

Gift of Healing

There is no question about healing being part of the ministry of Jesus. 'Nearly one-fifth of the entire Gospels is devoted to Jesus's healing and the discussions occasioned by it' (Morton Kelsey *Healing and Christianity*, Harper & Row, 1973, p. 54).

1 *Jesus healed in large numbers all kinds of diseases, etc.*
'Jesus went through Galilee . . . healing every disease and sickness among the people . . . people brought to him all who were ill with various diseases, those suffering severe pain, the demon-possessed, the epileptics and the paralytics, and he healed them' (Matthew 4: 23–24). This kind of mission is also reported in Matthew 8: 16; 9: 35; 14: 35,36.

2 *Jesus communicated his healing power by words and deeds*

On one occasion he took a deaf and dumb person aside from the crowd. He put his fingers in his ears and touched his tongue. He looked up to heaven with a deep sigh and said, 'Be opened!' At this the man's ears were opened, his tongue was loosed and he began to speak (Mark 7: 33–35).

Those experienced in using the 'power' gifts witness to an inner surge of compassion for the afflicted or anger against the afflictor (which accompanies this gift) and it may well be that the 'deep sigh' of Jesus in the above (Mark 7: 34) and his being 'deeply moved in spirit and troubled' (John 11: 33) at the mourning of Lazarus' friends are examples of this. Quite possibly the 'compassion' mentioned after healings in the gospels is of the same kind (Mark 1: 41; Luke 7: 12,13,14; Matthew 9: 36; 15: 32).

Gift of miracles

Jesus certainly used the 'gift of miracles' whenever he knew it was 'right' to do so. Most of the miracles are to do with healing or casting out demons, but Jesus also used the gift to manifest divine power over the forces of nature. He walked on water, stilled a storm, changed water into wine, fed multitudes out of minimal supplies, cursed a fig tree and helped catch fish. Jesus performed these by taking some action, giving a command, by blessing (the bread) or by cursing (the fig tree).

Gifts of Communication

Gift of prophecy

Jesus not only experienced the gift of prophecy, but he was recognised as a prophet by the crowds who came to hear him (John 6: 14). The Jews awaited the coming of 'the Prophet' foretold by Moses (Deuteronomy 18: 18) and Christ himself fulfilled that prophecy (Luke 4: 21; 24: 19).

Gift of tongues

With regard to 'tongues' and 'interpretation of tongues', we have no evidence that Jesus ever prayed in the way which Paul calls 'praying in the Spirit' or gave 'interpretations'.

Summary

Leaving aside the mystery of Christ's dereliction on the Cross, his communication with the Father was ever harmonious and totally unaffected by sin. Theologians have traditionally recognised a unique 'hypostatic union' between the nature of the Father and that of the Son.

It should be noted that whilst it is apparent from scripture that Jesus certainly operated in the gifts of the Spirit, it would be quite wrong to limit the unique Son of God to any modes which are necessarily comprehensible to man or to insist that he always operated in this way.

Doubtless he also healed out of his 'office' as a healer: 'I am the Lord who heals you' (Exodus 15: 26).

How did Jesus know who to heal?

Jesus said, 'The Son . . . can do only what he sees his Father doing' (John 5: 19). Then how did Jesus *see* what the Father was doing? The answer is: Through his open relationship with the Father.

1 He maintained a right relationship to his Father, which he had from the beginning (John 1: 2; Acts 10: 38).

2 Jesus had an unbroken relationship with the Father – he had no sin (1 John 3: 5), he knew no sin (2 Corinthians 5: 21), he did no sin (Hebrews 4; 15). He neither grieved, quenched nor resisted the Holy Spirit. The Spirit was in him 'without limit' (John 3: 34b).

3 Jesus spoke what he knew (John 3: 11). This knowledge, like his power, flowed out of his relationship with the Father and the Holy Spirit.

4 He worked together with the Father (John 5: 19).

5 He did nothing on his own initiative. He said and did only what he specifically saw and heard from the Father (John 5: 19).

6 The relationship was built on trust and commitment (John 8: 16, 26–29,38).

7 Jesus always did what pleased the Father (John 8: 29).

8 The Father and the Son were, as it were, continually in each other's presence, relating to each other – communicating. Jesus' prayer life was an integral part of this relationship (Luke 5: 16, etc.).

Whether it was through the revelatory gifts of 'word of
wisdom', 'word of knowledge', or prophecy or through the
unique 'only begotten Son' relationship (John 3: 16) which
he had with the Father, Jesus knew who and when to heal.

1 On some occasions Jesus healed all who came to him
(Matthew 4: 24; 8: 16). On others, as the pressure to
minister healing built up, Jesus withdrew (Matthew 8: 18).

2 At another time Jesus refused to attempt a healing
ministry at all, citing Elijah and Elisha as precedents (Luke
4: 23–27).

3 Jesus was very selective. He once visisted a local
'hospital', the Pool of Bethesda, and picked only one person
to heal (John 5: 1–9).

4 Jesus refused to be emotionally pressurised into
response, even when it came from his own mother (John 2:
4).

   a) A Canaanite woman pleaded with Jesus to cast out
the demon from her daughter. Matthew tells us 'Jesus did
not answer a word. So his disciples . . . urged him, "Send her
away"' (Matthew 15: 23).

   b) When the two sisters came to Jesus to tell him that
Lazarus was sick, John tells us that Jesus *stayed where he was
two more days* (John 11: 6).

In neither instance was Jesus going to be pressurised into
ministering. He did only what he saw the Father doing.
Once the Father had shown him his will, he healed the
demonised girl and raised Lazarus, though the latter had
been dead for four days.

Jesus was also shown *how* he was to heal specific cases
that were presented – whether to anoint with oil, lay on
hands, touch with his finger, spit upon, make clay and apply
to the affected part, cast out a demon, or forgive sin.

6

INTRODUCING THE GIFTS

Definition

The spiritual gifts in 1 Corinthians 12: 8–10 are the expression of God's grace at work, primarily in the Church, and are transrational manifestations of God's power dispensed by him in ministering for the common good.

Distinctions

There are *four main listings* of so-called gifts in the New Testament, with some apparent overlapping and no simple reconciliation. We place them in their biblical context and under headings according to their Greek word usage, adding a miscellaneous collection from other scriptures.

1 *Phanerosis – manifestation of the Spirit* (1 Corinthians 12: 8–10)
Word of wisdom, word of knowledge, faith, gifts of healings, miraculous powers, prophecy, discerning of spirits, kinds of tongues, interpretation of tongues.

2 *Diakoniai – ministries of the Spirit* (1 Corinthians 12: 28)
Apostles, prophets, teachers, miracles, gifts of healings, helps, administration, tongues.

3 *Charismata – gifts of grace* (Romans 12: 3–8)
Prophecy, serving, teaching, exhortation, giving, organising, mercy.

4 *Domata – equippers of the saints* (Ephesians 4: 8–14)
Apostles, prophets, evangelists, pastors/teachers.

5 *Miscellaneous*
Celibacy (1 Corinthians 7: 7,8), philanthropy (1 Corinthians 13: 3), hospitality (1 Peter 4: 9).

Manifestations of the Spirit

We are interested in the first list because of the *congregational setting* for the distribution of these gifts which seem to fall into three natural categories.

Category a: Gifts of revelation

1 Word of wisdom.
2 Word of knowledge.
3 Discerning of spirits.

Category b: Gifts of power

1 Gift of faith.
2 Gifts of healings.
3 Working of miracles.

Category c: Gifts of communication

1 Gift of prophecy.
2 Kinds of tongues.
3 Interpretation of tongues.

Setting for these gifts

These are gifts which are given to God's people *when they come together*. The context of the dispensing and exercising of these gifts is the congregation gathered for worship.
cf. 'When you *come together* as a church there are divisions . . .' (1 Corinthians 11: 18).
'When you *come together*, it is not the Lord's Supper you eat . . .' (1 Corinthians 11: 20).
'When you *come together* to eat, wait for each other' (1 Corinthians 11: 33).
'The body is a *unit*, though it it made up of many parts; and

though all its parts are many, they form one *body*' (1 Corinthians 12: 12).

'We are all baptised by one Spirit into one *body*' (1 Corinthians 12: 13).

'Now you are the *body* of Christ, and each one of you is a part of it' (1 Corinthians 12: 27).

'Try to excel in gifts that build up the *church*' (1 Corinthians 14: 12).

'In the *church* I would rather speak five intelligible words to instruct . . .' (1 Corinthians 14: 19).

'So if the *whole church comes together* . . .' (1 Corinthians 14: 23).

'When you *come together*, everyone has a hymn, or a word of instruction, a revelation, a tongue or an interpretation' (1 Corinthians 14: 26).

Using gifts for service

1 The gifts are given us *to use for others*. They are developed in a climate of risk-taking and a willingness to fail. They are developed in an atmosphere where others may be observed exercising the gifts. The gifts do not come in an academic setting; they are not a cerebral exercise. They are not discovered through research, but given sovereignly by God's grace.

2 The gifts are not *trophies* dispensed as prizes for faithful or long service, etc. Each believer receives at least one gift, irrespective of his maturity or responsibility in the church.

3 The gifts are the *tools* which enable the believer to effect the ministry required. Spiritual empowering equips the believer for service.

Gifts/ministries/workings (1 Corinthians 12: 4)

'There are different kinds of gifts – but the same Spirit.'

Gifts (charismata)

1 The gifts are released upon the believers whenever they come together in worship (cf. setting for gifts).

2 The gifts are dispensed sovereignly by God upon his gathered people (1 Corinthians 12: 11).

3 Each believer in the gathering receives a gift. 'Now to each one the manifestation of the Spirit is given' (1 Corinthians 12: 7).

4 It may not necessarily be the same gift each time.

5 The believer does not retain the gift as an endowment. The believer receives gifts for the common good when God requires that they should be used.

6 No believer can stand back and say 'I have nothing to contribute.' He should be asking for whatever gift God is pleased to give him. 'How much more will your Father in heaven give good gifts to those who ask him' (Matthew 7: 11).

7 As God sees the believer faithfully exercising the gift whenever God is pleased to dispense it, it may please him to dispense the same gift more frequently to that particular person.

8 This would become particularly noticeable with a gift such as prophecy or healing.

Ministries (diakoniai)

1 The other believers (the congregation) will soon discern that a particular believer is developing a ministry through his faithful exercise of a gift.

2 The church begins to look to that particular believer for that ministry in given situations. This is liable to be the case when the prophecies, for example, are clearly edifying to the church and people are blessed by them.

3 When this happens the gift has become a ministry. These ministries may be exercised among the assembled believers or out in the world. (This seems to be what the other list (diakonion) in 1 Corinthians 12 is all about – see page 57).

Workings or offices (energemata)

1 Just as God dispenses gifts to the believers, so he appoints ministries in the church as he wills.

2 God may 'work' these ministries in various ways (1 Corinthians 12: 5).

3 He may give the ministry he has developed in a believer greater or lesser significance (local, national, international, historical). The ministry becomes an office.

Conclusion

The dynamic of the gifts is treated in the following pages, dealing with each gift separately, always understanding that one believer may be functioning in the Spirit with two or more gifts simultaneously.

Because of the 'subjective' nature of the working out of these gifts, there is a natural tendency for the uninitiated to be fearful in handling something which has such potential for good use and easy abuse. Our limited experience would show that where there is sufficient freedom in the manifestation of all the gifts as and when God wills, there are ample checks and balances to prevent the church from being led astray by any particular abuse.

The church (or church cell, such as a house group) is the place to learn to use the gifts and to develop ministries which can then be used in the world to the glory of God and the extension of God's kingdom. The meeting place is the learning place for the market place.

Recommended reading:
Arnold Bittlinger *Gifts and Graces* Hodder & Stoughton 1967
Dennis and Rita Bennett, *The Holy Spirt and You* Logos International 1971
Reginald East *Heal the Sick* Hodder & Stoughton 1977
Donald Bridge and David Phypers *Spiritual Gifts and the Church* I.V.P. 1973
Larry Christenson *In the Spirit* Kingsway Publications 1979
Harold Horton *The Gifts of the Spirit* Assemblies of God Publishing House 1954

7

THE GIFT OF TONGUES

Definition

This is spontaneous inspired utterance by the Holy Spirit, where the normal voice organs are used, but the conscious mind plays no part. The languages spoken or sung are entirely unlearned by the speaker.

Introductory comments

1 'Speaking in tongues' or 'praying in the Spirit' is what happens when a Christian believer allows the indwelling Spirit to guide the form of words he utters. It is not an act of divine ventriloquism, but an act of collaboration. *'All of them ... began to speak* in other tongues as *the Spirit enabled* them' (Acts 2: 4).

2 We do not believe that the gift of tongues is necessary as the sign of being 'filled with the Spirit'. Neither do people who are filled with the Spirit necessarily manifest this gift, though we believe that everyone wanting it could have it.

3 We do not believe that tongue-speaking should be forced on anyone.

4 We do not believe that anyone can have the true gift of tongues without being born again by the Spirit of God.

5 This gift is not manifested in the Old Testament.

6 This is the only gift which the Christian believer can use at will when used for personal edification.

7 This gift is the only gift which edifies the individual user on his own.

8 The speaker in tongues may discover that he has been

given several tongues and he employs different tongues for different purposes.

The distinction of tongues

There are apparently three distinct manifestations in the area of 'tongues':

1 The use of 'tongues' where the utterance is not understood by the speaker, but overheard by members of the public, and, without interpretation, understood by those whose own language it is: 'How is it that each of us hears them in his own native language?' (Acts 2: 4–8).

2 The use of 'tongues' in public worship. The 'language' used is unknown and should be followed by an interpretation given by the Holy Spirit (1 Corinthians 14: 27).

3 The use of 'tongues' in private (1 Corinthians 14: 4a) which needs no interpretation, though apparently this could be asked for (1 Corinthians 14: 13). Most of those who use the gift in private have never exercised it in public worship. Public exercise is a distinct anointing, yet a link betwen the public and private use appears to exist, i.e. any person who exercises the gift of tongues in public almost invariably uses the gift in private.

The purpose of tongues in general

1 Where the tongue is not understood by the speaker, but understood by an unbelieving bystander, it is meant to be a 'sign' of the kingdom of God (1 Corinthians 14: 22; Acts 2: 12, etc.).

2 'Tongues' used in public enables the church to function as a body. Different members are involved. One speaks, another interprets (though others may also have been given the 'burden' of the interpretation if they have asked for it), and yet another person (or family or the church) is blessed through the interpretation, etc.

3 But the main purpose of tongues, whether for private or public use, is edification (Jude 20,21; 1 Corinthians 14: 4a,5b).

4 We believe that a 'tongue' is always speaking to God (1 Corinthians 14:2) and that the interpretation will be either praise or prayer addressed to him.

5 Because the use of tongues frequently 'triggers off' the other gifts, prophecy has often been uttered immediately following the 'tongue', but if this is believed to be the case, the leaders should repeat the call for an interpretation.

6. 'Tongues' are used for praise – a love language when one is 'lost in wonder, love and praise' and human words are inadequate or exhausted: 'We hear them declaring the *wonders* of God in our own tongues!' (Acts 2: 11); 'For they heard them speaking in tongues and *praising* God' (Acts 10: 46).

The efficacy of tongues in private

1 'Tongues' express a verbal intimacy with God (1 Corinthians 14: 2) – providing a whole new dimension in a person's prayer life.

How can I describe this heart language of the spirit, but as a love language for the Father's ear? An intimate language springing to the lips in times of pain, grief and fear, as well as joy.... It is not only a superb piece of practical equipment, but in its use there seems to be a pervasive and wholesome aroma of the Holy Spirit, a fragrance my Spirit breathes in. (Rosemary Attlee *Renewal* Oct/Nov, 1984).

2 'Tongues' is a prayer language which no man can understand, but only God, so such prayer cannot be hindered by opposing spiritual forces (as Daniel possibly experienced, see Daniel 10: 13).

3 'Tongues' is also used as a means of prayer and intercession: 'We do not know what we ought to pray, but the Spirit himself intercedes for us with groans that words cannot express' (Romans 8: 26).

There are occasions when I want to pray for a person but can't think of much to say about him. I can pray 'Lord, be with him in his problem and give him your grace' and that's all. If I go on puzzling what else to say, I tend to think about the person rather than pray for him. But with 'tongues' I can picture him in my mind's eye and lift him up to God for some time, asking the Lord to use what I say, that it may be the prayer that the Holy Spirit wants me to make in intercession for him. (John Gunstone *Renewal* Oct/Nov, 1984)

Our attention was first drawn to the help 'tongues' could be in intercession by John Sherrill's book *They Speak with other Tongues*, where he mentions the case of Carol, the victim of a car accident. Her pastor was called in. He did not know how to pray. The doctor warned that if she recovered she might be a 'cabbage' for the rest of her life. He prayed in tongues under his breath for fifteen to twenty minutes. At the end of this time one of the patient's eyelids flickered, which he felt was a sign from God. He encouraged the distressed relatives to believe she would recover. She did.

In an editorial in *Renewal* (Oct/Nov, 1984) Edward England wrote: 'Now I find myself praying in tongues when facing a perplexing problem. It is not a substitute for thinking, for analysis, clarification and proficiency, but such prayer does enable us to range beyond where reason extends.' Again: 'When I pray in tongues I believe I am praying for specific needs, known only to God.'

Paul Y Cho, writing on prayer, says: 'Sometimes I feel a burden of prayer: yet I may not know exactly what I should pray for; or I may not have exactly the words to express what I feel. This is the time when I enter my spiritual language and can pierce through my natural inability to articulate to God what I am feeling . . .' (Paul Y Cho *Prayer* Word Ltd. 1985 pp. 127)

4 'Tongues' is also used in spiritual warfare, during times of personal conflict, or when ministering to others in the area of deliverance or exorcism. Some have discerned a special sense of power and a different 'tongue' (very stern) given by God for this kind of ministry.

Paul encourages us to 'Pray in the Spirit on all occasions with all kinds of prayers and requests' (Ephesians 6: 18) when talking of the spiritual battle we are engaged in. This dimension, and the role of tongues is apparent in the following illustrations.

5 'Speaking in tongues' had beneficial effects on new converts amongst the drug addicts from the Triad gangs whom Jackie Pullinger met within the Walled City in Hong Kong. It appears that once such new converts began to pray in tongues some remarkable deliverances took place. (cf. J Pullinger *Chasing the Dragon*).

6 'Tongues' has also been most effectively used in praying for revival. This was the experience of the Rev. Dr WC Hoover of the Methodist Church at Valparaiso, Chile, in the early 1900s (WC Hoover *Historia del Avivamiento Pentecostal en Chile* Valparaiso 1948.)

7 'Tongues' brings inspiration.

It seemed to me more and more certain as time went on that this tongue was for the edification of the spirit, not of the conscious mind, for after I had ceased speaking inspiration would come to me. Indeed much of the latter part of 'Behold Your God' was given to me in this way, for I would ask a question concerning the mysteries of Jesus Christ and apparently while I was speaking in tongues, my spirit would receive inspiration, and I would write it down. (Agnes Sanford *Sealed Orders* Logos 1972 p. 223.)

I recall the initial glow in my life, walking along the road praising the Lord in a language I knew and in a language I didn't, knowing he was nearer than the near and dearer than the dearest. With a new openness to God I found all my creative faculties awakened. There was a freshness in my soul and in my daily work. I found myself praising God more and doing my work better. (Edward England *Renewal* Oct/Nov, 1984)

8 'Tongues' keeps one refreshed both physically and spiritually according to the testimony of David du Plessis: 'Often times ... I have to get my night's sleep sitting up in a Greyhound bus or a jet plane ... The minute I close my eyes I begin to pray in the Spirit. I pray all night that way, waking up and drifting back to sleep, always praying. I don't get much sleep, but I get a lot of rest. The next morning I'm fresh and strong and ready for a full day's work.'

9 'Tongues' can be used when praying for wisdom:

I also use this kind of prayer when brief petitions to God for help and guidance are required. One situation might be when someone is coming to see me, expecting to receive some instruction or advice. In the few minutes before they arrive (and when I am usually rushing to finish the job in hand) I pray quietly in tongues in God's presence. While they are with me I sometimes pray in tongues again (unknown to them) at appropriate moments in the conversation. If it is suitable to pray together at the end of the interview, I use the gift silently for a moment or two before launching into spontaneous prayer aloud in English. (John Gunstone *Renewal* Oct/Nov, 1984)

10 'Tongues' can have a role to play in personality integration.

It would seem ... that Jung believed 'tongues' could be a positive preparation for the integration of the personality. Most of Jung's followers have sustained the same view of 'tongues' as a genuine invasion into consciousness of contents from the deepest levels of collective unconscious. It would seem that, whilst speaking in tongues, many suppressed hurts are allowed to surface from the unconscious and in the process are healed, so that the subject's personality becomes more integrated. (Morton Kelsey *Tongue Speaking* Hodder & Stoughton, 1968, p. 199).

Receiving the gift

1 The gift was first given with an anointing of the Holy Spirit and this is usually the case today. This anointing for 'tongues' may come simultaneously with conversion, but usually subsequently. Where the gift is desired by the Christian, it may be asked for: 'Ask and it will be given to you' (Matthew 7: 7); 'How much more will your Father in heaven give good gifts to those who ask him' (Matthew 7: 11b).

2 It may be helpful to begin using the gift in song.

3 Having asked, it is important to be free from as much tension as possible as this can be inhibiting. A hot bath is an ideal place. We can praise God aloud in any way we like in the privacy of the bathroom and in a relaxed way just let the new language come.

4 The Christian desirous of receiving the gift may find it helpful to be prayed for by another with the laying on of hands as in Acts 19: 6 (see 2 Timothy 1: 6 – where a gift of some kind was imparted by the laying on of hands).

5 The gift of tongues is exercised on the human side by an act of will – both its starting and stopping – just as speech in any language would be.

6 The new language may initially 'pour out', but not necessarily so. The Bible does not tie this down to any particular form.

7 Even though the language may initially 'pour out', on subsequent occasions it comes in the same way as ordinary speech, though 'in the Spirit' and not with the mind.

8 Initially there may be ecstasy (joy) in the use of the gift, which would be the case on receiving any kind of gift or blessing from God, but it is not necessarily the experience of those who use the gift on subsequent occasions.

9 The new language may be released with a few stammering words (as a baby speaks) but the more these words are used so more words are added to our vocabulary.

10 The use of the gift in public should follow a special anointing each time.

11 Many, although not all, start praying in tongues in their private prayers.

12 It is only right to thank God for this gift of tongues when it is received, but it is probably unwise to announce to people that we have the gift, except perhaps those close friends who have prayed for us in this matter.

The exercise of the gift

1 The utterance, both in private and public, may be in a human language or that of angels (1 Corinthians 13: 1).

2 When used in public it should be spoken out loudly and

clearly for all to hear. 'If the trumpet does not make a clear call, who will get ready for battle?' (1 Corinthians 14: 8).

3 The human language will not be one learned by the speaker, but may be known to someone else present in the assembly or by one who overhears the language being used for personal edification.

4 A tongue-speaker may be aware that he has been given more than one tongue. He cannot understand them, but he recognises them: we have discussed their purpose earlier.

5 The gift of tongues in private can be exercised at will anywhere. Some people pray in tongues driving their car or washing up whilst their mind can be employed elsewhere.

6 Some, like Jackie Pullinger, have found it helpful to set apart a specific time of say fifteen minutes each morning to exercise the gift of tongues privately.

7 The gift of tongues in public is not a permanent ability, but is manifested as the Spirit anoints. Unlike the private use of the gift, the person cannot expect to open his mouth at any time he decides to do so and utter words which, when interpreted, will be significant to others present. There must be the anointing.

8 Tongues uttered in public need not be expressed emotionally and would normally better not be, as this tends to be counter-productive – certainly so in the more traditional churches.

9 The gift of tongues may be exercised publicly in song. This may be a corporate offering of praise: 'Sing and make music in your heart *to the Lord*' (Ephesians 5: 19). This may be an individual communicating a message from God: 'Speak *to one another* with ... spiritual songs' (Ephesians 5: 19).

10 John Sherrill describes his first experience of this:

As the music continued, several people ... began to sing 'in the Spirit'. Soon the whole room was singing a complicated heavenly harmony – without score, created spontaneously. It was eerie, but extraordinarily beautiful. The song leader was no longer trying to direct the music, but let the melodies create themselves: without prompting one quarter of the room would suddenly start to sing very loudly while others subsided. Harmonies and counter harmonies moved in and out of each other. (John

Sherrill *They Speak with other Tongues* Pyramid Books 1970 p. 118)

11 Those present who do not have the gift may also join in singing with 'Praise the Lord', 'Hallelujah', 'Hosanna', etc.

12 The gift may also be used privately in song (1 Corinthians 14: 15).

Two testimonies about speaking in tongues:

I awoke towards morning with a strange drawing feeling about my lips. I thought, 'Now what is happening to me?'... Then I remembered my friends saying something about 'the movement of the Spirit about the lips', and so I let my voice come forth and ... I found myself ... speaking in tongues. (Agnes Sanford *Sealed Orders* Logos 1972 pp. 221–222)

When I pray in tongues, I begin by murmuring quietly or saying silently sounds which quite quickly develop into a language-like flow. I've never understood the language (if language it be), nor, as far as I know, has anyone else ... I don't consciously control what I say. I don't think (to myself) 'I haven't used a "Zzzz" sound yet: I'll try and fit it in.' If there is any control by me on what sounds I make, it must happen at a deep conscious level. I'm not aware of it. (John Gunstone *Renewal* Oct/Nov, 1984)

Response to 'Tongues'

1 When used in public there should not be more than three individual 'tongues' at any one point in the meeting (1 Corinthians 14: 27).

2 There should be silence for an interpretation following each 'tongue' offered in this way. If there is no interpretation, the leader should not allow 'tongues' to continue as it does not edify the rest of the assembly (1 Corinthians 14: 19,28).

3 The congregation should *all* pray for the interpretation

when a 'tongue' is given, including the person who had the 'tongue' (1 Corinthians 14: 13).

4 It is obvious that when there is a general 'speaking in tongues' (1 Corinthians 14: 23) or 'singing in tongues' in the Spirit of praise or prayer, no interpretation is necessary because *all* are addressing God (1 Corinthians 14: 2). No one interpretation would be adequate in such a case. It's helpful for the leader to explain to all the congregation what is happening (if not on every occasion, then at least from time to time).

5 Experience in the public use of the gift seems to indicate that often the gifts of the Spirit are manifested in a sequence which begins with speaking in tongues and leads on to interpretation and then to other gifts. The same pattern appears to follow in the release of the gifts of the Spirit to individuals.

6 The leaders in the church will always aim to ensure that everything shall 'be done in a fitting and orderly way' (1 Corinthians 14: 40).

7 The use of 'tongues' at a public meeting will call into operation not only the gift of 'interpretation', but also the gift of 'discernment'. There are false 'tongues' as there are false prophets. The enemy will simulate every gift of God whenever he can. We all know that others use 'tongues' for enemy purposes.

In the South of Chile, the machis (witch doctors) amongst the Mapuche Indians all spoke in 'tongues' during their initiation rites. We have also met emotionally disturbed people who wander around 'speaking in tongues', which clearly do not originate from the Spirit of God.

Schizophrenics are sometimes given *deceptive tongues* which they cannot control themselves and cannot stop when they wish.

Final exhortation

'I would like every one of you to speak in tongues' (1 Corinthians 14: 5) may mean 'I want you all to continue to speak in tongues.' The emphasis here may be less on the 'any one' doing it, but rather be an encouragement to those who 'speak in tongues' to keep on doing so. Do not be put off! Keep it up!

Recommended reading:
Morton T Kelsey *Tongue Speaking* Hodder & Stoughton 1973
John L Sherrill *They Speak With Other Tongues* Pyramid Book 1970

8

THE GIFT OF INTERPRETATION

Definition

This gift is a supernatural revelation through the Holy Spirit which enables the Christian believer to communicate in the language of the listeners the dynamic equivalent of that which was spoken 'in tongues'.

Introductory comments

1 The interpretation is not an operation through the mind of the interpreter (except in the instance of the language being known) but of the mind of God.

2 The interpretation is just as much a supernatural manifestation as the original utterance in tongues: both are given 'in the Spirit'.

3 The congregation will remain unedified by 'a tongue' if there is no interpretation. Paul says that in public he would rather speak five intelligible words to instruct others than ten thousand words in a tongue (1 Corinthians 14: 19).

4 Paul forbids the continued use of tongues without an interpretation following such utterances (1 Corinthians 14: 28).

5 The interpreter receives the burden (dynamic equivalent) of the tongue and not a translation.

Purpose of the gift

This is to enable the church to *understand* the manifestation of the gift of *tongues* when it has been exercised in public through a solo utterance in speech or song.

How is the gift received?

1 A right relationship with God and with one's fellow beings must be maintained by the individual Christian believer.

2 The gift may be asked for whenever the need for it is felt, always remembering: a) that the Lord is soveriegn and distributes his gifts as he pleases, and b) that our heavenly Father will not give us a gift that is bad for us (Matthew 7: 11).

3 Some receive the gift without asking – the Lord bestows it sovereignly. One young person from an Anglican church near Viña del Mar (in Chile), all freshly renewed through the Holy Spirit, began to pray 'in tongues' for the first time. A girl in their number began to expostulate in amazement: 'He is saying this – now he is saying this, etc.' She had never asked for the gift, did not know of the gift's availability to her, and was not expecting it.

4 As with prophecy, the gift of interpretation may come with just a few words at first. The rest will follow as we speak out in faith.

5 The interpretation may also be given to us *in toto*.

6 The 'words' or 'burden' of interpretation may be accompanied by a sense of joyful ecstasy or some similar subjective feelings, such as a swelling sensation in the tongue or a tensing of the throat (as with prophecy) which seem to be urging speech. Christine Huggett gets a 'thumb' in the stomach as a sign that God wants her to speak out a tongue during a meeting. (J C Huggett *It Hurts to Heal* Kingsway Publications 1984 p. 58)

7 As the 'tongue' speaker continues, the interpretation

may come to another in words, pictures of symbols or through an inspired thought.

8 Alternatively, the person being given the interpretation may hear the message of the person speaking 'in tongues' as though the person were speaking directly to him in his own language or in some other language with which he is familiar.

9 If the 'tongue' is a sung solo, the interpretation may be given in song as well, but not necessarily so. It is profoundly beautiful when it is – especially when it is the same melody, which sometimes happens.

10 On the other hand, the interpretation may be given in very different form from that of the original utterance. Without violating its meaning, it may be given in pictorial, parabolic, descriptive or literal language, according to the dictates of the Spirit or the character of the one interpreting. The Spirit is at liberty to operate as he wills.

11 It is not necessary for a person who has a 'tongue' which he uses for private prayer to have an interpretation, but it seems it may be given if it is desired/needed and asked for (1 Corinthians 14: 13).

12 Neither is it necessary for there to be an interpretation when many are singing together 'in the Spirit', because the purpose is that *all* should join in, each offering his own praises and thanksgiving and intercession as the Lord gives the utterance. No interpretation would be possible since each person is saying/singing something different in praise to God.

Exercise of the gift

1 Greater faith is needed for interpretation than for speaking in 'tongues'. Whereas the tongue is usually unintelligible, the interpretation is given publicly for the edification of the whole congregation and must be understood and tested.

2 The person who speaks 'in tongues' should also pray for the interpretation, but this is not limited solely to the

person who spoke 'the tongue'. All those others who speak 'in tongues' should also be praying for the interpretation.

3 It is a very affirming experience to pray for and receive an interpretation, and, before one has opened one's mouth, to hear someone else utter exactly the same words one has been given oneself. The sense of the Spirit's presence and moving becomes wonderfully real.

4 At times one person may be given the first part of the interpretation and another given the words to continue or terminate. But care must be taken here because: it may become tempting for people to 'outdo' each other in interpretation. It should be noted that 'someone must interpret' (1 Corinthians 14: 27) may also be translated as 'Let one interpret' (as RSV), which would mean, therefore, that it is only permissible for one person to interpret, effectively ruling out such 'serial interpretations'.

5 Since it is the Lord who gives the interpretation, the length of time speaking may not correspond to the time spent over the actual speaking 'in tongues'. The interpretation may seem to be longer or shorter in length than the original utterance. There is nothing strange about this. It would be the case also for an Englishman translating/ interpreting for a Spaniard.

6 It would seem better that the one who speaks should stand (1 Corinthians 14: 30).

7 It is wise for the one who speaks to speak out 'loud and clear'.

8 Initially interpretations may be a little 'muddy' due to nervousness.

Points of order

1 Where 'tongues' are legitimately employed the leader should ensure that time is given for interpretation.

2 Someone should interpret each separate utterance.

3 There must be no competition among interpreters. Several present may sense they have an 'interpretation' revealing the Spirit's meaning (1 Corinthians 14: 26) when in fact they may be being given prophecies.

4 Some may feel that they have been given a more

adequate unfolding of the message 'in tongues', which often could be the case, but they must 'hold their peace'.

5 On the other hand, if someone has a further revelation along the same lines as that already given, this may be a call to 'complete the interpretation' (1 Corinthians 14: 30). A secondary 'interpretation' may *complement*, but may not *contradict* what has been said.

6 If there is a genuine call to 'contradict' an 'interpretation', this will come through the 'gift of discernment' and must not be introduced under the guise of interpretation, which would tend to debase this gift and cause confusion.

7 If the leadership discerned that 'a tongue' was ill-conceived, obviously any interpretation of that particular utterance would only add to the confusion, and this should be explained, otherwise there should be no more utterances 'in tongues' at that time.

8 Similarly it may be that an 'interpretation' is ill-conceived and discernment must be exercised. This is illustrated by the Huggetts at a healing service at a Pentecostal Church in the Midlands when a lady spoke 'in tongues':

Immediately John saw a picture of a fireplace. But at the same moment a man screeched out an interpretation in very emotional tones. It included quotations from Scripture and mention of the blood of the Lamb. But I discerned that it was motivated by a religious evil spirit. It left many of us feeling cold and we found it difficult to get back into an atmosphere of worship.

The pastor was leading this part of the service, and when he eventually handed over to John, my husband shared how he had seen a fireplace with coals in the grate but no fire. It was a picture of the church there. God was calling the people to return to him before he would rekindle the fire of his Spirit in that place... I believed John's fireplace was the *true* interpretation of the 'tongue' given earlier in the service. (J and C Huggett: *It Hurts to Heal*, Kingsway, 1984, p. 173/4)

9 In a very large meeting with many visitors present it

may be right to allow only those known to the leadership the liberty to interpret.

10 No amount of 'anointing' can allow anyone to go beyond the word of God. No more than three 'tongues' and three interpretations at the most in one 'spot' at a meeting are permitted (1 Corinthians 14: 27).

9

THE GIFT OF PROPHECY

Definition

'The gift of prophecy (1 Corinthians 12: 10; 14: 1) is the special ability that God gives to members of the Body of Christ to receive and communicate an immediate message of God to his gathered people, a group among them or any one of his people individually, through a divinely anointed utterance.'

Peter Wagner (adapted).

Introductory comments

1 In its general sense prophecy covers a spiritual ministry by any servant of the Lord. In the Old Testament this was usually something distinct from the priesthood, though some priests also prophesied (e.g. Ezekiel). In the Old Testament, prophets were preachers, seers and miracle workers – a wide ranging ministry.

2 In its more specific sense 'prophecy' covers two areas: forthtelling and foretelling:

a) *Forthtelling*, such as preaching, teaching and evangelism, which could be through speaking, writing, drama and music, etc. A prophet may also be a person with a special burden for social justice (like Amos) who identifies areas in need of reform and who is emboldened to denounce the forces or sources of the evil. Such forthtelling usually emanates from, and appeals to, both the intellect and compassion of man. This office is recognised as authentic for the church today (see Ephesians 4: 11).

   b) *Foretelling* some event(s) of the future such as John
did broadly in the book of Revelation or Agabus did
specifically and personally in the book of Acts (21: 10,11).
Such foretelling emanates from the Spirit (Revelation 1:
10).

3 The gift of prophecy is not confined to recognised
prophets (Ephesians 4: 11), but is more widely distributed in
the church in fulfilment of Joel 2: 28. So we read 'For you
can all prophesy in turn' (1 Corinthians 14: 31).

In apostolic teaching there is a distinguishing line drawn
between the gift and the ministry of prophecy. Though all
can prophesy, by virtue of the Holy Spirit's anointing, not
all are prophets. Though all can 'manifest' the gift of
prophecy, only some are 'appointed' to the ministry of a
prophet (cf. 1 Corinthians 12: 7,28,29; 14: 29–33a). So
Agabus arrived at Caesarea to meet Paul, who was lodging
with Philip the evangelist and his four daughters. Although
these four girls had the gift of prophecy, Agabus had the
ministry of a prophet (the only one featured as such in the
Acts of the Apostles). It was Agabus, not one of the four
girls, who was entrusted with a major directive prophecy
for Paul (Acts 21: 8–11).

The purpose of prophecy

1 Prophecy brings glory to Jesus Christ (Revelation
19: 10c).

2 Prophecy builds up, encourages (this could include
warnings) and consoles (1 Corinthians 14: 3).

3 Prophecy serves as a sign for unbelievers to convince
them (1 Corinthians 14: 24,25).

3 'Prophecy is not the equivalent of Scripture. Prophecy
is a particular word for a particular congregation at a
particular time through a particular person. Scripture is for
all Christians in all places at all times. That is the difference'
(Michael Green *To Corinth with Love* Hodder and Stoughton
1982 p. 75).

5 Paul wrote to the Corinthian church that this gift was
for the positive *building up* of the church (1 Corinthians 14:

3), whereas the prophets had also to 'pull down' and
'denounce' (Jeremiah 1: 10).

6 This gift may also be used to foretell (John 16: 13; Acts
11: 28; 21: 10,11), but care should be exercised both in
giving and receiving this (see Deuteronomy 18: 20–22).

7 Though prophecy may be given to warn, it is not
necessarily irrevocable – see Jeremiah 18: 7,8.

The exercise of prophecy

1 In the exercise of all the gifts 'Follow the way of love'
(1 Corinthians 14: 1). Love must always be the motive.

2 This gift is to be eagerly desired (1 Corinthians 14:
1,39) and could be exercised by any anointed believers.

3 Prophecies should be restricted to two or three at any
one time (1 Corinthians 14: 29).

4 The supernatural revelation behind the message may
come to one prophesying through meditating on scripture,
visions (Acts 18: 9), dreams (Matthew 2: 13), trances (Acts
22: 17), impressions (i.e. a word or a picture), an audible
voice or even an angelic visitation.

5 The gift may come to an individual Christian in times
of prayer concerning himself (Acts 2: 17–18). It may come in
an obscure manner and he will need to leave time for the
Lord to confirm it.

6 The words or visions for a prophecy are most likely to
come in an atmosphere of prayer and adoration (Acts 13: 2).

7 The prophecy may be uttered loudly or quietly, in
song, poetry, prose or mime, or any combination of these,
but notice, as Michael Green says, 'Prophecy does not rant.'

8 Having asked for the gift, while consciously seeking to
maintain a right and open relationship to the Lord, one may
sense an anointing for the utterance of the prophecy – a
witness of the Spirit in one's own heart. There may be
physical sensations, often related to the mouth area –
dryness, tingling, slight swelling. An anointed person will
begin to recognise the peculiar ways God is urging him to
speak.

9 A person receiving an anointing for prophecy is not
bound to utter it instantaneously. The prophecy may be
appropriate for use on a later occasion. The prophet can
wait. 'The spirits of the prophets are subject to the control

of prophets' (1 Corinthians 14: 32). There need be no fear of forgetfulness: 'The Holy Spirit ... will remind you of everything I have said to you' (John 14: 26).

10 The one prophesying should always be fully in control of himself (1 Corinthians 14: 32), and to express himself with too much emotion will be counter-productive (cf. 7 above).

11 The one who anticipates the gift may be given the first two or three words only. He speaks these out as an act of faith. Often he will not know how it will continue or end. The first words are like a stopper in the bottle. Once they are out the rest will follow. 'It's just like opening a packet of tissues' says John Huggett, 'I receive a few words in my mind and as I speak them out I'm given a few more, and so on, until it suddenly stops.' (J and C Huggett *It Hurts to Heal* Kingsway, 1984, p. 57)

12 Or he may simply sense a burden or see a picture in his mind's eye.

13 Don't be surprised if the prophecy is brief. (cf. Haggai 1: 13. '"I am with you" declares the Lord.' Very short, but very comforting!)

14 Beware of continuing in the flesh when the anointing has lifted. Cease immediately the anointing ceases even if it appears to leave things in the air. It may well be all that God wants to say or he may intend someone else to continue it (1 Corinthians 14: 30).

15 There may be a great sense of ecstasy (especially initially) in the exercise of this gift, but it is not necessarily the experience of those who continue in the use of it.

16 The introductory style of commencing may be formal and biblical, such as: 'I am the Lord' or 'Thus says the Holy Spirit' or even possibly 'Lo! I tell you a mystery' (1 Corinthians 15: 51 RSV). Or it may be reported in a more relaxed way, such as 'I believe the Holy Spirit/the Lord is saying/telling us/you that ...' Plenty of room for variety in God's leading should be allowed and expected.

17 The prophecy itself may be couched in biblical language or quotations of scriptural texts. The book of Revelation is a prophecy (Revelation 1: 3), which contains over 400 citations from the Old Testament.

18 The fact that the speaker may use Elizabethan English should not surprise anyone. If someone has soaked his mind in such language through reading the King James version and been accustomed to hearing God speak in that way it will not be surprising if the Holy Spirit causes him to recall God's word in such old fashioned language.

19 There is no need for prophecy to be given in a strange voice. Neither should it be discredited on that account since this strangeness may be due to nervousness.

20 The gift of prophecy should always be sought and offered in great humility. 'It is not an ego-trip for the person concerned' (Michael Green). Frequent misuse will quickly bring prophecy into disrepute.

21 This is a purely human and subjective observation, but probably in the most pure prophecy eighty percent is of God and twenty percent human. In some cases it could be twenty percent of God and eighty percent human, but it would be sad to reject the latter completely when God really has something he wants to communicate.

22 Let the church be aware that some so-called 'prophecy' may be uttered out of wishful thinking, vested interests, because of a 'chip on the shoulder', or simply a lying spirit. (Ezekiel chapters 13 and 14 give some important warnings in this regard.)

23 It is best to limit the use of this gift to members of the local church asking visitors to refrain from utterance so that good order may be maintained.

The setting for prophecy

This will normally be when people are 'gathered together' (1 Corinthians 14: 23) for worship. Probably Paul had in mind a small group because he seemed to envisage participation by all present. Thus we could expect to find prophecy being used in a small gathering ('home group' cells are the best places to learn how to exercise it), but it will also be used in a larger congregational setting.

Response to prophecy

1 All prophecy should be carefully weighed (1 Corinthians 14: 29). Prophecy is uttered by humans who could be misled. No one should engage in prophecy who is not willing that his prophecy should be tested. Here another example may help:

> At a rally in London a Christian woman gave a 'prophecy'. It was couched in religious phraseology, but delivered in a wailing tone and quickly I discerned it was not from the Lord. We were in an Anglican Church and after the woman had sat down the vicar stood up to say that he thought that the 'gift' should be tested. A number of folk in the congregation raised their hands to agree that God had not spoken. Then John swiftly encouraged people to turn their eyes back to Jesus (J and C Huggett *It Hurts to Heal* Kingsway, 1984, p. 173).

But we should be swift to hear and slow to speak and not rush into publically correcting prophecy in case when we root out the weeds we may root up the wheat with them (cf. Matthew 13: 29). When prophecy is of God there is a general consensus that it is so. When it is 'of the flesh' nearly everybody knows it except possibly the person prophesying who may have been deceived.

2 The 'spiritual gift of discernment' should be exercised.

3 The prophecy should be tested against the touchstone of scripture (2 Peter 1: 20).

4 The prophecy should be tested by whether it confirms what God is already doing.

5 The prophecy should be tested by determining its benefit.

6 It may be best, like Mary, simply to store up the words of a prophecy in our hearts (Luke 2: 51). No other immediate action should normally be taken unless the prophecy itself is a clear confirmation of what the Lord has already revealed in some other way.

The Huggetts were living in the North of England. One night Christine Huggett saw a picture of Dick Whittington with his little bag slung over his shoulder. 'It means we are going back down London way' said John, quoting from the old rhyme, 'Turn again Whittington... Lord Mayor of London'. 'During the next few days we asked friends to pray about a possible move. One of them was given the word "Sussex". We decided to store these things in our minds. If they were from the Lord they would come to fruition' (p. 133). In the autumn Christine 'began to get the impression of a very long building set in extensive grounds' (p. 151). After advertisements in the *Church Times*, they were led to Southwater, a village near Horsham in West Sussex (p. 152) to a place which exactly fitted all the details of their vision (see J and C Huggett, *It Hurts to Heal*).

7 There must be a witness of the Spirit in the heart of the one to whom the prophecy is addressed, or if it is in public we would expect a degree of acceptance by others (if not at the time, then later).

8 The character of the one giving the prophecy is relevant. 'By their fruit you will recognise them.' We must be alert because Jesus warned us that there are false prophets (Matthew 7: 20).

9 Do not over-rate this gift, because, at the moment, 'we know in part and we prophesy in part' (1 Corinthians 13: 9) – only later will we know in full.

10 Do not under-rate this gift either, as some of the Thessalonians were wont to do – 'do not treat prophecies with contempt' (1 Thessalonians 5: 20).

11 It is helpful at the end of a period when the gifts of the Spirit have been manifested for one of the leadership to summarise briefly the burden of what he feels the Lord has been saying to the church through the Spirit: 'He who has an ear to hear, let him hear what the Spirit says to the churches' (Revelation 2: 7).

12 It may be appropriate to invite the Holy Spirit to apply the burden of the prophecies to the hearts of the congregation then and there.

Conclusion

If both those who exercise the gift and those to whom the prophecy is directed make love their aim, there will be a conducive climate for the gift to emerge and flourish. 'Love will be welcoming towards embryonic prophecy. Love will be forgiving when mistakes are made. Love will bind those with this gift and those without it into an interdependent unity' (Michael Green).

Recommended reading:
Donald Bridge *Signs & Wonders Today* I.V.P. (Appendix 3)
George Mallone *Those Controversial Gifts* Hodder and Stoughton (Ch. 2)
Michael Cassidy *Bursting the Wine Skins* Hodder and Stoughton (Appendix B)
Michael Green *To Corinth with Love* Hodder and Stoughton (Ch. 8)

10

THE GIFT OF DISCERNMENT

Definition

This is a supernatural gift of perception given sovereignly by God to enable individuals in the church to distinguish the motivating spirit behind certain words or deeds.

General comments

1 In the world of painting and antiques there is a gift called 'jizz' which instinctively conveys instant recognition of the indefinable. The gift of discernment operates in a similar way through the Spirit. It is transrational.

2 Some suggest that this gift is always paired with the gift of prophecy as 'tongues' is paired with interpretation.

3 But just as the gift of interpretation, according to scripture, is not linked exclusively with 'tongues' – both Joseph and Daniel could 'interpret' dreams – so we believe the gift of discernment has wider application.

4 Any Christian, through the Spirit, is able to evaluate according to the true light of Christ (1 Corinthians 2: 4).

5 Any mature Christian who is trained in the word of God is able to distinguish between good and evil (Hebrews 5: 14).

6 A demonised person can discern a good spirit. The most obvious example is that of Legion confessing who Christ really was (Mark 5: 7), but there is also the case of the slave girl who shouted at Paul (Acts 16: 17).

7 In extreme cases of some demonised persons, even the

general public may be aware of satanic activity. (Mark 5: 2–5).

8 We believe the gift of discernment is something more than this. It is a revelatory gift from God.

9 Beware of being deceived even in this. Some have imagined they were operating with a gift of perception when in fact it was a degree of suspicion.

The use of the gift in weighing prophecy

1 The Church is told to test 'all things'. The context of this implies the testing of prophetic utterances (1 Thessalonians 5: 21).

2 The Church is told to test the 'spirit' of the one prophesying (1 John 4: 1–6).

3 Paul seems to be saying that in the church gathering several should use this gift of discernment simultaneously, 'the others should weigh carefully what is said' (1 Corinthians 14: 29).

The use of the gift in other areas

1 In the deliverance ministry for those afflicted, oppressed, tormented and demonised, such as Gehazi (2 Kings 5: 26). (cf. chapter 27 'Healing the oppressed')

2 In unmasking a worker of evil, such as Elymas (Acts 13: 10).

3 For exposing the source of error in believers, as in the case of Peter (Matthew 15: 16; 16: 23).

4 The gift of discernment is required for recognising 'all kinds of counterfeit miracles, signs and wonders' and 'every sort of evil that deceives those who are perishing' (2 Thessalonians 2: 9,10).

5 For discerning a good spirit in a man, as with Christ in the case of Nathaniel (John 1: 47): as the psalmist says, 'Deep calls to deep.'

6 For discerning someone else's spiritual states.

George Fox, the founder of the Quakers, or the Society of Friends, believed he had this gift. 'The Lord had given me a Spirit of Discerning by which I many times saw the states and conditions of people and could try their spirits whether they were of God.'

How does the gift operate?

There will, of course, be great variety here as the subjective impressions will differ from person to person, but it may be helpful to detail how it works for some with experience in this area. Human behaviour is normally motivated by the human spirit which may be influenced by a demonic/satanic spirit or it may be influenced by the Holy Spirit. The true spiritual source of motivation may be discerned in the look of a person. There is a sense of transparency or opacity about him/her. Jesus said 'Your eye is the lamp of your body. When your eyes are good, your whole body also is full of light. But when they are bad, your body also is full of darkness, see to it then... (Luke 11: 34,35).

Demonic:

Discernment of a demonised person may sometimes be confirmed by one of the following:

1 A tell-tale word superimposed over a face may be seen.

2 A second face (like an old wizened one) may intermittently appear superimposed over a younger one.

3 Shadows or darkened passages on a face reveal the presence of afflicting spirits.

4 Shapes superimposed over parts of the anatomy, such as a sinister creature.

5 In extreme cases of demonic possession a supernatural gift of discernment may not be necessary at all. Even the general public recognised the case of Legion (Mark 5). (cf. the section on the discernment in 'Healing the oppressed', chapter 27.)

Divine:

1 A person under the anointing of the Holy Spirit may appear to have a light above his head like a flame (a tongue), or round the head like a halo or sometimes an aura outlining the whole body.

A friend known to us was looking at a godly preacher and saw an 'aura' surrounding his body, except for one part of it – the left shoulder. She commented on this to the person beside her, asking what she thought it meant. The reply came 'I don't know, but I think it may be the enemy and we should pray against it.' This they did as the preacher continued. Suddenly a woman in the front row shrieked diabolically and ran out. The broken aura once again completed the outline of the preacher.

2 As we minister with eyes open, we begin to discern physical manifestations which indicate that the Spirit of God is *on* someone. The following may be observed: A 'look' of being engaged with God; eyelids fluttering almost uncontrollably; flushing coming up the neck; shaking or trembling; weeping or laughing, etc.

What to do when something sinister is revealed

1 Trust; we believe that what God by his Spirit is revealing can only be for good (Romans 8: 28).

2 Pray; we ask God what to do; we ask for the gift of wisdom etc. (James 1: 5).

3 We should never suggest even the hint of an infesting spirit without very clear confirmation through some manifestation in the person being ministered to, and also from those in the ministry team who have experience in this area.

4 Share; we seek to share what we believe God may be saying humbly and simply with those we are ministering with and look for some kind of confirmation or check from them.

5 They may encourage us by saying they too have sensed the same or by saying that though they were not themselves shown it, their spirit affirms that what we are saying is true.

6 If an 'external' afflicting spirit is discerned, it may be commanded to go immediately in Christ's name.

7 It may be more appropriate to arrange for a deliverance ministry at a separate time and place.

8 If there appears to be a need for an exorcism, (see

chapter 26 'Healing the oppressed') the evil spirit should be bound in the name of Christ and the case referred to the church leadership.

What to do when something else is revealed

1 The Holy Spirit may sometimes be surfacing emotional pain for healing which may produce physical manifestations similar to those of demonisation.

2 Bless the person concerned with God's peace.

3 Arrange for the person to have counselling and ministry in the area of inner healing (see chapter 28).

11
WORDS OF WISDOM

Definition

The gift of the word of wisdom is the special ability that God gives to members of the body of Christ to receive instant insight on how a given revelation (word of knowledge, prophecy) may best be applied to a specific situation or need arising in the body of Christ, or how a given situation or need is to be resolved or helped or healed.

Introductory comments

In the divine storehouse of God's infinite mind he holds all the fruits of time and eternity. Four kinds of wisdom are distinguishable:

1 There is normal human wisdom which is naturally applied knowledge/sagacity. Such wisdom, rightly used, can contribute much to human progress – however it also panders to man's pride. For that reason the scripture says 'I will destroy the wisdom of the wise; and the intelligence of the intelligent I will frustrate' (1 Corinthians 1: 19).

2 There is this fallen world's supernatural wisdom. This was one basis of the first temptation when the woman saw that the forbidden fruit was 'desirable for gaining wisdom' and 'took some and ate it' (Genesis 3: 6). Such wisdom was strictly forbidden by God.

3 There is the spiritual wisdom, such as is exemplified by the book of Proverbs, etc., and we are told to seek to acquire this kind of wisdom. Ultimately, Christ is the wisdom of

God (1 Corinthians 1: 24). Scripture says that 'if any of you lacks wisdom, he should ask God ... and it will be given to him' (James 1: 5). Paul prayed that the Colossian believers would be filled 'with the knowledge of his will through all spiritual wisdom and understanding' (Colossians 1: 9).

4 Then there is the word of wisdom – which is the sudden miraculous giving of wisdom to meet a given situation, answer a particular question or utilise a particular piece of knowledge, natural or supernatural (see Dennis and Rita Bennett *The Holy Spirit and You* Logos International 1971 p. 162–3).

The purpose of the word of wisdom

Scriptural examples

1 Solomon prayed 'Give thy servant therefore an understanding mind to govern thy people, that I may discern between good and evil...' (1 Kings 3: 9 RSV) His possession of this gift was manifest when two women came to him with their babies, one dead and one alive. Each mother claimed the living child to be her own. Through a 'word of knowledge' Solomon was shown who was the mother of the living child and by a 'word of wisdom' he was able publicly to resolve the problems by suggesting the living child be cut in two! Whilst one mother agreed, the other pleaded that the first mother keep the baby. Solomon ordered the baby to be given to the latter (1 Kings 3: 16–28).

2 In the New Testament Jesus warned his disciples of persecution to come, but promised them 'I will give you words and wisdom that none of your adversaries will be able to resist or contradict' (Luke 21: 15).

3 Jesus himself manifested this wisdom in the way he taught his parables; in the way he answered his accusers over the matter of authority (Matthew 21: 23–27); in the question of paying taxes (Matthew 22: 15–22); in the way he obtained the tax money by acting on a 'word of knowledge' and sending Peter to fish for it (Matthew 17: 27); in the way he answered trick questions about the commandments (Mark 2: 27, John 8: 7); and in the way he responded to the Chief Priest, Pilate and Herod.

Modern Day Examples

A mental breakdown.

In January, 1984, the wife of a pastor in Colorado was struck with a complete mental breakdown. Although she remained at home, she was under the supervision of a psychiatrist in their congregation, and she required the constant attention of her pastor-husband. It became necessary for him to be with her at all times, except for Sunday mornings, when a woman from the congregation would stay with her so that he could preach. This condition persisted without any measurable release for two and a half months, effectively curtailing the ministry of the pastor, and limiting his activity to grieving over and praying for the release of his wife.

I was present at an elders' meeting (during) the last week in March, in which an extensive time of prayer was held for the wife of the pastor. As I was on my way home from that meeting, the Lord suddenly revealed to me that the condition of the pastor's wife was due to the resistance of the elders to the moving of the Holy Spirit, particularly with reference to speaking in tongues and ministering healing to the sick. Through the ministry of the Spirit, I saw that the relationship of the pastor to his wife was a picture of the relationship of the Holy Spirit to this particular congregation, and even to the denomination as a whole, and that because of their resistance to the moving of the Holy Spirit, he was grieving and weeping over the incompetence of the congregation, even as the pastor was in grief over the incompetence of his wife.

Sensing the heaviness of this insight, I began to ask for confirmation, which I received two days later through reading Ezekiel 24. In this chapter, the Lord uses the death of the prophet's wife as a message to his people concerning the state of their relationship with him. With this passage as confirmation, I shared the word with the elders and the pastor and one elder heard it as from the Lord. They called a special session of the elders to discuss the matter, and the following week made a decision to give priority time in the elders' meeting to prayer for the congregation, and to the exploration of how to begin to pray for the sick. Upon hearing of this decision, I was greatly encouraged, sensing an imminent break-through of the move of the Spirit.

Within one week of the decision to accept this word as from God, the wife of the pastor began to show marked improvement, and as I write this, some six weeks later, she is fully recovered and functioning normally in the role of church member and pastor's wife. Her psychiatrist has termed her recovery 'unusual, even miraculous', and is in the process of removing her from all medication.

I praise God for his persistence, for his severe mercy, and for his grace in showing his people that to walk in obedience and responsiveness to him is indeed health and peace.

(Taken from an article by Gary Wiens in *First Fruits* September, 1984 Vineyard Ministries International)

A case of arthritis. Some two years ago a lady from Wales came to kneel at the communion rails after the service at St Andrew's, Chorleywood (probably in response to a word of knowledge for someone with rheumatoid arthritis in the hands). As she was being prayed for, nothing seemed to be happening. After a while one of the team praying offered the suggestion (word of knowledge) that it was due to something which happened in her teens. The leader of the group, asked her (word of wisdom) if she could recall any trauma or problem to do with her 'teens'. She looked quite blank. 'Do you mind if we pray over these years?' she was asked. She readily consented and the Lord was asked to heal whatever it was. As this was done the sufferer suddenly began to weep profusely. The tears fell on her hands. Suddenly the fingers loosened up and she was healed. She has returned since to give thanks to God. She is even typing again quite normally.

The 'word of wisdom' revealed how to minister. The 'sufferer' herself had no idea what the trauma was she had suffered as a teenager even after the healing had taken place.

Irrational fear of death (An example of a word of wisdom being given showing how to act on word of knowledge.)

A pastor was praying for a man named Bill, who had an irrational fear of illness and death. A word (of knowledge) came into his mind. It was a very embarrassing word. He dismissed it, but it kept coming back. He climbed into his car and drove across to Bill's house. As there was no possible way to be tactful about it, he took Bill aside and simply said the word. Bill began to tremble. He poured out a story, which, until that moment, his conscious mind had resolutely refused to remember.

When Bill was a young boy, an uncle had made sexual advances to him. The frightened boy ran away and told no one, but loathed the uncle from that day forward. A little later the uncle died. The boy was made to look at his uncle in the coffin (exactly as in 'The Three Faces of Eve'). Staring at the corpse, he was filled with glee that his uncle was dead . . . and then appalled at the thought. Any psychiatrist could piece together the rest of the story. A boy growing into manhood had carried the conviction that he was to blame for his uncle's death. Had he not wished it and gloated over it?

Here was the situation into which Jesus could come. 'The same yesterday, today and forever', he could come now into Bill's life, and sponge it away. They knelt and asked him. The fear of death was washed away. (D Bridge and D Phypers *More than Tongues can Tell* Hodder and Stoughton 1982. p. 42).

Practical effects

1 The 'word of wisdom' indicates how to apply the insights revealed through words of knowledge, prophecy, etc.

2 It indicates how to pray for a person, especially when one is ministering healing to him/her.

3 It helps to avoid some dangers which might possibly confront one in life or that might affect others.

4 It helps to know how to speak constructively in a difficult situation.

5 It causes mankind to wonder and give glory to God.

How is the gift received?

1 It may be given sovereignly by God. One discovers one has been given it.

2 It may be requested from God: 'Eagerly desire spiritual gifts' (1 Corinthians 14: 1); 'Ask and it will be given to you and you will receive . . . How much more will your Father in heaven give good gifts to those who ask him' (Matthew 7: 7,11b).

3 It may be imparted through another who has the gift. Paul wrote 'I long to see you so that I may impart to you some spiritual gift . . .' (Romans 1: 11).

How 'words of wisdom' are exercised

1 The recipient seeks to be in a right, open and prayerful relationship with the Lord.

2 In the context of a healing ministry the gift is usually exercised with others present.

3 The recipient is given a spiritual revelation – God's perspective in a situation. This revelation could take a number of forms: by receiving a mind's-eye picture or word, by hearing with his 'inner ear', etc. God, being sovereign, can reveal this in any way he wills.

4 It is sometimes accompanied by a 'word of knowledge', revealing some fact previously unknown to the persons ministering and possibly the person being ministered to.

5 A word of wisdom is sometimes given as a prophetic utterance and has all the characteristics of prophecy.

6 Words of wisdom almost always come in the exchange of what is happening.

7 In the context of ministry someone may be shown how to respond to some unexpected situation. Having been given miraculously some 'word of knowledge' oneself, or this being revealed to someone else who shares it with the rest of the ministering group, it becomes clear how to minister, pray, speak, or otherwise act.

Responses to 'words of wisdom'

This will be manifest in three areas:

1 The perceptive way in which others present discern its spiritual origin.

2 The practical way the person ministering uses the wisdom. He/she can cover areas in the life of the person ministered to, not in an accusing or condemning way, but wisely, compassionately and positively.

3 The positive way the person being ministered to reacts.

Results from acting on 'words of wisdom'

1 There will be blessing to the person receiving such ministry.

2 Healing, release or help of some kind to the person ministered to, or a solution to a problem, which may also include the blessings of new faith.

3 Amazement expressed by the onlookers.

4 Glory should be given to God by all.

Conclusion

The Spirit searches all things, even the deep things of God. For who among men knows the thoughts of a man except the man's spirit within him? In the same way no-one knows the thoughts of God except the Spirit of God. We have not received the spirit of the world but the Spirit who is from God, that we may understand what God has freely given us. This is what we speak, not in words taught us by human wisdom but in words taught by the Spirit, expressing spiritual truths in spiritual words (1 Corinthians 2: 10–13).

12
WORDS OF KNOWLEDGE

Definition

This is the supernatural revelation of facts about a person or situation, which is not learned through the efforts of the natural mind, but is a fragment of knowledge freely given by God, disclosing the truth which the Spirit wishes to be made known concerning a particular person or situation. (Adopted from John Wimber.)

General comments

A *warning*: There have been heretical, fringe Christian groups/sects who have pretended to special revelations or secret knowledge ever since the first-century Gnostics.

A *corrective*: Any 'knowledge' or new revelation concerning the person of the Godhead or the way of salvation which goes beyond, distorts, or is contrary to Holy Scripture must always be rejected.

A *blessing*: Any knowledge which gives insight for the benefit of an individual or body of people concerning their own health, safety or blessing which does not violate scripture and brings glory to God is good.

Distinction in kinds of knowledge

1 Natural human knowledge. The incredible scientific

advances in the West in the last century are proof erough of
the benefits (and otherwise) of such knowledge, but this
has been naturally acquired, not spiritually discerned. Paul
shows the difference: 'The man without the Spirit does not
accept the things that come from the Spirit of God, for they
are foolishness to him and he cannot understand them,
because they are spiritually discerned' (1 Corinthians 2: 14).

2 This fallen world's supernatural knowledge is the
natural man's attempt to gain knowledge by supernatural
means other than through the Holy Spirit. It includes the
occult, the psychic and the metaphysical investigations
which Satan uses to ensnare, and is forbidden by God.

3 True spiritual knowledge starts by knowing God
personally through Jesus Christ (John 17: 3). This is
increased through prayer and the study of Holy Scripture.

4 Word of knowledge. This gift comes from and through
the Holy Spirit to our spirit and reveals something of the
mind of God to profit and benefit one another. It may
concern the past, the present or the future.

Some biblical examples of the 'word of knowledge' in operation

1 A warning of an enemy's plan for destruction (2 Kings
6: 9–12).

2 An encouraging insight (1 Kings 18: 41; 19: 15–18).

3 A disclosure of hypocrisy (2 Kings 5: 20–27).

4 A revelation to convince a wayward woman that her
secret sins were known by God (John 4: 18,19,29).

5 A revelation of the whereabouts of a man in hiding (1
Samuel 10: 22).

6 An indication of a man's need (Acts 9: 11).

7 An insight into the source of corruption in the church
(Acts 5: 3).

8 An indication of a suitable meeting place for God's
people (Mark 14: 13–15).

9 An insight into other men's thoughts (John 2: 24 and 1
Samuel 9: 19).

10 A revelation of the presence of a four-drachma coin in

a fish's mouth, which Peter would catch (Matthew 17: 27).

11 A revelation of a visitor to one's home who would call later (Acts 10: 17–23).

12 A revelation of the kind of demon troubling an epileptic boy. The father had said it was dumb (Mark 9: 17) – Christ said it was also deaf (Mark 9: 25).

13 There is an interesting crisis situation where Elisha was waiting for a 'word of knowledge' which had not yet been given him (2 Kings 4: 27).

Some modern-day examples of the gift in operation

Faith-building

W V Grant has a regular ministry which can be seen on TV in California. In the crowded auditorium he greets sick people he has never met before. He is 'given' the person's name, the spouse's name, sometimes the names and numbers of their children, the family doctor's name, the particular ailment and length of time it has been troubling the sufferer, etc.

During this interview he asks the person if they have met before and when the answer is in the negative he asks if the sick person believes Jesus can heal him/her. If the answer is 'yes', he touches the person on the forehead and says 'In the name of Jesus be healed.' In every case the person appeared to be miraculously healed and glory was given to God.

Bringing repentance

John Wimber, who heads up the Vineyard Fellowships from California, is on record as saying 'We've had numerous occasions where God has revealed sins of people either through a word of knowledge or a combination of that and a word of wisdom or prophecy. For example, I was once on an airplane when I turned and looked at a passenger across the aisle to see the word "adultery" written across his face in big letters. The letters, of course, were only perceptible to spiritual eyes. He caught me looking at him (gaping might be more descriptive) and said, "What do you want?" As he asked that, a woman's name came clearly into my mind. I

leaned over the aisle and asked if the name meant anything
to him. His face turned pale and he asked if he could talk to
me.

'It was a large plane with a bar so we went there to talk.
On the way the Lord spoke to me again, saying "Tell him to
turn from this adulterous affair or I am going to take him."
When we got to the bar I told him that God had told me he
was committing adultery with the woman whose name
God had revealed to me and that God would take him if he
did not repent. He melted on the spot, and asked what he
should do. I led him through a prayer of repentance and he
received Christ. This was in front of a stewardess and two
other passengers, who were shocked, but then also began
to cry.

'Then he said that his wife was downstairs in the seat
next to his. I told him to go and tell her the entire story,
which he did. He led her to Christ.'

Finding a house to live in

Esme Russell, a missionary with the South American
Missionary Society, who had gone to work in Peru after
several years work in Chile received a letter from a
Christian couple in Chile, asking her prayers as they were
looking for a home on a housing estate where accommodation was particularly difficult to find, but (since they
were going to have responsibility in the church there) it was
urgent that something suitable might be found to rent.
Whilst praying for them Esme saw a large cedar tree in her
mind's eye. She wrote back suggesting they went to call on
the occupants of any house close to a cedar tree (there was
one obvious tree). This they did and found to their joy a
man who was thinking of putting his house up for rent, but
had not advertised his intention as yet. He let them have
this house, which was most suitable, at a very reasonable
rent.

A warning

Dr John White, a well-known Christian psychiatrist and
writer, tells in his *The Cost of Commitment* of what he calls a
'premonition' of his wife and family's danger when they

were travelling to Bolivia on an alternative route to his own. This was, I believe, a 'word of knowledge'. He felt too foolish to tell her, but went through agony after he had left her. He had a tremendous struggle in prayer with God, who clearly told him simply to trust him. The plane crashed. Everyone on board was killed. A terrible disaster. 'But my wife had also had a "premonition" and cut their journey short, getting off the plane the stop before the tragedy occurred.' (John White, *The Cost of Commitment*, I.V.P., 1976, p. 64)

Identifying a source of technical trouble in a machine

Harold Hill's firm had furnished the heavy machinery for a power station in Baltimore. Part of the contract included checking before finally handing it over. One morning he received an urgent phone call: 'At one o'clock this afternoon this power station has to be turned over to the mayor and the city council – and it will not function.' 'They had had the technicians from the General Electric and our own technicians working on it for about two weeks, but they were all stumped,' he explained.

'I began to pray and immediately while I was praying I knew exactly what was wrong... I saw it as clearly as a picture on a TV screen. This was my first experience with diagnosing a serious and complicated electronic problem strictly by the Holy Spirit.' He was strongly tempted to doubt as he drove down to the power station, but as he walked onto the premises he *knew* the Lord would direct him. 'I walked over to the spot that I had seen in the Spirit as being the trouble source and issued instructions to the technicians as to what to do to cure it. They said, "Hell, we've been through all that, we've checked it all out." I said, "You called me in here as a consultant. Are you going to carry out my instructions? If not, I'm going back to the office." One of them said "Yes, sir", although what I suggested seemed absurd. They had nothing else to try. So they did what I told them, pushed the button, threw the switches and the thing took off like it was supposed to do – to my amazement and theirs.'

He said he didn't realise till afterwards quite how

ridiculous it looked for him to walk onto the scene with
about twenty highly trained engineers and technicians who
had been baffled for weeks and put his finger on the trouble
immediately.

(Harold Hill *How to live like a King's Kid* Logos International
1974 pp. 158–160).

Guidance about one's future

As a young girl, Jackie Pullinger was praying about what
she should do with her life, but she seemed to be getting no
clear answers. She hoped perhaps a letter would come by
the post bringing God's guidance through someone or from
some organisation. 'One night' she writes, 'I had a dream in
which the family were all crowded round the dining room
table looking at a map of Africa. In the middle of the
different coloured countries was a pink one. I leaned over to
see what it was called. It said "Hong Kong". I did not really
believe that, but I did not want to show my ignorance.
"Aah", I tried to sound nonchalant, "I never knew Hong
Kong was there."

"Yes, of course it is, didn't you know?" said my Aunt
Dotty in a superior tone and I did not dare argue.' When
Jackie woke up she first wrote to the Hong Kong
Government and then a missionary society, with frus-
trating results. She felt she must have misinterpreted her
dream. She found a tiny peaceful village church in which to
pray. 'Then I saw a vision of a woman – holding out her
arms beseechingly as on a refugee poster. I wondered what
she wanted – she looked desperate for something. Was it
Christian Aid? Oxfam? Then words moved past like a
television credit "WHAT CAN YOU GIVE US?" What did I
honestly think I could give her?... Then it came to me that
what she needed was the love of Jesus.' This was the
background to Jackie's journey to Hong Kong and her most
effective ministry in the Walled City.

(Jackie Pullinger *Chasing the Dragon* Hodder & Stoughton
1980 pp. 28–29)

An answer to prayer about a dying son

Rosemary Attlee had a seventeen-year-old son dying with
leukaemia. She went into church desperately imploring

God to let her know the time span of the illness. Then she realised that if she happened to be standing on a memorial stone she could read that as a sign. Slowly she looked down to a nineteenth-century inscription at her feet. The stone commemorated a man who had died aged twenty and a few weeks. She took that as God's answer. And so it turned out to be. Later when she revisited the same church with her husband to look once again at the stone they searched the whole floor, but there was no stone (*William's Story* Marshall's 1983 p. 5). Clearly God had given her a word of knowledge through a vision in a similar way to the inscription on the wall of King Belshazzar's banqueting hall (Daniel 5: 25).

How is this gift received?

1 It may be given sovereignly by God: 'He gives them (gifts) to each man, just as he determines' (1 Corinthians 12: 11).

2 It may be requested from God: 'How much more will your Father in heaven give good gifts to those who ask him' (Matthew 7: 11); 'Ask and it will be given to you' (Luke 11: 9). In ministering to others it may be right to ask God to show the secrets of people's hearts.

3 It may be imparted through another who has this gift, as Paul wrote to the Christians in Rome, 'I long to see you so that I may impart to you some spiritual gift to make you strong' (Romans 1: 11). Paul wrote to Timothy, urging him to 'fan into flame the gift of God, which is in you through the laying on of my hands' (2 Timothy 1: 6). This may not refer to the 'word of knowledge' in particular, but the principle is the same for gifts of the Spirit in general.

4 The gift (as in 1 Corinthians 12) is understood as a 'gracelet' given in the situation for the blessing of someone else and is not necessarily a permanent endowment.

5 The gift of 'word of knowledge' is to be encouraged, expected and exercised as a gift which is clearly scriptural and emanates from God.

6 The gift may come to someone in the Body of Christ at a service of worship, or to someone in a small group meeting in prayer or ministering to another person.

How is the gift exercised?

We seek to be in a right, open and prayerful relationship with the Lord. Ministering to others in this attitude we pray 'What is it, Lord? What is it, Lord?' We keep asking. Then we wait and listen.

We may suddenly sense the real truth about a problem, a simple fact or the whereabouts of something lost; or we may sense a power to minister which prompts us to ask who may be in particular need.

1 We may see a picture (vision or dream) or word in the mind's eye or superimposed over a person's face or the affected part of his/her body.

2 We may 'hear' a word or phrase in the mind's ear.

3 We may feel that another person is afflicted in some way by feeling an unaccustomed pain or strange physical sensations in our own body.

4 We may sense power coming upon us, alerting us that God wants to minister to someone present.

5 We may sense heat, heaviness or tingling in the hands, alerting us to lay them on someone for healing.

6 Whenever supernatural knowledge is revealed, we may not necessarily feel constrained to speak the 'word' out aloud immediately, if at all. Supposing God revealed that a person had cancer, we would need to pray for a 'word of wisdom' as to what to do with such knowledge. We might then be led to ask that person how he had been feeling lately. If he mentioned some troubling symptom, we would suggest we prayed about that.

7 Ideally we would first share a 'word' (such as in (6)) with a sympathetic third party, preferably one known to have been given gifts of discernment. Words from God can be 'sharper than a double edged sword' and must be handled with great care.

8 Opportunity should be given for the gathered church to share 'words of knowledge'.

9 Words of knowledge indicate the direction in which God is working.

10 Words of knowledge are faith builders.

11 When God reveals something in this way, it is because God wants something done with such knowledge.

12 Sometimes a person in the team may begin to act out something. A team member was once observed adopting a crouching position, crying and hammering on an imaginary door with two fists, by which the Lord was showing that the person being prayed for suffered trauma by being shut up in a cupboard as a child – the revelation was absolutely right. However, such persons should wait for God's enabling to vocalise the 'word of knowledge' properly. Bizarre models cannot become standardised as normal practice.

13 We may be given a spontaneous utterance which comes without our own volition. We may open our mouth to say something on our mind and find ourselves saying something quite different.

14 So we 'see' it, 'know' it, 'read' it, 'feel' it, 'say' it or 'hear' it.

15 It is possible that a number of 'words of knowledge' may all apply to one and the same person – perhaps someone absent – but the 'words' all clearly describe a person known to someone present.

16 People frequently fail to respond when 'words' are shared out of embarrassment or fear, lack of faith, the nature of the 'word', or genuine wariness lest they cause concern to loved ones present who have been kept unaware of the condition or affliction.

Cautions and dangers

Whatever God does the enemy will attempt to simulate.

1 It is possible to have false impulses – contradictory to the line God is indicating.

2 Extreme care must be taken in the case of secrets revealed. A person being ministered to could so easily be destroyed by the improper and insensitive use of knowledge. On receiving such a 'word', we would then say 'I think God may be saying...' or 'Shall we now pray into your relationship with...', etc. Jesus 'knew' that the woman of Samaria was an adulteress: The way he dealt with the problem was first to ask her to call her husband – a word of wisdom?

3 We try to be wary about entering into directive counselling of any kind, unless, of course, it is God clearly telling us to do this. We do not normally tell people what they *ought* or *should* be doing about any revelations from God. We help to clarify issues and leave people to form their own conclusions. It is important that they make their own decisions.

Conclusion

Pastor Paul Y Cho, founder of the world's largest church, in Seoul, Korea, found he was receiving strange impulses as he preached from his pulpit. He would 'see' twisted ankles, stiff joints, internal organs of the human body, apparently burning or decaying. He thought these must be from Satan or he was going mad.

He discovered soon after that these were 'words of knowledge' when he passed on a 'crazy' thought to a crippled woman in a wheelchair – 'God wants me to tell you that you can walk. He has touched your body and commands you to stand up and walk.' Not daring to wait and see what happened, Cho turned and walked away. But the crowd started shouting. What was the commotion? The woman was standing up and walking to and fro in front of the platform. It *was* God who had been speaking to him after all.

13
THE GIFT OF FAITH

Definition

This gift is a supernatural surge of confidence from the
Spirit of God which arises within a person faced with a
specific situation or need whereby that person receives a
transrational certainty and assurance that God is about to
act through a word or action. This miracle utterance covers
creation or destruction, blessing or cursing, removal or
alteration.

'It is both the irresistible knowledge of God's intervention at a certain point and the authority to effect his
intervention through the power of the Holy Spirit'
(Grossman).

General comments

There are four kinds of faith in the New Testament.

1 There is faith which is a *creed* – the doctrine we profess
to believe (Ephesians 4: 13; 1 Timothy 6: 20–21; Jude 3).

2 There is faith which is the basic *trust* which one has in
God for salvation (John 3: 16; Ephesians 2: 8; Hebrews 11:
1–4,6).

3 There is faith which is a *fruit* of the Spirit – a loyalty
which is produced by the Holy Spirit and cultivated by the
believer, i.e. faithfulness (Galatians 5: 22).

4 There is a faith which is a *gift* of the Spirit – a mountain-
moving surge to which both Jesus and Paul refer (Matthew
17: 20; Matthew 21: 21 and 1 Corinthians 13: 2).

This last category is the one which Paul has in mind when he speaks of the gift of faith. James also implies this kind of faith – 'the prayer of faith' which will heal the sick. This kind of faith (like saving faith) is given sovereignly by God. Scripture sometimes appears to merge the two, for example in Hebrews 11.

We may have the gift of faith (4) without the fruit of faith (3), or the fruit of faith (3) without the gift of faith (4). We can have neither (3) nor (4) without saving faith (2), which should never be separated from sound doctrine, 'the faith that was once entrusted to the saints' (1).

The area of operation as observed in scripture
(selecting from and adding to Harold Horton in *The Gifts of the Spirit* Assemblies of God Publishing House 1954 p. 141, etc.)

1 The gift of faith was used for direct supernatural blessing in fulfilment of human utterance. Thus Isaac blessed Jacob, 'May God give you of heaven's dew and of earth's richness – an abundance of corn and new wine' (Genesis 27: 28). The writer to the Hebrews lists a number of similar instances, including the one above:'By faith Isaac blessed Jacob and Esau in regard to their future. By faith Jacob, when he was dying, blessed each of Joseph's sons . . .' (Hebrews 11: 20,21).

2 The gift of faith was employed for personal protection in perilous circumstances. Thus we see Daniel in the lions' den. 'When Daniel was lifted from the den, no wound was found on him, because he had trusted in his God' (Daniel 6: 23). Again, Jesus, whilst tempted in the desert, 'was with the wild animals, and angels attended him' (Mark 1: 13). Also in the case of Paul's snake-bitten hand 'Paul shook the snake off into the fire and suffered no ill effects' (Acts 28: 5, cf. also, Mark 16: 18).

3 The gift of faith was employed for supernatural sustenance in famine or fasting. Thus we see Elijah being told by the Lord to hide by the brook of Kerith, with the assurance of adequate food since 'I have ordered the ravens to feed you there', and we learn that 'The ravens brought

him bread and meat in the morning and bread and meat in the evening' (1 Kings 17: 4,6).

Secondly we see Elijah raising to life the son of the woman of Zarephath 'O Lord my God, let this boy's life return to him ... The Lord heard ... and he lived' (1 Kings 17: 21,22).

Again in the desert, we see Jesus sustained by faith in the word of God. Jesus replied to the devil's temptation to make bread from stones 'It is written "Man does not live on bread alone, but on every word that comes from the mouth of God"' (Matthew 4: 4).

4 The gift of faith operated in bringing about some of the astounding promises of God. Thus we read of Sarah, who was old and past the age of child-bearing, becoming pregnant and bearing a son at the very time God promised (Genesis 21: 2). Paul drew attention to Abraham's part in this 'Yet he did not waver through unbelief regarding the promise of God, but was strengthened in his faith and gave glory to God, being fully persuaded that God had power to do what he had promised' (Romans 4: 20,21).

5 The gift of faith operated in the administration of spiritual discipline to grossly moral offenders.

Paul speaks about how the Corinthian Christians were to discipline a particular individual acting immorally. 'When you are assembled in the name of our Lord Jesus and I am with you in spirit, and the power of our Lord Jesus is present, hand this man over to Satan, so that the sinful nature may be destroyed and his spirit saved on the day of the Lord' (1 Corinthians 4: 4,5).

6 The gift of faith was exercised in the victory of the Israelites over the Amalekites at Rephidim. 'As long as Moses held up his hands, the Israelites were winning, but whenever he lowered his hands, the Amalekites were winning' (Exodus 17: 11).

7 The gift of faith was seen to operate in solving domestic and economic problems. Elisha told the woman in debt to 'Go round and ask all your neighbours for empty jars. Don't ask for just a few. Then go inside and shut the door ... Pour oil (from the little she had remaining) into all the jars, and as each is filled, put it to one side' (2 Kings 4: 3,4).

8 The gift of faith operated in raising the dead. Bound in grave-clothes, the four-days-decomposed dead body of Lazarus was resuscitated when Jesus called in a loud voice 'Lazarus, come out' (John 11: 43).

9 The gift of faith operated in curses. We see this in the case of the fig-tree, following Jesus' words 'May you never bear fruit again!' – the tree withered immediately (Matthew 21: 19).

Again there is the case of Sapphira, the wife of Ananias, who lied to the Holy Spirit. 'Peter said to her, "The feet of the men who buried your husband are at the door, and they will carry you out also." At that moment she fell down at his feet and died' (Acts 5: 9,10).

Examples from latter days

1 George Müller operated his Bristol orphanage with the gift of faith. With hundreds of hungry children, he prayed God's blessing on their empty cups and plates and as he prayed churns of milk came in at one door and baskets of bread at another.

2 The Rev. Eric Townson (formerly with the Church Missionary Society) tells of an experience which he had as a fairly new missionary. He attended an open-air meeting in East Africa when the rain began to fall. This was going to ruin plans for an open-air conference. Eric felt an urge to rebuke the rain, which he did loudly in Christ's name. The rain stopped instantly!

3 A dramatic example of the use of the gift of faith comes from Bud Sickler, an Elim missionary in Tanzania. An enraged lioness dashed out of the jungle killing domestic animals, a woman and a child, and headed directly towards a congregation gathered to celebrate Easter. Seeing the danger, the native pastor shouted to the crowd 'Don't be afraid – the God who saved Daniel from the lions is here – the Risen Christ of Easter is here.' He turned to the lioness and cried 'You lion. I curse you in the name of Jesus Christ.' Then the most amazing thing happened – a bolt of lightning from the sky struck the lioness dead.

The response to this gift

1 Glory to God.
2 Amazement from the disciples (Matthew 21: 20).
3 New faith. 'Many of the Jews who had seen what Jesus did, put their faith in him' (John 11: 45).
4 The church is affirmed in the value of this gift.

Conclusion

1 The operation is often less spectacular than other power gifts because it frequently achieves the objective secretly or silently over a long period. It is usually a process, whereas the gift of miracles is a crisis.
2 There is often considerable overlapping in the use of the power gifts of the Spirit. For example, in the raising of Lazaras it might be said that the gift of faith operated with the gift of healing, since not only was the man raised, but he was healed – he had been sick before he died and his body was decomposed after his death, but he came back to life whole. But no one could doubt that the gift of miracles had been called into operation too!

14

THE GIFT OF MIRACULOUS POWERS

Definition

The gift of miraculous powers operates through individual persons by the supernatural intervention of the Holy Spirit in the natural order.

Introductory comments

1 A miracle is a supernatural act; a temporary suspension of the accustomed order; an intervention into the course of nature as it is normally understood.

2 Jesus' own miracles were performed primarily out of his *compassion*, both to meet human needs and for practical purposes.

   a) He walked on water to comfort his disciples.

   b) He fed the multitude because food was otherwise unavailable.

   c) He turned water into wine to solve a crisis at a wedding.

3 It is difficult to draw any clear line between the gift of miracles and the gifts of healings.

   a) Healing includes those acts of power which produce an abatement of the symptoms or a cure in a living body.

   b) Other events which show miraculous manifestations of power beyond healings are plain miracles.

4 Signs and wonders are included in God's programme for extending the kingdom of God. The preaching of the kingdom was affirmed by manifestations of God's power

which would serve as signs and wonders to the world.
Miracles vindicate the name of God and the gospel, and
cause all those who witness them to reflect.

5 Christians suffering persecution and Christians
pioneering the gospel have always been more aware of this
gift than their contemporary believers in other situations.

The purpose of miracles in scripture

1 The gift was used for the miraculous deliverance of
God's people (Psalm 136: 10–22).

2 To provide for those in want (Exodus 17 and Mark 6:
13,30–44).

3 To carry out divine judgments and disciplines (the
plagues in Exodus 7–11; Ananias and Sapphira in Acts 5).

4 To confirm the word preached (Acts 13: 11,12).

5 To deliver out of unavoidable danger (Matthew 8:
24–26; Acts 12: 4–11).

6 To raise the dead (John 11: 38–44).

7 To display God's power and magnificence (Psalm 145:
3–7).

How the gift operates

It is of course impossible to know how God works miracles
but it is possible to know something about how the gift
operates.

1 Whilst we can never demand a miracle, we may be
authorised to command a miracle wrought by the power of
God.

2 There are signs which accompany the working of
miracles:

a) Deep compassion or anger (John 11: 33,38).

b) An accompanying gift of faith – an absolute
conviction that this is God's will now (Mark 10: 46–52).

3 The miracle worker then says the word or performs
the act (or does both) which effects the miracle (Mark 7:
33–35).

Response to the exercise of this gift

  1 Glory to God.
  2 Amazement from the disciples (Matthew 21: 20).
  3 New faith (John 11: 45).
  4 Each exercise of the gift affirms the Church in the further use of it.

15
THE GIFTS OF HEALING

Definition

These gifts are channelled through human agents for the supernatural healing of diseases and infirmities to the glory of God.

Introductory comments

1 Healing proceeds from God (Exodus 15: 26) and is available through the atoning work of Jesus Christ (Isaiah 53: 4, Matthew 8: 16,17 and 1 Peter 2: 24).

2 The gifts of healings are listed among the power gifts mentioned in 1 Corinthians 12: 7–11 – the others being *faith* and *miracles*.

3 Although the gifts of *faith* and *miracles* extend beyond the realm of healing, they are often integrated into the ministry of healing.

4 The gifts of healing also operate in conjunction with other gifts of the Spirit such as words of knowledge.

5 Fundamental to the gifts of healing is the principle upon which Jesus operated: 'The Son can do nothing by himself; he can do only what he sees his Father doing' (John 5: 19).

Some distinctive ministries of healing

1 There is, of course, a vast ministry of healing through

the medical services. All scientific knowledge comes from the sovereign Lord and we thank God and pray for those who minister to us in this way.

2 There is a sacramental ministry of healing exercised by church elders/priests (James 5: 14).

3 There are anointed Christians in the Body of Christ who exercise a legitimate itinerant healing ministry with a genuine gift from the Lord, to whom they give the glory.

4 Such individuals have often discovered that their ministry is especially blessed in certain areas, using a special methodology. One such would be Kathryn Kuhlman operating through 'words of knowledge' and 'gifts of faith and miracles'. This ministry flows out of the frequent and faithful use of the gifts of healing.

5 There are some compassionate warm-hearted Christian people who are sensitive and understanding, who have natural healing abilities which accompany their prayers for the sick and communicate a degree of healing.

6 There are those who minister with other 'spirits' and although miracles and healings occur, there is a serious danger that the person thus ministered to will take on board more subtle spirits to deceive and ultimately destroy him.

7 Paul, in 1 Corinthians 12, is addressing himself to the healing gifts (amongst others) which are bestowed by the Holy Spirit upon the Body of Christ – the gathering of church members – when they minister to each other and to visitors in their company *in the church*. This is what interests us particularly. The meeting place is the learning place for the market place.

The purpose of healing

It is intended:

1 To contribute towards the process of wholeness in the individual.

2 To alleviate physical suffering through a cure or the abatement of symptoms.

3 To cleanse the soul.

4 To release the emotions.

5 To edify those believers made aware of the Holy Spirit's healing ministry.

6 To be a sign in an unbelieving world of the kingdom which has come with Christ.

7 To bring glory to God.

Healing is spiritual warfare

1 Sickness is clearly the domain of the devil (cf. Acts 10: 38).

2 Any who become involved in the healing ministry will find themselves involved in active spiritual conflict.

3 The enemy attacks both before, during and after any healing ministry.

The most common kinds of attacks experienced by those involved.

Before ministry:

1 Sudden depression.

2 Disinterested feeling and tiredness.

3 Anger and frustration.

4 Some strife or tension with others close by.

5 Sense of blockage through some specific incident or circumstance.

6 Sense of unworthiness.

During ministry:

1 Distractions.

2 Doubts, confused and unedifying thoughts.

3 Feelings of ebbing faith and lack of anointing.

4 Temptation to override one's faith.

5 Temptation to stop listening to God and take over 'in the flesh'.

6 Tendency to focus on the condition (especially if it is drastic).

7 Discouraging, negative thoughts – 'nothing is happening'.

8 Desire to speed up the ministry and finish quickly.

After ministry

The commonest subsequent experiences sensed by those who have been ministering are:
1 Sudden depression.
2 Sense of failure (especially when people do not *appear* to be healed).
3 Sense of exhaustion.
4 Confused and mixed feelings. (Of course, one may have good reasons for feeling a failure if one has mismanaged the situation, but some mistakes are almost inevitable.)
5 Temptation to pride – a desire to boast following clear manifestation of the power of God.

The values to be accepted by those involved in healing

1 The ministry of the Holy Spirit (Acts 13: 1–3; 16: 6–10; 18: 9).
   a) He empowers to heal.
   b) He will reveal how to minister through words of knowledge, etc.
   c) He is invited to come upon the person to be healed.
   d) Those ministering should watch, observe and listen to what the Holy Spirit is doing and saying. Recognise when the Spirit is *on* a person. Learn to interpret the afflicted person's responses.
   e) The Holy Spirit should be honoured and blessed in the process for what he does to the person being ministered to for healing.
2 The authority of Jesus. He has commissioned us to heal.
3 The relationship between those ministering and those being ministered to must be:
   a) Adult to adult (where the afflicted is adult) rather than parent to child.
   b) Honesty and truth from both parties.
   c) Devoid of manipulation by either party.

d) Based on compassion and respect for the individual's dignity.

e) There must be a willingness to take time.

f) We must display concern for the whole person – all aspects of his/her life.

g) We must also avoid emotionalism from the ministers of healing.

h) Care must be taken to ensure the afflicted person is not brought into bondage (some mistakenly bind people to themselves through their ministry, whereas Christ sets us free – John 8: 36).

i) Care must be taken to ensure the afflicted person is not put under condemnation.

j) Care must be taken to ensure that all personal disclosures are kept confidential.

The setting for healing

1 A helpful setting could be a home group cell or the gathering of believers at church, but it could be wherever the need arises.

2 a) Worship is the ideal context for healing. This prepares both the afflicted persons, and those involved in their healing, to be open to God's Spirit.

b) Such a context builds faith. A negative atmosphere is counter-productive (Mark 6: 5,6).

c) Healing (whenever there is such ministry) should go hand in hand with the preaching of the kingdom. It is a sign of God's power and approval.

3 This ministry may take place during the main part of a service of worship, and from time to time it should, so that all the church members may see and learn how it is exercised.

4 Because time is needed to be relaxed, it may normally be best to minister at the end of the service when friends and relatives may stay, but others with other commitments can leave.

5 The person being ministered to may stand, or kneel at the communion rails, or sit in the pews or be taken to another room if more privacy is required.

6 It is important that the person being prayed for should

be as relaxed as possible and protected from all unnecessary embarrassment.

7 An unhurried ministry at the front of the church (with friends and relatives apart praying silently) and other church members chatting at the back creates a relaxed atmosphere and also provides some privacy.

8 Two or three will gather round the sick person to minister.

Preparation before ministry to others

1 We seek to remind ourselves of who Jesus is, what he has done and what he has told us to do.

2 We also seek to empty ourselves of 'self', remembering that of ourselves we can do nothing (John 15: 5).

3 We check that the armour of God is in place (Ephesians 6: 14–18).

4 We try to empty the mind of preconceptions and presumption. No two cases are alike in the ministry required.

5 We then ask for a fresh infilling of the Holy Spirit.

6 We ask God what he wants to do (John 5: 19,20).

7 We frequently pray in tongues.

8 We try to envisage the affected part of the body well and functioning properly.

How the ministry of healing begins

1 Through inviting and honouring the ministry of the Holy Spirit: 'If the Spirit of him who raised Jesus from the dead is living in you, he who raised Christ from the dead will also give life to your mortal bodies through his Spirit, who lives in you' (Romans 8: 11).

2 Through inspiration – a sudden flood of thoughts describing the situation.

3 Through a vision/picture.

4 Through an impression – a deep *knowing* in the Spirit.

5 Through a scripture verse coming to mind.

6 Through a word or beginning of a sentence describing a condition.

How the power for healing comes

1 An annointing – a sudden infusing of power or heat (tingling) or heaviness in the hands, a feeling of compassion or a full assurance that it will be done.
2 Detachment – a standing back and sensing something beyond ourselves happening through us.
3 Words of knowledge, wisdom or faith which we had not expected to say proceed from the mouth.
4 A vision or a picture in the mind's eye of the healing miracle taking place.

The place of faith in healing

There must be faith – positive expectancy. This may be:
1 in the person ministering (John 11: 22) (This is the gift of faith);
2 or in the person being ministered to (Mark 5: 34; Luke 7: 9; Luke 17: 19);
3 or in the friends or relatives who bring their afflicted (Mark 2: 5).
4 At some stage it is good to encourage some faith response in the person to whom ministry is being given. It seems important to encourage the person's faith.
5 It may be necessary to remove obstacles which may hinder faith.
   a) Jesus did not do many mighty works in Nazareth because of their unbelief (Mark 6: 5,6).
   b) Jesus put out unbelieving mourners from the room of a dead girl and took in just the parents and his disciples (Mark 5: 40).

The place of active faith in the person gifted with healing

Jesus spoke, with the gift of faith, to the condition of the

sick. We are also encouraged to exercise our faith: 'If
anyone says to this mountain, "Go, throw yourself into the
sea," and does not doubt in his heart but believes that what
he says will happen, it will be done for him' (Mark 11: 23).
Note that he is not told to 'pray', but 'say' – commanding the
mountain to do something.

The place of active faith in the one being healed

We have found it helpful sometimes to encourage the sick
person to 'see' his disease *on* Jesus for 'He took our
infirmities and carried our diseases' (Matthew 8: 17).

1 Jesus was specific in his requests for a faith response
and said 'Stretch our your hand' (Mark 3: 5); 'Get up! Pick
up your mat and walk (John 5: 8); 'Go, wash in the pool of
Siloam' (John 9: 7); 'Go, show yourselves to the priests'
(Luke 17: 14).

2 The Hunters say: 'We tell them we are going to lay
hands on their necks (or knees) and as we do we ask them to
move their necks' (C and F Hunter *How to Heal the Sick*, p.
124).

The place of forgiveness in healing

Those ministering need to know God's forgiveness.

Those ministering need to maintain a forgiving spirit in
all areas of their lives.

Those being ministered to need to experience God's
forgiveness and to be forgiving in all other areas, though
where the afflicted are not Christians this may follow
rather than precede their healing. An unforgiving spirit
may cause an affliction to return: 'Forgive us our sins, for
we also forgive everyone who sins against us' (Luke 11: 4).
(This is dealt with more thoroughly in chapter 24.) Often
the 'real' reason God moves people to present themselves
for healing is to bring them to salvation. 'It is better for you
to enter life crippled than to have two feet and be thrown
into hell' (Mark 9: 45).

Phenomena often experienced by those involved in healing

A sense of heaviness or heat in the hands or power flowing out of them; a tingling feeling/goose pimples; trembling/shaking of the hands; a sense of anointing. The inward witness of the Lord's presence to heal; a sense of electrical currents through the body; a sense of 'knowing'; a sense of detachment – standing back to see the Lord operating. Sometimes there is no feeling at all – in which case we minister out of our authority on the basis of what we know.

This last point may be illustrated from a personal experience. I was once walking to church in a poor area in the hills above Viña del Mar, Chile, when a woman rushed up and begged me to pray for her baby, who, she said, was dying. (The doctor at the hospital had said there was nothing more that could be done for her baby). She pushed a bundle of rags with a baby in them towards me. I remember thinking at the time how very inappropriate it seemed (to do this in the street) and felt slightly annoyed, being in a hurry to get to church! I certainly didn't sense any anointing, but, because she insisted, I prayed for the child and walked on. My companion asked me if I had noticed how the baby's breathing had changed, but I had to admit I had not. I completely forgot about the whole event until three days later when passing the same way again the mother rushed out to thank me – the baby was completely well and eating normally. We gave God the glory for what he had done.

Phenomena often experienced by people being ministered to

Sense of heat or cold on the body. (The latter may indicate deliverance is taking place.)

Hot flushes on certain parts of the body, e.g. neck, hands, back, etc.

Ripples on the skin/movement under the skin, especially over lower chest and stomach area, or various other related phenomena: a radiance on the face; the flickering of the eyelids; a sense of electrical current; trembling and shaking; stiffness of the body or particular parts of the body; light-headedness; a sense of weariness; a sense of deep peace; deep breathing; tenderness and tears; brokenness and sobbing; moaning and groaning; laughter and joy; falling down under the power of the Spirit ('resting in the Spirit'); prostrate body 'bouncing' (sometimes like a fish on dry land); or the body being laid out looking deathly (especially after a demon is cast out spontaneously).

An *observation*: Any of these sensations or experiences may be manifest. Whilst they may be signs of God at work, they are never proofs of healing. To quote the Hunters again:

'We have seen people go under the power of God and be instantly healed while lying on the floor. We have seen people go under the power of God and not get healed. We have seen people who did not go under the power and were healed standing up. We have seen people who did not go under the power and did not get healed.' (C and F Hunter *How to Heal the Sick*)

Points to ponder

1 We endeavour to give all the glory to God.

2 We seek to beware of the enemy's counterattacks. 'Resist the devil, and he will flee from you' (James 4: 7).

3 We never rely on our own emotions, nor do we ignore them.

4 We note that the more we minister healing, the more results we see.

5 We have discovered that some of us have periods of anointing for different conditions/occasions.

6 Some of us develop faith for one area of healing, which we anticipate will become a recognisable ministry.

7 Sometimes there are special anointings and whatever we do brings the desired result.

8 Even though we may feel nothing (no virtue going out), healings can take place, effected on the basis of authority and obedience to the Scriptures.

9 Sometimes someone in a ministry team may be given a word of prophecy for the person healed.

10 We have found that this ministry tends to go in waves. It's easy to get proud when God uses us. The temptation is to take the glory to ourselves. There is a constant need to humble ourselves and to be continually repenting. (This applies both to churches and individuals).

The Welshman Stephen Jeffreys had a remarkable healing ministry and thousands were blessed through it – especially those suffering from rheumatoid arthritis – until one day at a huge meeting in South Africa, where hundreds were being healed, he exalted himself and declared 'The world is at my feet.' His ministry ended there. He became ill and eventually died. Rheumatoid arthritis destroyed him!

16

DREAMS, VISIONS AND 'ENIGMATIC SPEECH'

Introduction to dreams

Dreams, visions and 'enigmatic speech' are not included among the gifts of the Spirit, but are frequently integral to the work of the Holy Spirit. (See chapter 12 for the significance of a dream given to Jackie Pullinger.) Here are important media for revelations from God which the Church has ignored to her cost.

Christian study sources

Morton Kelsey: *God, Dreams and Revelations*, Minneapolis, Augsburg, 1974.
Catherine Marshall: *Something More*, McGraw Hill Book Company, 1974.
John and Paula Sandford: *The Elijah Task*, Logos International, 1977.
George Mallone: *Those Controversial Gifts*, Hodder and Stoughton, 1983.

Setting for the gifts

There is a degree of overlap in the Bible between visions and dreams (Daniel 7: 1) and yet there is a distinction, as, of course, there is with 'enigmatic speech' (Numbers 12: 8).

Such revelations (as with the gifts of the Spirit) are linked with the outpouring of the Holy Spirit (Joel 2: 28) and can be the setting for a simultaneous manifestation of a gift, e.g.:

1 A word of knowledge came through a vision (Acts 27: 23–26).

2 A gift of healing came through a vision (Acts 9: 10–12).

'One picture is worth a thousand words'

When a non-visual means of revelation fails to convey a message, a picture will communicate freely, effectively and immediately. Because of our fears, pain, preconceived ideas, and stubbornness, a direct revelation may sometimes be counter-productive, whereas an indirect revelation which requires some praying through and puzzling out by ourselves may yet become effective. Since these come to us apart from, or even despite, the controlled conscious mind, dreams, visions and 'enigmatic speech' have ways of by-passing other blockages and gaining our attention.

Dreams in scripture

1 A prophet was known as a 'dreamer of dreams' (Deuteronomy 13: 1 RSV).

2 At many major turning points in biblical history God has guided his people by dreams.

In the Old Testament:

a) God warned King Abimelech through a dream that Sarah was Abraham's wife and caused him to send Abraham away a wealthy man (Genesis 20).

b) Jacob had a dream as he fled from Esau (Genesis 28: 10–22).

c) The Lord appeared to Jacob in a dream and told him how to outwit Laban (Genesis 31: 10–13).

d) The Lord appeared to Jacob in a dream when he told him to flee from Laban and return to Canaan (Genesis 31: 3).

e) Joseph had two dreams which foretold his leadership over his brothers (Genesis 37: 1–11).

f) Having been sold into slavery in Egypt, Joseph rose to power as an interpreter of dreams (Genesis 40–41).

g) Daniel rose to power in Babylon interpreting the dreams of Nebuchadnezzar. In both the king's dream and Daniel's vision the coming of Jesus Christ was foretold (Daniel chapters 2,7).

In the New Testament:

a) Joseph was told in a dream to keep Mary as his wife (Matthew 1: 20).

b) Joseph was told in a dream to flee to Egypt with the child Jesus (Matthew 2: 13).

c) The wise men were warned by God in a dream not to return to Herod (Matthew 2: 12).

d) Joseph knew when to return to Nazareth through a dream (Matthew 2: 19).

If every instance involving dreams was removed from the Bible, large chunks would be missing, including most of its important revelations and events.

Dreams are a primary consequence of the outpouring of the Holy Spirit. (Joel 2: 28)

Dream categories

Dreams can be external or internal in their significance.

An *external* dream reveals information which has little to do with our own personality or character, but may involve people we will meet or minister to in the near future; they may also reveal some coming events.

An *internal* dream reveals information about our own inner being – an insight through the Holy Spirit on the condition of our own heart and soul. These revelations of the truth about ourselves are one of the kindest and most private ways our heavenly Father uses to warn us, guide us, or bring about our healing.

Nearly every Christian believer can record some instance of being 'told' something in a dream but, common as informative dreams are, ignorance about what to do with such dreams is widespread.

1 Dreams foretelling death or disaster do not have to be received as something inevitable. The Christian faith is not

fatalistic. God did not send his Son... to condemn the
world, but to save the world (John 3: 17). We can pray and
God will hear us as he heard Abraham when he pleaded for
Sodom and Gomorrah (Genesis 18: 22–33).

2 Not all informative dreams warn of evil. God also
speaks to us in dreams that we might pray for the blessing a
dream depicts or foretells.

3 Some dreams are encouragements to us to embark
upon, or hold to, a course which significantly affects his
purposes for us within the kingdom of God.

Dream language

We must all learn by experience what our dream language is
and what the symbols, the peculiar language of dreams,
mean.

Some symbols have universal meanings and some have
individual, local, social or cultural meanings. So much will
depend upon our personal background.

Animals and objects

Like any other symbols these can have double meanings.
For example, the lion stands for both royalty, power and
courage; also for destructive carnal violence. If a man is
walking with Jesus Christ, then the Lion of Judah
(Revelation 5: 5) is his strength. If a man is walking apart
from God, the devil comes like a roaring lion to destroy (1
Peter 5: 8). A serpent on a pole may symbolise healing
(Numbers 21: 8,9) but the serpent of Genesis 3 and
Revelation 20 represents Satan. Chains can stand either for
negative things that bind us or bonds of love which, though
binding, set us free. The cross, an object of disgrace and
cruel death, can be used by God to mean redemption and
victory.

People

The most important dream symbols are people. Dreams of a
parent, relatives and friends are more *internal* than external
in significance, but can have double meanings. Dreams

involving mothers, grandmothers, aunts or sisters – any woman – often tell us about the *feminine side* of our nature. Dreams about fathers, grandfathers, uncles or brothers – any man – reveal truth about our *masculine side*. Dreams about babies and children may be communicating something important about our *inner child*. There may be an *external* meaning where such dreams are informing the dreamer about someone else; how to help someone we are praying for or going to help through ministry for example.

Happenings

A dream of giving birth often means the Holy Spirit is speaking of something new happening or about to happen to us in life. Dreams of the death of a person may represent the dying of some aspect of our nature. A dream of someone being ill can be informing us of some inner sickness in our own soul. Such dreams in themselves are neither good nor bad. They may apply to ourselves or to someone else we know of or are about to meet or minister to.

  Though knowing about symbols is helpful, we can never develop our perceptions into fixed formulae. We must always be open to whatever God, through the Holy Spirit, is trying to teach us.

Introduction to visions

So much of what has been said already about dreams applies also to visions. The main difference between dreams and visions is that visions come to us in our waking hours. Visions are much more under our control than dreams. The Holy Spirit can work more freely through dreams. Our thoughts can so easily intrude into our visions. But the Lord speaks to man through both.

Visions in Scripture

Both in the Old Testament and in the New most of the vital

turning points in mankind's history were marked by dreams.

After the coming of the Holy Spirit at Pentecost these turning points came more commonly by visions:

1 Paul's conversion (Acts 9: 3–7).

2 Peter's commission to minister to Gentiles (Acts 10: 9–16; 11: 4–18).

3 Paul's call to go to Macedonia (Acts 16: 6–10).

(John's vision of the apocalypse (the book of Revelation) certainly portrays a turning point in the future.)

Various degrees of vision

1 Sometimes the Holy Spirit flashes a picture across the inner screen of our mind with or without the intrusion of conscious thoughts, even when we are not in a particularly spiritual frame of mind.

2 Sometimes the visions are products of our imagination. We should not discount these because the Holy Spirit also operates through imagination.

We frequently discard such pictures which commonly come to mind because:

   a) Our own minds seem to be producing them.

   b) They seem too quick and simple.

   c) We assume that because we were not in an attitude of prayer when the vision came, it could not be God trying to show us anything.

3 Sometimes a vision flashes vividly across the inner screen when we are in the act of prayer with no conscious prompting, often catching us by surprise. We know we have done nothing to induce it. As if watching a TV screen, we find ourselves involuntarily observing something that is happening.

4 Sometimes we may sense we are actually seeing a reality beyond ourselves with more than physical eyes. We are awake, alert and in full control.

   a) Paul had such a vision of Jesus on the Damascus road (Acts 9: 1–9).

   b) Ananias received specific instructions from the Lord through a vision about ministering to Paul (Acts 9: 10–18).

c) Stephen saw a vision of the glory of God and Jesus at his right hand as he was being martyred by his enemies (Acts 7: 55–60).

5 Finally some visions occur in trances. As in a dream, the conscious mind is not in operation. We cannot deliberately enter a trance: it happens to us with an overwhelming of the senses without any overpowering of the will. It may accompany a physical falling under the power of God (see chapter 18). An entranced person can bring himself out of a trance if he wishes.

a) Peter was thus 'overwhelmed' when he 'fell into a trance' (Acts 10: 10).

b) John was thus 'overwhelmed' when he 'fell at his (Jesus's) feet as though dead' on the Lord's day (Revelation 1: 17).

c) Daniel was 'troubled' by a vision (Daniel 7: 15) and later overwhelmed' – 'As he came near the place where I was standing, I was terrified and *fell* prostrate' (Daniel 8: 17).

Response to visions

Paul said, 'I was not disobedient to the vision from heaven' (Acts 26: 19). There is no excuse! Visions must be obeyed. Dreams can easily be forgotten. Our minds and wills are not fully engaged in a dream and we are not fully responsible. But in visions we are fully awake and, therefore, are fully responsible. But how shall we obey if the meaning is obscure? We will be obliged to pray, ponder, share with other believers, and wait for the Lord to show us.

We should not strive to interpret, for in that way we easily open the door to the flesh and the devil to intervene. We should tell the Lord of our desire to understand, and be relaxed as we ponder and pray.

1 Sometimes the Lord will respond promptly. But often that would short-circuit the process of discovery that began with a dream or vision which was allegorical or figurative. He gives us visions to move us to thought and will reveal their meanings at the right time.

2 Sometimes the Lord will respond directly. Ananias had no doubt and no delay in understanding the Lord's command to him in a vision. 'Go to the house of Judas on Straight Street and ask for a man from Tarsus named Saul... In a vision he has seen a man named Ananias... restore his sight' (Acts 9: 11,12).

3 Sometimes God will show us something by vision or dream which we shall store up for the future and when it pleases God, he will prompt us to seek its meaning and act on it.

General comment

1 Some people have recurring childhood dreams. The Holy Spirit prompts us to open up because the time is ripe for the 'child' in this vision to be healed.

2 Some revelations may be warnings to us or for our guidance. Some are vital clues for our healing and deliverance which has now become imminent.

3 Not all daydreams are visions, but any recurring dream or daydream is worth examining.

4 Sometimes a dream or vision may be given to a non-believer (Matthew 27: 19) and sometimes the inter-pretation of an unbeliever's dream may be given to a believer, e.g. Joseph and Daniel.

5 Often the Lord will give a vision or dream years in advance to prepare one of his servants for work. Joseph dreamed of his pre-eminence over his brothers long before it became reality (Genesis 37). Or to prepare God's people for a future event (Daniel 12).

6 Sometimes it is difficult, when confronted with opposition, to know if God is saying 'You are being misled' or 'Take heart, this is a sign from me.' Being placed within the Body of Christ, we can share it with others to check it: 'Every matter must be established by the testimony of two or three witnesses' (2 Corinthians 13: 1). However, let us beware, because our closest friends are not always the best able to help us here. Their judgment may easily be obscured by their own interests, especially if it is something they do not want to hear. Frequently the Lord will confirm it

through a total stranger.

7 We may sometimes be mistaken even so, but the Lord will honour the intention and forgive the mistake and help us through the turmoil if we have sincerely felt we were doing it for him (Psalm 91: 15b).

8 Another problem with visions arises from our sinful dispositions. When we think God is speaking to us, or through us, we quickly get puffed-up and big-headed. Paul warns us: 'Do not let anyone who delights in false humility and the worship of angels disqualify you for the prize. Such a person goes into great detail about what he has seen, and *his unspiritual mind puffs him up with idle notions*. He has lost connection with the Head, from whom the whole body, supported and held together by its ligaments and sinews, grows as God causes it to grow' (Colossians 2: 18,19).

Dreams and visions are integral to God's ministry to us and through us. Frequently God gives us prophecies, words of knowledge, words of wisdom and discernment in this manner. Such revelations are for our own wholeness or to help towards the 'wholeness' of others (Proverbs 29: 18).

Everyone of us who dreams or receives a vision should always be sure to follow the Lord and not the vision. If the revelation is from God, he will bring it to pass.

A case in point

Visions played a significant part in the beginnings of the Welsh Revival which culminated in 1904. In one Evan Roberts saw the moon in ever increasing brilliance and size. In a matter of moments the moon seemed to reflect the divine presence and there appeared an arm outstretched towards the world claiming something for itself before it was withdrawn. At another time the arm and hand were indistinct, but the piece of paper which it held had the figures *100,000* written on it. Afterwards, whenever Evan Roberts prayed he had no peace until he had asked God specifically for that number of souls.

Each vision was presented in biblical categories such as the victory of Christ's Kingdom, the spiritual conflict with Satan and the power of God in salvation. They were also prophetic in nature, because each found in the subsequent revival, which spread not only over Wales but also across the world, its literal and complete fulfilment. However, although their details were startling and their meaning unmistakable, Roberts dared not act until the way had become clear.

Eifion Evans: *The Welsh Revival of 1904*. (Evangelical Press of Wales, 1984, p. 79).

Introduction to 'enigmatic speech'

The Bible shows us that from time to time God employs 'enigmatic speech' in communicating to his people. The classic example is God using the prophet Nathan to rebuke David for his adultery with Bathsheba. Nathan told him a story about a rich man who took a poor man's only lamb to feast a visiting traveller. Whilst the offender remained unidentified, the injustice was so blatant that David unwittingly found himself to be judging himself! There are infinite varities of use and purpose to which such enigmatic speech can be put. It could be used (as in the case above) to compel us to recognise in ourselves something we readily justify and would unwillingly admit; it could be used to reveal an area of our life which requires inner healing. It could be showing us a person we are to meet shortly and minister to; it could be a lesson for the Church of God 'where, for instance, God uses the sickness of the vicar's wife to show there is sickness in the church, (cf. our example on page 94) or it could refer to a coming event (Daniel 12: 11, cf. Matthew 24: 15).

Bible references

1 'When a prophet of the Lord is among you, I reveal myself to him in visions, I speak to him in dreams', but with Moses, 'I speak face to face, clearly and not in riddles' (NIV), 'not in *dark* speeches' (AV and RV), 'not in *dark speech*' (RSV) – Numbers 12: 6,7).

2 'I will open my mouth in parables, I will utter things hidden from of old' (Psalm 78: 2).

3 'Jesus ... did not say anything to them without using a parable' (Matthew 13: 34).

4 'Now we see *in a glass even in a dark speaking*' (Wm. Tyndale), '*but a poor reflection*' (NIV), '*a glass darkly*' (AV), '*in a mirror dimly*' (RSV), '*a mirror darkly*' (RV) – but then face to face (1 Corinthians 13: 12).

Some reasons why God communicates in this way

Why should God choose this way of speaking to us when he is capable of speaking directly? Consider:

1 The superior effectiveness of circuitous communication under certain conditions in particular situations. We value so much more highly what we puzzle out for ourselves.

2 The politeness and less threatening nature of such a roundabout approach.

3 The Lord's desire for us, his children, to mature by learning to discover God's will for ourselves.

4 God remains hidden for our good. A full and direct revelation of God would be more than we could take (John 16: 12).

How it works

Concerning some situations it may please God to speak to us in a pun, a riddle or a parable. While he allows us to suppose that he is thinking about what we are thinking about, in reality he is telling us something quite different. He knows we will come round to understanding it eventually.

Old Testament illustration

Sometimes Old Testament prophets thought they were speaking about imminent events whereas the Holy Spirit was speaking about matters of far greater significance than they ever knew.

We also notice the Lord leading the prophets to perceive deeper meanings in common things:

1 *Jeremiah* watched the potter at the wheel and prophesied '"O house of Israel, can I not do with you as this potter does?" declares the Lord' (Jeremiah 18: 6).

2 *Amos* was shown a plumb-line (Amos 7: 7,8) and the Lord said 'I am setting a plumb-line among my people Israel; I will spare them no longer' (verse 8b).

3 *Saul* in his anxiety tore Samuel's cloak, 'Samuel said to him, "The Lord has torn the kingdom of Israel from you today"' (1 Samuel 15: 28).

4 *Daniel*, in answer to the question 'How long will it be before these astonishing things are fulfilled?' was given the mysterious reply 'It will be for a time, times and half a time' and was then told: 'The words are closed up and sealed until the time of the end.' (Daniel 12: 6,7,9).

New Testament illustration

Nicodemus (in John 3) and the woman of Samaria (in John 4) both thought they were speaking of one thing – 'being born of a woman' or 'getting a drink of water' – when in reality the Lord had used the conversation to draw out deeper spiritual truths.

Role of the mind

Dreams happen when the mind is asleep. Visions occur when the mind is awake. 'Enigmatic speech' comes through 'hearing' the voice of God, but the mind cannot immediately fathom its meaning.

Not face to face

'Moses was a very humble man, more humble than anyone else on the face of the earth' (Numbers 12: 3) and could be spoken to 'face to face, clearly and not in riddles' (Numbers 12: 8). The Lord had so prepared Moses that he could trust

Moses to remain faithful when he spoke to him plainly. Most of us would be quite unprepared for this. 'Enigmatic speech' with its degree of obscurity is, by God's grace and wisdom, a protection for us. Too much clarity, too quickly, could be overpowering. 'Enigmatic speech' gives us time to receive the grace to quieten our protesting hearts and listen.

Permission to be inconsistent

'Enigmatic speech' teaches us that human knowledge cannot encompass reality, and, therefore, we do not follow our rational mind, but the Spirit. We may learn to be relaxed with inconsistencies. The world and the devil hate illogicalities and inconsistencies. The guilty try to cover every loophole and ensure that everything looks sane and logical. The Lord's people know they are sinful and inconsistent: they are no longer under compulsion to make everything conform to a consistent standard. Satan seeks to establish a totalitarian regime where everything and everyone must conform to some pattern. But when we are 'walking in the Spirit' carnal logic no longer lords itself over us. We are free from the demands of uniformity and consistency.

Believers need to start along the road of rediscovery in this area of communication from God. We must be open to what God in his sovereignty wants to reveal to us through dreams, visions and 'enigmatic speech'; to begin to be relaxed with our God, whose thoughts transcend ours (Isaiah 55: 9), but who wants to reveal some truth about ourselves or others which will help us in our ministry for him.

As Christians, we need to develop a new sensitivity to dreams, visions and 'enigmatic speech', but we also need to know the proper safeguards if such means of communication from God are not to be distorted or exploited.

Six tests

Since there will always be some ambivalence about the

source of these communications, human or superhuman (if the latter, either divine or devilish) – we shall need to have some tests. As the Bible warns against false prophets so it also warns us against false dreams (Jeremiah 14: 14; 23: 32; Ezekiel 13: 3–7; Zechariah 10: 2). There is one instance in the Bible where we see how bodily needs may prompt a dream which upon awakening proves to be unreal (Isaiah 29: 8). Solomon wisely warns: 'Much dreaming and many words are meaningless. Therefore stand in awe of God' (Ecclesiastes 5: 7). The more heavenly the revelation may seem, the more carefully it needs to be tested (2 Corinthians 11: 4; 2 Thessalonians 2: 2).

Scripture

Does the revelation agree with Scripture? It may not have biblical symbolism, but it must be dismissed if it disagrees with scripture, sound doctrine or established Christian principles – 'We do not know the voice of strangers' (cf. John 10: 5).

1 Mormonism, for example, founded by Joseph Smith on his visions, contradicts the authority of scripture and the doctrine of God, besides containing other heresies.

2 Christian Science was founded in the same way by Mary Baker Eddy, who taught erroneously that sin and death were mere illusions.

Our heavenly Father

Does the revelation draw us closer to God the Father through Jesus Christ? Does it lead to peace or panic? Factual accuracy is not in itself proof of divine origin. The Bible warns against prophets whose words came to pass and said 'Let us follow other gods' (Deuteronomy 13: 1–5).

Occult

It is relevant to know if the recipient of the revelation has had any contact with the occult. If such contact has not been renounced and repented of, there is risk and we must 'test the spirits' anyway (1 John 4: 1–3).

Glory

Who gets the glory? The Bible is insistent that God must be the one glorified. Who is exalted by the revelation? The giver or the receiver? It is easy for the recipient of a revelation to get puffed up and assume that it is a sign of spirituality (Colossians 2: 18). Paul was given a 'thorn in the flesh' specifically to hold him in check at this level (2 Corinthians 12: 7).

Confirmation

There should normally be some kind of confirmation. Either the revelation itself confirms what we see God doing or some subsequent event should confirm the revelation. But let us beware that a sign which comes to pass does not in itself authenticate a revelation. We know that such signs can emanate from the enemy who always seeks to lead us astray (Deuteronomy 13: 1–3) and the devil can work wonders (Revelation 16: 14). When the angel Gabriel appeared to Mary in a vision he gave her clear signs so that she would *know* he was from God (Luke 1: 26–38).

Submission

When a revelation is believed to be from God for his Church, the recipient should offer it in a submissive spirit. Through the Body of Christ, the Holy Spirit will help us discern the source and purpose of any revelation; and sometimes with it the interpretation. Paul says 'I pray that you ... may have power, *together with all the saints*, to grasp how wide and long and high and deep is the love of Christ' (Ephesians 3: 17,18,19).

17

INVITING THE HOLY SPIRIT

Introduction

There are occasions when a leader who is open to God may sense that it is right and proper to invoke the Holy Spirit in the name of Jesus onto the people of God assembled in worship, or invite the Father to send his Holy Spirit to do this.

Reasons from scripture

Although at times the Spirit fell sovereignly and spontaneously (Acts 2: 2; Acts 10: 44), there were times when the disciples prayed for the Holy Spirit. 'After they prayed, the place where they were meeting was shaken. And they were all filled with the Holy Spirit' (Acts 4: 31).

We may proceed to do this, therefore, with confidence because:

1 The scriptures teach that we can ask for the Holy Spirit (Luke 11: 13).

2 The Church needs power. The Church was first *empowered* through the falling of the Holy Spirit on the disciples (Acts 1: 8, Acts 2: 4).

3 So often in the book of Acts, Church growth was triggered off with a manifestation of God's power through signs and wonders (e.g. Acts 5: 12,14).

4 Paul, in spite of brilliant reasoning, rated demonstrations of God's power more highly when preaching the gospel (1 Corinthians 2: 4).

5 Miracles, signs and wonders were wrought by the power of God to confirm the preaching of the gospel (Mark

16: 20; Acts 14: 3; Hebrews 2: 3,4).

6 The anointing of power through the Holy Spirit accomplishes the release of the gifts of the Spirit and allows God to initiate spiritual ministry (1 Corinthians 12: 11).

7 Such anointing blesses those who receive the Holy Spirit and those subsequently being ministered to by them. The gospel is confirmed, the kingdom of God is thereby extended and the name of Jesus glorified.

Reasons from tradition

There is a hint of the invocation of the Holy Spirit even in the early liturgies for the Holy Communion celebration. Today we pray, 'Grant that these gifts of bread and wine may be to us His body and His blood' (The First and Second Eucharistic Prayers of the *Alternative Service Book*) and that they 'may be to us the body and blood of our Lord Jesus Christ' (Third Eucharistic Prayer of the ASB).

The invocation to the Father to send the Holy Spirit upon the bread and wine is known liturgically as the 'epiclesis'. The 'epiclesis' has been regarded by some as support for the teaching that the bread and the wine are changed into the very body and blood of Christ. Whilst we ourselves could not go as far as this, we note how the practice of the Church has gradually changed. 'Evidence suggests that at one time *the Holy Spirit was invoked upon the communicants* that they might enjoy the benefits of Communion' (F L Cross *The Oxford Dictionary of the Christian Church* OUP 1961 p. 456).

The invocation of the Holy Spirit upon the congregation in the various modes (including hymns) during worship is common to the whole Christian Church. The difference between what we see in the scriptures and what we experience in practice is in the level of expectation. Too often we do not in fact expect God to do anything. The principle of 'according to your faith be it unto you' operates every time. And if God did manifest himself in most churches there would be great confusion because at all costs the programme devised by man must go on!

The manner of invocation

1 The congregation may be asked to stand to welcome the Holy Spirit.

2 Some such invocation may follow:

'Come now Holy Spirit. Anoint your people waiting here'; or 'Heavenly Father, we invite your Holy Spirit to fall on these your people gathered in the name of Jesus'; or (using a familiar bidding such as) 'The Lord is here', which evokes the liturgical response, 'His Spirit is with us.' Then say, 'Let the Holy Spirit now minister to each of you. Welcome His presence in your life.' As an alternative one could sing a familiar invocation, such as 'Spirit of the Living God, Fall afresh on me.'

3 Everyone should be encouraged to put his own will to this by welcoming the Holy Spirit into his life and by thanking him for coming.

4 Allow time for the Holy Spirit to do his own work. Do not be tempted to rush, but be prepared to tarry in silence. Be assured the Holy Spirit is active.

Some signs of the Holy Spirit's anointing

As we await the Holy Spirit's working, we may begin to observe one or more of the following phenomena being simultaneously manifest on the same person: fluttering of the eyelashes; appearance of engagement with God; 'sheen' on the face; flushes around the neck; feeling of heat; shaking or trembling; deep breathing; weeping – even very gently; laughing; peace; falling and even bouncing on the floor. Those ministering may be given discernment of what God is doing – a sense of 'knowing' of God's presence.

Although we know of similar manifestations occuring under other circumstances, our experience is that these frequently occur under an anointing of the Holy Spirit.

What to do next?

1 A prepared team may go to those who are manifestly being anointed.

2 It may be wise to take some people to another room for the sake of their personal dignity.

3 Those ministering should always keep their eyes open and observe what God is doing.

4 Those ministering can bless and honour what God is doing for his people. Lay a hand lightly upon the person under the power of the Holy Spirit, using such words as 'We bless you, Lord, for what you are doing in this person', 'We honour the work of the Holy Spirit in this person now, Lord' or 'Increase your power, Lord, upon this person.'

5 Those ministering should seek for 'words of knowledge' or other gifts of the Spirit, to show them what more God wants to do. Through a 'word of knowledge' the Lord may reveal a problem which is preventing the power of God reaching a certain area of life in the person being ministered to.

6 Those ministering should be relaxed and alert – seeking to minister quietly, gently and unemotionally.

How to conclude?

The leadership must always be open to the Holy Spirit, who suggests an amazing variety of alternatives. There is no correct pattern with the Holy Spirit and frequently no known pathway. 'The wind blows wherever it pleases'! (John 3: 8). When the leader senses that this phase of the ministry is complete, he may suggest that everyone sits down.

1 A 'Thanksgiving' to God may be offered.

2 Some of those anointed may feel 'power', or tingling in their hands; even extreme heaviness in the arms. This will often reveal that there are other people present who need healing. Those anointed for healing may gather round to minister to those who indicate a need for healing. Alternatively they may go to another room to minister as the worship continues in the church.

An uncomfortable ministry

1 Accept that this is an uncomfortable ministry.

2 God is unpredictable.
3 God can often be untidy.
4 We must let God be God.

18

'FALLING' UNDER THE POWER OF GOD

Introduction

Sooner or later involvement in this ministry will lead to a person being prayed for falling to the ground under the power of the Holy Spirit. This may come as quite a shock to those ministering if they have never experienced it before, especially when they know they have done nothing deliberately to induce it except invite the Holy Spirit to come. It can also cause considerable concern to any congregation which has never seen the like in their church before. Because this phenomenon seems to be increasingly common and because of lack of literature readily available on the subject, it may be helpful to see the falling manifestation in perspective.

Material available

Fr Francis MacNutt has included material on this subject in his book, *The Power to Heal*, written in 1977. Fr George Malmey has produced a leaflet entitled 'How to understand and evaluate the Charismatics' newest experience – Slaying in the Spirit.' There is reference to it also in the Rev. Colin Urquhart's *Faith for the Future*, the Rev. Trevor Dearing's *Supernatural Healing*, Pastor Trevor Martin's *Kingdom Healing*. The Rev. John Richards had an article entitled 'Out to Heal' in *Theological Renewal* (No. 13), 1975, and also dealt with the subject in a review of the Rev. Trevor Dearing's book *Supernatural Healing Today* in Renewal (No. 83) in 1979. Also relevant is Cecil Cousins' review of MacNutt's book *The Power to Heal* entitled 'Dilemmas of the Healing Ministries' in *Renewal* (No. 72), December, 1977, followed by a letter in response to this by Mrs Shepherd entitled 'Resting in the Spirit', *Renewal* (No. 74), April, 1978. Evangelist Don Double wrote an article, 'Slain in the Spirit', which was published in *Renewal* (No. 80) in April, 1979. Most Catholic writers on the subject have turned to the mystical writings of St John of the Cross and St Teresa for insight into assessing the phenomenon. Cardinal Suenens wrote an article on the subject in *Ecumenical and Charismatic Renewal: Theological and Pastoral Orientations*, published by Darton, Longman and Todd, and reprinted, with permission, in 1979 by *Renewal*. The Rev. John Richards published a pamphlet (reprinted in April, 1983) on the subject entitled *Resting in the Spirit* available from Renewal Servicing, P.O. Box 366, Addlestone, Weybridge, Surrey, from which pamphlet much has been drawn here.

Common description

Phrases such as 'falling under the Power', 'resting in the Spirit', 'being slain by the Spirit', 'being overcome by the Spirit', prostrations, paroxysms, swooning, fainting, 'flaking out', being 'zapped' or 'having a glory fit' have commonly been used to describe the phenomenon. Some of them are helpful – others are much less so and may even be misleading.

Scriptural references to 'Falling'

1 The *prophets* sometimes fell as the Spirit came upon them, giving them a vision or a burden or a message from God. 'When I saw it (the likeness of the glory of the Lord), I fell face down, and I heard the voice of one speaking' (Ezekiel 1: 28) – 'Then I heard him speaking, and as I listened to him, I fell into a deep sleep, my face to the ground' (Daniel 10: 9) and John the Divine in Revelation 1: 17 – 'When I saw him, I fell at his feet as though dead' (Revelation 1: 17).

2 The *priests* in the Old Testament appear to have fallen

under the overwhelming 'cloud of God's presence' as they worshipped the Lord at the time of the Temple rededication (2 Chronicles 5: 14).

3 The *disciples* who accompanied Christ fell on their faces before their transfigured Lord (Matthew 17: 6).

4 Some *people* being delivered of demons fell under God's power, it seems. 'Whenever the evil spirits saw him (Jesus), they fell down before him and cried out "You are the Son of God"' (Mark 3: 11). When the epileptic boy was delivered of a demon at the command of Jesus, 'The spirit shrieked, convulsed him violently and came out. The boy looked so much like a corpse that many said, "He's dead." But Jesus . . . lifted him to his feet, and he stood up' (Mark 9: 26,27).

5 *Saul* (who became the apostle Paul) was thrown to the ground with *all his companions* when he saw a light from heaven on his journey to Damascus – 'We all fell to the ground, and I heard a voice . . .' (Acts 26: 14; cf. Acts 9: 4).

6 *An unbeliever* coming into the company of believers where the gifts of the Spirit are manifested 'will fall down and worship God, exclaiming, "God is really among you!"' (1 Corinthians 14: 25).

7 *The crowd* at Jesus' arrest drew back when Jesus said 'I am he' and fell to the ground (John 18: 6).

The 'Falling' phenomenon in history

St Teresa of Avila in sixteenth century Spain was caught up in the Counter-Reformation taking place in the Roman Catholic Church. Discussing 'trances' in her book on prayer *Interior Castle*, she was aware of some abuses, but viewed them positively. Revivals in the eighteenth and nineteenth century have been notable for manifestations of power, among which were 'prostrations'. John Wesley, in his Journal, records a meeting where: 'One and then another sunk to the earth. They dropped on every side as thunderstruck.' The phenomenon was also common in many Welsh revivals between 1762 and 1905.

What happens when people fall?

Unbelievers sometimes get converted when their experience of God's power is accompanied by such prostrations (1 Corinthians 14: 25), though not necessarily everyone who 'falls' finds it a life changing experience. There is no evidence for anything of spiritual value happening either to the crowds who came to arrest Jesus (John 18: 6) or to the crowd around Saul, who all fell to the ground (Acts 26: 14). The phenomenon may be a manifestation of a 'power encounter' between light and darkness. 'Falling' accompanied the deliverance ministry observed in the case of the crowds in Mark 3 and the epileptic boy in Mark 9.

Some believers (cf. the priests worshipping God) have been prostrated by the power of God in the course of public worship and others individually in private, cf. Ezekiel, Daniel and John the Divine.

Reading back into the phenomenon from our own experience today, it may be a type of conversion experience a revelation from God, an anointing for the believers to a ministry, an inner healing of some kind, or a form of spiritual deliverance.

In conclusion we may say, after talking to hundreds who have experienced it, that falling to the ground after an encounter with the power of God in a special way seems to be a perfectly wholesome experience. (It is important to note here that there may be a variety of other manifestations besides falling during such 'power encounters'.)

Dilemmas

John Richards warns us that this 'falling down' is a snare to four kinds of people:

1 Those within the Church who wish to make the unusual the focus of their thinking.

2 Those outside who single out any unusual phenomena which perplex or even frighten and make such the focus of their thinking.

3 Those who are 'soulish' and go for every kind of

spiritual manifestation as a kind of boost to spiritual pride. Such may easily affect such a manifestation for the wrong reasons.

4 Those who are looking for some way of drawing attention to their ministry and will even appear at times to be pushing people physically to make them fall. We may have seen this sort of thing (on the TV even) and many believe that people only 'fall' as a result of a human push.

It is inevitable that some form of crowd dynamics will always be operative when Christian people gather in large numbers for worship. There is no need to try to eliminate this. In fact it would be impossible. We need simply to be aware of such psychological factors so that we do not create the phenomenon, but allow God to create it if he so wills (as, according to scripture, he is well able to do). The unconscious desire to fall can effect it. There may be many reasons for such a desire. If, for example, we believe mistakenly that it is a greater blessing than not falling, or if we believe that God is visibly demonstrating his blessing on our life, or if we mistakenly believe it is a badge of God's approval.

Ministry to those who have 'fallen'

1 Wherever possible, someone should stay beside those who have fallen until they want to sit or get up.

2 There is no need to do anything except watch and pray quietly (in tongues too) and bless what God is doing.

3 If any further ministry is needed, the Lord will make it plain in his own way, and at the right time.

Perception of the phenomenon

It is important to recognise that our own fears and feelings of insecurity may be more prominent than the real nature of the phenomenon itself. It is good to share our feelings and reactions with our church minister, or some other respected Christian in the congregation.

Conclusion

It is often helpful to talk to people 'overcome', following such an experience. Usually the response will be a feeling of deep peace and calm. We have talked to many, so it may be helpful to share some feed-back from our own ministries at this point. We give a few examples in conclusion.

About six months ago a lady came forward following evening worship in the church and knelt at the rails. She asked for prayer concerning a thyroid condition. My wife encouraged her to relax and invoked the Holy Spirit to come and minister to her. A few seconds later she was falling backwards. Her husband came forward believing she had fainted and wanted to put her head betwen her knees to revive her, but was deterred when trying to touch her head and he felt 'currents' of power coming from her. She remained on the floor for some fifteen minutes or so, after which she got to her feet, thanked those who had prayed for her and departed. The following day she phoned up, identifying herself as the one prayed for who had keeled over. She said 'Hullo, my name is . . . I am a Jewess, but I want to be baptised. I have become a believer in Jesus.' She was recently confirmed by the Bishop of St Alban's. Glory be to God!

Some two years ago a boy came forward for prayer in St Andrew's. He had a history of epilepsy, was small, hyperactive and behind in his school work due to this affliction. The Holy Spirit was invoked to come upon him, and a few seconds later he fell to the floor. He looked so white and still that at least one person thought he had died and was only comforted by reflecting that when Jesus ministered to an epileptic he fell and appeared 'like a corpse' (Mark 9: 26). After a while the boy seemed to revive and his parents took him home and put him to bed. He slept for fourteen hours; in fact he slept so much the following week that he could not go to school. Since that day he has never had a single 'fit'. He has grown several inches. By the time this is in print he will have taken several O-levels at school. His doctor has just seen him and says there is no reason why he should not drive a motor bike. This was the Lord's doing and is marvellous in our eyes!

We have recently heard of a ministry similar to that of Jackie Pullinger in Hong Kong (who found that once a new convert was speaking in tongues it was relatively easy to break the grip which drugs had over him). In this case the ministry is also being developed in the Far East, but the power of drugs seems often to be broken following a manifestation of the Holy Spirit which has 'prostrated' the addict first.

19

VALUES IN THE HEALING MINISTRY

Values are the foundation upon which any ministry is based. The stronger these values, the more enduring the ministry will be. From the values we hold we rate our priorities, and our priorities obviously become our practices. There are five main values which undergird our ministry of healing, since we discovered them from the Vineyard Christian Fellowship at Anaheim, Los Angeles.

We value the work of the Holy Spirit

The book of Acts provides excellent examples of the ministry of the Holy Spirit being properly valued and of the beneficial consequences accompanying his work.

1 The Holy Spirit is revealed to be the active administrator of the Church (Acts 13: 1–4). How often do we think the Church should be run by the minister, the elders, the deacons, or the Parochial Church Council, etc.? It is a novel concept today to regard the Holy Spirit as the administrator of the Church. What was a normal value in the book of Acts has been absent for so long that any direct intervention by the Holy Spirit in the life of a Church is too often dismissed as abnormal.

2 The Holy Spirit acts dynamically among God's people and gives gifts generally and generously (1 Corinthians 12: 11).

3 The Holy Spirit always comes when requested (Luke 11: 9–13), especially when two or three are agreed about inviting him (Matthew 18: 19), though of course there is no

guarantee that the person being ministered to will welcome the Holy Spirit specifically into his life.

4 It is vital to observe and learn from what the Holy Spirit is doing in a person as we minister to him.

a) For this reason we minister with our eyes open – to see what the Spirit is doing.

b) We also minister with openness to the Holy Spirit – listening to what the Holy Spirit may be telling us or others involved with us in praying, through words of knowledge or wisdom, etc.

5 We need to allow the Holy Spirit *time* to do his own work – to let God be God.

6 It is wise to *say as little as possible* when ministering in the Spirit. It is good simply to bless and honour what God is doing at that moment in the life of the person to whom ministry is being given.

We value harmony in relationships

1 Relationships are of primary importance. Healing flows where relationships are harmonised and reconciled. Sickness is often a by-product of a bad or broken relationship.

2 Our relationship with God the Father, the Son and the Holy Spirit needs to be fostered in worship and prayer, repentance, confession of sin and forgiveness (Galatians 6: 1–10).

3 Our relationships within the Christian family need constant attention. We are taught to pray 'Forgive us our sins, for we forgive everyone who sins against us' (Luke 11: 4). Matthew gives practical guidance about dealing with sins in the Christian fellowship in Matthew 18: 15–17, and Paul instructs us to 'Be devoted to one another in brotherly love. Honour one another above yourselves' (Romans 12: 10), the latter part being expounded in Ephesians 5: 21: 'Submit to one another out of reverence for Christ.'

4 The relationship of the one ministered to and all with whom he has been involved in life may need to be 'harmonised' very early in the ministry of healing (Romans 12: 18; and 14: 17) (see chapter 23 on forgiveness).

5 The relationship between those ministering and those being ministered to should be governed by truth, love, purity (Ephesians 5: 3) and humility. We should never be ministering 'down' to people. We will not manipulate those to whom we are ministering into saying things they are not experiencing. Nor will we pressure people to say things intended only to feed our pride.

We value the individual person

The kingdom of God is made up of individuals.

1 Man enters the kingdom of God as an individual; 'Unless a man is born again, he cannot see (or enter) the kingdom of God' (John 3: 3,5).

2 Although we all need to belong to a church family, God still cares for the individual. Jesus taught 'Whatever you did for one of the least of these brothers of mine, you did for me' (Matthew 25: 40). God counts our tears (Psalm 56: 8) and even the hairs on our head (Matthew 10: 30). The good shepherd calls his own (individual) sheep by name (John 10: 3). He knows his sheep and they know him (John 10: 14). He leaves the ninety and nine to find the individual lost sheep (Luke 15: 4). We shall all stand before the judgment seat of God as individuals (Hebrews 9: 27; Romans 14: 12).

3 Jesus picked out a disabled individual at the Pool of Bethesda and said: 'Do you want to get well?' (John 5: 6) (see chapter 3, 'Wholeness'). We minister to the spiritual, emotional, physical, mental and social areas of the individual's life – his whole being.

Love

In ministry we will want the afflicted person to feel loved. This is not, however, the place to minister sympathy. Sick people do often cry out for sympathy, but love may override sympathy when it is plain that this will prevent the healing which is necessary. A sufferer sometimes is tempted to befriend his sickness to gain more sympathy.

Dignity

If on occasion it is necessary to hear some shameful

confession in the process of a man's repentance, it is important to demonstrate to the individual that he is still worthy of dignity and love. To ensure this we should avoid ministering in an accusing way, imposing guilt, bondage or embarrassment. We must never send someone away feeling that it's all his fault, that he has too much sin or too little faith.

Sensitivity

We shall be especially sensitive in the way we offer what we feel God is telling us through words of knowledge or wisdom. If, for instance, God reveals that the problem is related to a previous marriage we could say something such as: 'What I seem to be getting at the moment is that before any healing can begin there is something blocking God's grace' – give the person time to make his own observation – 'Could it be anything unresolved from your first marriage? How do you feel about this?' Such an approach is less accusing or dogmatic and allows space for the other person to disagree with dignity. It leaves him free to exercise his own will, which is an essential element in any healing from God. The imposition of the will of the one ministering can be very counter-productive in this area.

We value biblical authority

1 The Bible teaches that it is God's nature to heal. 'I am the Lord who heals you' (Exodus 15: 26). We should look again at the ministry of Jesus. The gospel shows that Jesus not only healed the sick, taught about it and commissioned others to heal, but that he never turned anyone away who came to him for healing.

2 We need to remind ourselves that it is our calling to be involved in the healing ministry. This was part of Jesus's commission to the twelve in Luke 9 and later to the seventy-two in Luke 10. It must have been included in the Great Commission (Matthew 28 and Mark 16). It was continued by the early disciples (Philip in Acts 8: 6 and Stephen in Acts 6: 8).

3 We need to be sure that the ministry of healing is

anchored in the truth of the Bible. We should constantly check the biblical evidence.

4 Healing is a way of proclaiming the mercy, the love and the glory of God.

5 This ministry must never be abused. There may be the temptation to exploit it for money (Acts 8: 18,19) or to achieve special status through it for ourselves (2 Corinthians 2: 17).

6 Healing is part of a process towards wholeness (see chapter 3). With every exchange there is a measure of healing. We must never assume that nothing has taken place when we minister 'in the Spirit'. It is impossible to measure what God is doing.

We value the Body of Christ

1 The Body of Christ is the spiritual and social family to which we belong and we isolate ourselves from it at our cost. The place to learn is within the Body of Christ – the people of God (1 Corinthians 14: 23–24). The meeting place is the learning place for the market-place.

2 The congregation meets under authority (Hebrews 13: 17). Whilst the ministry of healing is kept within the body there will be many inbuilt checks against abuse – both the authority of the church and the variety of the gifts. Body ministry (rather than a superstar activity) helps to preserve a greater humility amongst those ministering and the glory will properly be given to God. We can recount the mighty works of God we have witnessed to the church and avoid the elevation of any particular individual to a position of status for what is attributable solely to God.

3 Gifts are distributed to each member of the congregation whenever it meets for the common good (1 Corinthians 12: 7; 1 Corinthians 14: 12; 1 Peter 2: 9). Those who exercise the gifts dispensed to them may find they receive the same gift more and more often and in time the church will recognise they have a particular ministry along the lines of this or that gift. Ideally every believer can become part of a team involved in healing the sick.

4 Those who develop this kind of work should also be

helping to train others by having them alongside as they minister so that the number of those ministering is always increasing. Ministry in the power of God's Spirit is taken out into the world for the extension of God's kingdom and the excellence of his glory (1 Peter 4: 10).

20

REASONS WHY WE HAVE NOT HEALED THE SICK

This study presents reasons why we do not pray for the sick, reasons why we should and questions which arise on the subject.

Reasons why people do not pray for the sick

1 A faulty world view. Some have a rational view of the world. Others assume that because they have never seen such healing it doesn't happen.

2 A lack of power. Where we make our goal the acquisition of knowledge we will never experience the power.

3 The absence of an acceptable model. Most of us have never seen effective healing ministered in a way that we could relate to.

4 A concern for God's reputation or our own, should healing not occur in the way expected.

5 A restricted theology of healing, discernible in such rationalisations as 'It is not that I think that God can't heal; it's just that I believe he doesn't usually do it. Anyway, I don't think we should bother God about such a small thing as a headache when there are so many problems in the world which are vast and horrific.'

6 A fear of how others will react once we begin praying for healing. This could be a fear of ending up friendless or a fear of being regarded as fanatical.

7 A lack of encouragement from the rest of the Body of Christ.

Reasons why people do pray for the sick

Reasons from common sense

1 If God were only a good human friend he would want me well.

2 A normal person wants to be healthy and will take practical steps to stay healthy.

3 It is an obvious way to spread the gospel. It is often easier to pray for someone's healing than to share the gospel with them – especially when we think they have heard it all before.

4 It is not necessary to have a developed theology to believe that God can think the same way.

Reasons from scripture

It is the Lord who heals: 'He said, "If you listen carefully to the voice of the Lord your God and do what is right in his eyes, if you pay attention to his commands and keep all his decrees, I will not bring on you any of the diseases I brought on the Egyptians, for I am the Lord who heals you"' (Exodus 15: 26). 'If you pay attention to these laws and are careful to follow them then the Lord your God ... will keep you free from every disease' (Deuteronomy 7: 12–15).

1 The command to heal was always integral to the total commission of Christ to his disciples (Luke 9: 1; 10: 9; Matthew 28: 20).

2 This commission is amplified: 'They will place their hands on sick people, and they will get well' (Mark 16: 18).

3 Gifts of healings (1 Corinthians 12) come from God. If he gives such gifts, they should not be buried, but used.

4 Sick people are encouraged to call for the elders to minister healing to them. Prayer offered in faith will make the sick person well; the Lord will raise him up (James 5: 15).

Reasons from Church history

1 In the first one hundred years (the apostolic area) of the Church healing was a common activity. A by-word among Christians was, 'If you see a brother who is sick and do not heal him, his blood will be on your hands.' Healings,

signs and wonders were an integral part of the proclamation of the gospel in the early Church.

2 It is surprising to see how many references to healing
miracles occur in the ministry of the early Church fathers,
e.g. Irenaeus (140–202), Origen (185–254), Ambrose
(340–97), Athanasius (296–373), Basil (329–79), Gregory of
Nazianzus (329–89), Macrina (327–379), Augustine of
Hippo (354–430), Benedict (480–547), Gregory of Tours
(538–594) Pope Gregory I (540–604), Bede (673–735),
Malarchy of Ireland (1094–1149), Antony of Padua
(1195–1231), Edmund of Canterbury (1180–1240), Richard
of Chichester (1193–1253), Dominic (1170–1221), Francis
of Assisi (1182–1226), Thomas of Hereford (1218–1282)
and Catherine of Siena (1333–1380).

3 Healing was taken over into the Reformist Movement;
cf. the life and work of Peter Waldo of Lyons (died
1217), founder of the Waldensians, Martin Luther (1483–
1546), and Blaise Paschal, a leading Jansenist (from 1656
onwards).

4 Healing has always accompanied the great religious
revivals: John Wesley (1703–91), Prince Alexander of
Hohenlohe (c.1815), Johann Cristoph Blumhardt (Black
Forest – 1842), Dorothy Trudel (USA) (1850), Alexander
Dowie (1847–1906), Mary Woodworth-Etter (1876), Smith
Wigglesworth (1860–1947).

5 Healing has been a common phenomenon in the
proclamation of the gospel by many missionaries during the
history of the Protestant missionary movement com-
menced by William Carey (1761–1834).

6 In this present century William Branham, Smith
Wigglesworth, Alexander Peddie, F L Wyman, Kathryn
Kuhlman, Oral Roberts, Francis MacNutt, Jim Glennon –
and a vast number of others have become increasingly
involved.

Matters arising

It is natural for questions to arise as the church moves into
the ministry of praying for the sick. Often questions can
inhibit us and prevent our ever getting involved in a healing
ministry. We need have no fear about facing up to the
problems involved if we are open to God.

Does everyone get healed?

Let us notice:

1 Jesus healed *all* who came to him (Matthew 4: 24; 8: 16; Mark 1: 32; Luke 6: 18,19). In the case of Peter's shadow and Paul's handkerchiefs, all were healed (Acts 5: 15,16; 19: 11,12).

2 There were clearly special times of anointing, e.g. 'The power of the Lord was present for him to heal the sick' (Luke 5: 17).

3 But Jesus healed only *one* man at the pool of Bethesda, which was a kind of hospital where many sick were assembled for healing in the pool (John 5: 2,3). Jesus explains that 'the Son... can do only what he sees his Father doing' (John 5: 19).

4 As crowds were coming to be healed, Jesus would often withdraw to lonely places for prayer (Luke 5: 15,16).

5 We may conclude that though Jesus healed all who actually came to him everyone in need was not healed. Though our desire is for all to be healed today we may only minister as the Father reveals.

Does every healing happen immediately?

1 Most of the healings recorded in the New Testament seem to have happened immediately (cf. Mark 1: 31,42).

2 Jesus prayed twice for a blind man. Then he saw men like trees walking about (Mark 8: 24).

3 Physical healing may sometimes be delayed because other matters need to be dealt with first. As a man's spiritual health improves, so it beneficially affects his physical state (3 John 2).

What about the use of medicine?

1 Asa is criticised because he sought a physician and not the Lord (2 Chronicles 16: 12). This cannot be used as proof that we should not go to the doctor. Physicians in those days frequently resorted to occult practices.

2 Paul encouraged Timothy to use a little wine for his stomach because of its medicinal benefits (1 Timothy 5: 23).

3 Jesus used spittle (John 9: 6; Mark 7: 33; 8: 33) and the disciples used oil (Mark 6: 13). Both were considered to have

healing qualities. However, the issue is not whether these elements had healing qualities or not, but that Jesus did not disassociate himself from medicine. In fact he seemed to sanction it. The priests to whom he sent the ten lepers represented the health officials of the day (Luke 17: 14).

4 God is the source of all healing, but he uses various means to heal.

What about dying?

1 We must accept that there is a time to die (Ecclesiastes 3: 2; Hebrews 9: 27).

2 We cannot control the moment when this should be.

3 However, we do not have to die before our time through sin, sickness or judgment (1 Corinthians 11: 30).

4 Sickness does not have to be the cause of death, and even then Jesus has control over death and can raise the dead (John 11: 1, 40–44).

5 Therefore we need to discern when a sickness is 'unto death' and minister comfort and courage to the dying.

Is sickness always caused by sin?

1 In the Old Testament there appears to be a direct relationship between sin and sickness (Deuteronomy 28: 15,21) whereas in the New Testament the emphasis is on the healing power of Jesus over the works of the devil (Acts 10: 38).

2 Jesus was asked about the blind man he was about to heal in John 9, 'who sinned this man or his parents, that he was born blind?' Jesus replied that this blindness was not due to sin in either the blind man or his parents.

3 However, in the case of the lame man at the Bethesda pool being healed, Jesus warned the man not to continue in the sin (which seems to have caused his lameness) lest something worse should happen (John 5: 14).

4 In conclusion, it seems that although all sickness comes originally through the curse of sin, not all sickness is caused by specific sins in the afflicted individual.

How do we account for Christian believers who do not get well?

1 Paul had an eye affliction for some reason not cited (Galatians 4: 13–16).

2 Trophimus was left sick at Miletus and no explanation is given (2 Timothy 4: 20).

3 Epaphroditus was ill and almost died, but God had mercy (Philippians 2: 26,27).

4 Timothy had a persistent stomach complaint for which Paul prescribed some wine (1 Timothy 5: 23).

5 It should be pointed out that Paul's thorn in the flesh (2 Corinthians 12: 7–10) was not sickness, but from both the context and cross reference with the Old Testament it is clear that it was opposition from other people.

6 Where someone is not healed it could be worthwhile checking on such areas as unforgiveness, deeper emotional hurts, unbelief or faithlessness, but in the final analysis it must always be recognised that our sovereign God may have some inscrutable reasons which he is not willing to disclose (Isaiah 55: 9). God may permit the sickness for some greater objective. He may delay the healing because it is not in his time (John 8: 8; 11: 6). He may choose to use another human instrument for his sovereign purposes.

7 It is very important that no one is left feeling accused by us that he must have some hidden sin or condemned that he did not have enough faith.

Does sickness and suffering come from God?

1 In the Christian life sickness and suffering are not synonymous. There is no indication in the New Testament that suffering means or involves sickness. Christ was never sick, but he suffered gruesomely (Acts 10: 39, cf. Philippians 1: 29).

There are beatitudes for those who are poor in spirit (Matthew 5: 3) those who mourn (Matthew 5: 4) and for those who are persecuted (Matthew 5: 10) but there is no beatitude for those who are sick!

2 It is God's nature to heal. It is not his purpose to teach us through sickness. Sickness is never made to appear beneficial in the New Testament. The lame man at the pool of Bethesda had been robbed of his freedom for thirty-eight years.

3 Indisputably, people have been drawn nearer to God through sickness, but the virtue lies in God's goodness,

which leads to repentance and acceptance rather than in what the sickness has done (Romans 2: 4, cf. 1 Corinthians 11: 29–32).

4 'Unnecessary suffering' in innocent children and helpless people cannot be blamed on God, who is 'love' (1 John 4: 8). The curse of sin in the world results in constant war, famine, poverty, etc.; and sometimes the effect of the sins of parents remain in the bloodline of a family to the third and fourth generations (Exodus 20: 5b; 34: 6,7; Psalm 51: 5).

21

WHO SHOULD MINISTER?

Introduction

Question: If this ministry is potentially for all, how mature, whole and holy does a person need to be before he/she can be trusted with it?

Answer: 'As mature, whole and holy as the disciples were when Jesus trusted them with such ministry.'

Focus on the disciples

We notice the following remarkable *deficiencies* in the characters of certain of the disciples of Jesus:

1 *Ambitious:* They wanted to be great (Mark 9: 34).

2 *Argumentative:* They argued (Mark 9: 33).

3 *Cowardly:* Peter disowned Jesus three times (Matthew 26: 70,72,74).

4 *Critical:* The disciples questioned the waste of expensive perfume used for anointing Jesus (Matthew 26: 8).

5 *Deceived:* The disciples experienced failure in their ministry (Matthew 17: 16).

6 *Deserters:* Everyone deserted Jesus and fled (Mark 14: 50).

7 *Doubtful:* The disciples doubted Christ's ability to repeat a miracle (Mark 8: 4, cf. Mark 6: 37). Thomas temporarily doubted Christ's resurrection (John 20: 25).

8 *Dull:* They did not understand his teaching (Matthew 15: 16).

9 *Faithless:* They were lacking faith (Matthew 17: 20), and asked Jesus to increase it (Luke 17: 5).

10 *Greedy:* Judas was a thief (John 12: 6) and betrayed Jesus for money (Matthew 26: 14,15).

11 *Misunderstanding:* Peter rebuked Jesus (Matthew 16: 22).

12 *Prayerless*: They were lacking in prayer (Mark 9: 28,29). They asked Jesus to teach them how to pray (Luke 11: 1).

13 *Revengeful:* They wanted to call down fire on unbelieving villagers (Luke 9: 54).

14 *Unforgiving:* Peter lacked understanding about forgiveness (Matthew 18: 21).

15 *Unloving:* The disciples rebuked those who brought babes to Jesus for blessing (Mark 10: 13).

These were the people Jesus appointed to minister in his name (Luke 9: 1–6 and 10: 1–12). Clearly these men were not yet mature, whole or holy, yet Jesus chose to commission them to preach and heal, etc.

Focus on the church at Corinth

1 The past character records of the members in the Church at Corinth were not good (1 Corinthians 6: 9–10). Paul gives a shocking list, but adds 'And that is what some of you were. But you were washed, you were sanctified, you were justified in the name of the Lord Jesus Christ and by the Spirit of our God' (1 Corinthians 6: 11).

2 The present conduct of the church members at Corinth was not good either. Paul criticises their compromise in lifestyle (1 Corinthians 10: 21), the conduct of their meetings (1 Corinthians 11: 17), warns of divisions in the Church (1 Corinthians 11: 18) and abuses (self-centredness and irreverence) of the Lord's supper (1 Corinthians 11: 21,27).

3 Yet he says: 'To *each one* the manifestation of the Spirit is given for the common good' (1 Corinthians 12: 7). God gives the gifts of the Spirit 'to *each man*, just as he determines' (1 Corinthians 12: 11). The important point to notice is that in the same letter Paul tries both to correct

their faults and to help them in the use of their gifts. 'When you come together, everyone has a hymn, or a word of instruction, a revelation, a tongue or an interpretation. All of these must be done for the strengthening of the church' (1 Corinthians 14: 26).

4 The conditions of this ministry:

a) The operation of the gifts of the Spirit should go hand in hand with the cultivation of the fruits of the Spirit.

b) In the middle of Paul's description of the nine gifts of the Spirit (1 Corinthians 12) and explanations of how to use them (1 Corinthians 14) is that sublime chapter on love (1 Corinthians 13).

c) This should not be surprising as Jesus is often recorded as ministering out of compassion (Matthew 15: 32; Mark 8: 2; Matthew 20: 34; Mark 5: 19; Luke 7: 13).

d) A close examination of 1 Corinthians 13 would seem to show that love is the mother of all the fruits of the Spirit found in Galatians 5: 22.

5 The heart of this ministry:

a) *Love:* This abides in conjunction with faith and hope and is the greatest of the three (1 Corinthians 13: 13);

b) *Joy:* Love rejoices with the truth (13: 6);

c) *Peace:* Love is not easily angered (13: 5), does not envy, nor boast (13: 4);

d) *Patience:* Love is patient (13: 4);

e) *Kindness:* Love is kind (13: 4);

f) *Goodness:* Love is not proud (13: 4), does not delight in evil (13: 6);

g) *Faithfulness:* Love always trusts, always hopes (13: 7);

h) *Gentleness:* Love always protects (13: 7), keeps no record of wrongs, is not rude (13: 5);

i) *Self-control:* Love is not self-seeking and perseveres (13: 5 and 7).

Focus on Paul

1 'We put no stumbling block in anyone's path, so that our ministry will not be discredited' (2 Corinthians 6: 3).

2 Paul commends his own ministry: 'We commend

ourselves in every way' and discusses his lifestyle (2 Corinthians 6: 4) as follows:

a) *Self-control:* 'in great endurance; in troubles, hardships and distresses; in beatings, imprisonments and riots; in hard work, in sleepless nights and hunger';

b) *Goodness:* 'in purity, understanding';

c) *Patience:* 'patience';

d) *Kindness:* 'kindness', 'in the Holy Spirit';

e) *Love:* 'in sincere love';

f) *Peace:* 'in truthful speech and in the power of God';

g) *Gentleness:* 'with weapons of righteousness in the right hand and in the left';

h) *Faithfulness:* 'through glory and dishonour, bad report and good report; genuine, yet regarded as imposters; known, yet regarded as unknown; dying, and yet we live on; beaten, and yet not killed';

i) *Joy:* 'sorrowful, yet always rejoicing; poor, yet making many rich; having nothing, and yet possessing everything'.

Paul did not claim to be perfect, but he ministered powerfully as he pressed on towards the high calling of God in Christ Jesus (Philippians 3: 14).

Focus on the church at Ephesus

All God's people should be being prepared for ministry.

1 Paul writes to the Ephesian Christians that God 'gave some to be apostles, some to be prophets, some to be evangelists, and some to be pastors and teachers, *to prepare God's people for work of service* (ministry), so that the body of Christ may be built up' (Ephesians 4: 11, 12).

2 Maturity comes through ministry, 'until we all reach unity in the faith and in the knowledge of the Son of God and become mature, attaining to the whole measure of the fulness of Christ' (Ephesians 4: 13). The unity, the knowledge, the maturity and the wholeness came *through* ministry.

Focus on the Church today

Clearly the evidence of serious deficiencies in the disciples
and the churches did not prevent their receiving God's
commission. It is equally clear that God's commission to
minister is no excuse for not going on to maturity. Spiritual
maturity is not the key to ministry though it is the key to
quality ministry. We must not hold back out of our sense of
unworthiness, but we should not continue in ministry
without seeking God's grace to help us in the area of our
obvious deficiencies.

As soon as a church becomes aware of the potential in
this ministry, the question arises as to who should be
involved 'up front'. He should be:

Subject to faith

Here we are not talking about the gift of faith – we are
talking about the relationship of faith – trusting in God the
Father and knowing his Son, Jesus, believing that Christ
died for our sins on the cross. This is basic to becoming a
disciple of Jesus. 'Without faith it is impossible to please
God, because anyone who comes to him must believe that
he exists' (Hebrews 11: 6).

Subject to prayer

Having begun in faith, we continue in faith. A child simply
trusts. But it would be unusual if the child did not begin to
relate to his parents. The relationship of faith is developed
through prayer. It would be possible to minister power in a
limited way without prayer, but sooner or later the disciple
will realise how futile such a ministry is without the prayer
relationship. When the disciples failed to heal the epileptic
boy, Jesus pointed out that 'This kind can come out only by
prayer' (Mark 9: 29). James said that it was the prayer of a
righteous man that was powerful and effective (James 5:
16). Prayer is the communication line in our faith
relationship with God, through Jesus Christ, who has
plainly said, 'No-one comes to the Father except through
me' (John 14: 6) and 'Apart from me you can do nothing'
(John 15: 5).

Subject to anointing

Those who minister must know God's anointing. Jesus said to the disciples that they would receive power after the Holy Spirit had come upon them (Acts 1: 8). The first requisite for those wanting to minister is that they are disciples who have experienced God's anointing of power through the Holy Spirit.

The ministry is God's. He shows us what he wants us to do. He shows us how to minister his power. *He* does it. There is no magic formula, no technique, beyond allowing God, through His Holy Spirit, to take over and do what he chooses.

Subject to authority

Those who minister must be subject to authority in the church. Church leaders may not know all there is to know about this ministry, but they do know what their own responsibility is in the Body of Christ (Hebrews 13: 17).

Any person with experience in ministering knows what a great help it is to be under authority in the church. The rest of the Body of Christ senses the rightness of the ministry when it is properly authorised and overseen.

This does not mean that mistakes can never happen this way. They will often happen on the way along our learning curve, but it does mean that if and when they do happen the church knows that there is authority for sorting things out and that the same mistakes are not repeated over and over again by the same people.

Subject to being taught

Those who minister must have a teachable spirit. If they are authorised and then won't listen to those over them, the whole ministry will be threatened. Those in authority may not always know the answers, but they can lead those involved in this ministry in seeking answers from the Lord. There must be submission to them as they seek to check any apparent abuse or misuse of the ministry. It is to be hoped that leaders will be very wise as they share their concerns and very careful not to quench the Spirit.

Subject to being healed

If we are wanting to minister to others, we need to be quite sure we ourselves are not overlooking something obvious which needs attention in our own lives. So long as we are unwilling to be open to wholeness, it is hypocritical to try to bring healing to others. This is the 'plank' principle Jesus spoke about: 'How can you say to your brother "Let me take the speck out of your eye," when all the time there is a plank in your own eye? You hypocrite, first take the *plank* out of your own eye, and then you will see clearly to remove the *speck* from your brother's eye' (Matthew 7: 4,5). We may not yet have got the whole 'plank' removed, but it must be being attended to if we are aware of it.

God called a redundant accountant, Ian Andrews, 'Go and preach the gospel and heal the sick.' Here was a real problem. Ian had suffered with a severe stammer for most of his life. He replied, 'What me, Lord? I'd be thrilled to preach the gospel and pray for the sick – only heal me first.' But God said, 'No! – I will heal you gradually as you go.' And that's just what happened. God healed him as he went out to minister to others. (Ian Andrews: *God Can Do It For You*, Marshall, 1982, p. 12).

God matures us through experience of life in the church. God heals in the processes of ministry, both to us and through us. As we go on in obedience to his call to minister, so we should grow in maturity, wholeness and holiness of life.

22

EQUIPMENT FOR THOSE MINISTERING

Introduction — Weapons and Armour for Spiritual Warfare (Ephesians 6: 10–18)

Obviously it is desirable to be properly equipped at all times. But we can get taken unawares when called in to a deliverance situation which needs our immediate attention. We should not allow ourselves to feel condemned because of this. God is greater than all our techniques and rituals. But if we are caught unawares and the spirit being cast out subtly enters one of those ministering who is unprepared then he can turn to his partners and seek their help in ministering release and cleansing in the name of Jesus.

Canon Jim Glennon of Sydney, Australia, openly describes his own early experience following prayer in Jesus's name for a young woman who was depressed and confused as a result of occult involvement and who was wonderfully released after the prayer. But he soon found himself in black despair which he could not understand until it dawned upon him that the darkness had followed his ministry to the young woman so afflicted. He turned to a prayer partner to minister to him and the spirit of heaviness left him.

The authority of the armour

1 People are recognised by the uniforms they wear; a

policeman, a traffic warden, a nurse, a fireman, a ticket collector, a soldier, etc.

2 The uniform itself conveys authority. This may, of course, be deceiving if the man in the uniform is not in fact entitled to wear it.

3 But if he *is* a policeman, the policeman's uniform endorses his authority.

4 No one can actually put on the armour of God who is not entitled to it. No one can take the shield of faith if he does not in fact believe in Jesus Christ. It is spiritual armour for spiritual warfare against a spiritual enemy. The enemy does not see any armour on one not entitled to wear it (Acts 19: 13–16).

The necessity of the armour

1 The soldier's armour is only essential when engaged in warfare.

2 The Christian soldier is constantly called to engage in spiritual warfare: offensively, in driving back the enemy, and defensively, in withstanding the enemy's attacks.

3 The weapons have divine power and are for the demolishing of the enemy's strongholds (2 Corinthians 10: 3,4), and for the Christian soldier's personal spiritual protection.

An inventory of the armour

Once a soldier has been in the front line he begins to appreciate every piece of his armour – both for defence and attack.

Paul details six main pieces of the soldier's equipment: the belt, the breastplate, the boots, the shield, the helmet and the sword. Some would include 'all prayer' as the antitype of the javelin to make the total up to seven. Paul uses the different items as pictures of truth, righteousness, good news of peace, faith, salvation, the word of God and prayer.

We need every piece of God's armour. We cannot pick and choose which we like and leave off the others. 'Put on the full armour of God'.

The belt of truth   (Ephesians 6: 14)

1 Jesus warned that the enemy is the Father of lies (John 8: 44) who from the beginning has cast doubt on the truth – 'Did God really say . . . ?' (Genesis 3: 1).

2 Jesus told his disciples 'I am the . . . truth' (John 14: 6) and also said 'Your word (Father) is truth' (John 17: 17). The Christian soldier should enjoy an open trusting relationship with his captain, Jesus Christ, and have the regular discipline of reading 'standing orders' (God's word in the Bible).

3 The belt of truth, by holding the outer garments in place and ensuring that the 'sword' is at hand for instant unsheathing, this belt, reminds the Christian soldier that he must also have truth in the 'inner parts'. 'If we claim to be without sin, we deceive ourselves and the truth is not in us. If we confess our sins, he is faithful and just and will forgive us our sins and purify us from all unrighteousness' (1 John 1: 8,9).

4 There is a powerful significance in the belt of truth for the enemy. On one occasion a married woman, converted to Christ two or three years earlier, came asking prayer for deliverance from certain psychic powers. Three or four of us gathered in chairs around her. We were still for a moment before God and I said: 'As we prepare for this ministry, let us simply put on the whole armour of God. First we put on the belt of truth.' At this she jumped up, shouting 'Belt of truth – who wants the belt of truth? I don't want that!' and before we knew it she had unbuckled her own belt and flung it away in the corner. It was a spirit in her speaking. When she was delivered we gave her back her belt to put on. She looked at it in genuine surprise. 'Wherever did that come from?', she asked, 'It's *my* belt!'

The breastplate of righteousness   (Ephesians 6: 14)

1 'Satan, whose name means accuser or slanderer (Job 1: 6) comes to challenge the Christian soldier's fitness to stand in the ranks of the King's army.

2 He will try to condemn the soldier and all his accusations may well be true, but the Lord's soldier puts on the breastplate of righteousness.

3 This is the Lord's righteousness (even his judge, Pilate, could find no fault in him). This righteousness is issued as standard equipment to every soldier (Romans 3: 22). This is essential defence against an accusing conscience and the slanderous attacks of the evil one.

4 Sometimes demons will speak out loud and threaten to disclose the sins of those ministering. It is important to ensure that as far as possible all known sin is confessed and those ministering are right with Christ. With sin cleansed and forgiven, the demons can have no hold on us and must obey our command in Jesus's name to be silent.

The gospel boots (Ephesians 6: 15)

1 Some commentators suggest that Paul has the *caliga* in mind, the Roman legionnaire's 'half-boot' made of leather. These had heavily studded soles, and were tied to the ankles with leather straps. They left the toes free.

2 This equipped the soldier for long marches and gave a sure foothold. With these boots on, the soldier did not easily tire or slip.

3 These boots came with the gospel of peace. The Christian soldier stands firmly on the gospel which declares peace with God. Christ is the Prince of Peace. He made peace through the blood of his cross (Colossians 1: 20). He gives a peace which the world cannot give (John 14: 27). This is the moral justification for spiritual warfare. The true objective is peace with God.

The enemy is a warmonger – his speciality is making war on the saints (Revelations 13: 7). Christ's soldiers are peace-makers (Matthew 5: 9). Whatever house the soldier enters he should first say 'Peace to this house' (Luke 10: 5).

The shield of faith (Ephesians 6: 16)

1 This *scutum* consisted of two layers of wood glued together, covered with linen and then hide, and banded with iron. It was specially designed to quench flaming arrows dipped in pitch.

2 The devil has many flaming arrows (doubts, accusations, etc.), but they can all be quenched with the 'shield of faith'.

3 The soldier involved in spiritual warfare soon becomes aware of the variety of foul thoughts that may assail him, but he recognises from whence they come and catches them in the shield of faith to quench them.

The helmet of salvation (Ephesians 6: 17)

1 Roman helmets were usually made of a tough metal like bronze or iron. Helmets are worn over the head – the housing for the mind.

2 The mind is the 'operations room' of every spiritual campaign and needs to understand clearly the grounds of man's salvation through the shed blood of Christ on the cross of Calvary.

3 'The weapons we fight with are not the weapons of this world. On the contrary, they have divine power to demolish strongholds. We *demolish arguments* and every pretension that sets itself up against the knowledge of God, and we *take captive every thought* to make it obedient to Christ' (2 Corinthians 10: 4,5).

The Sword of the Spirit (Ephesians 6: 17)

1 This weapon is both for defence and attack. The *machaira* is a sword used for close encounters. The *machaira* of the Spirit is the word of God. The word of God has cutting power sharper than any two-edged sword. (Hebrews 4: 12)

2 Jesus repulsed Satan's wilderness attacks each time with scripture – 'It is written,' he said (cf. Matthew 4 and Luke 4).

3 In the book of Revelation a two-edged sword issues from the mouth of Christ (Revelations 1: 16; 2: 12; 19: 15). This weapon, which comes from God, may well include the words which Jesus promises that the Spirit will put in the mouths of his disciples in difficult circumstances when they do not know what to say (Matthew 10: 17–20).

All kinds of prayer (Ephesians 6: 18)

1 This is to be used at all times with all perseverance for all the saints, and is to be 'in the Spirit'. Without pressing

the point too hard, this is probably 'praying in tongues'. It certainly includes it. There is praying with the mind and praying with the spirit (1 Corinthians 14: 15). Both are approved ways of prayer. Praying in the Spirit is certainly an effective weapon in spiritual warfare. 'The Spirit helps us in our weakness. We do not know what we ought to pray, but the Spirit himself intercedes for us with groans that words cannot express' (Romans 8: 26).

2 Included in 'all kinds of prayer' is praise, which is an integral part of prayer, 'in everything, by prayer and petition, with thanksgiving, present your request to God' (Philippians 4: 6). When the people of Israel were sent into battle for the Lord, men were appointed to go out at the head of the army, singing praise to God (2 Chronicles 20: 21–22).

Summary

With this armour the Christian soldier can stand. The word 'stand' comes four times in the passage (verses 11, 13, 14). The Christian soldier must keep rank. As the devil is resisted, he flees (James 4: 7).

Recommended reading:
David Watson *How to Win the War* Harold Shaw Publishers 1979

23

HEALTH AND FORGIVENESS

Introduction

1 One paramount value in the kingdom of God is forgiveness.

2 Forgiveness is clearly linked with healing in the Bible.

3 The Old Testament psalmist wrote 'He (the Lord) forgives all my sins and heals all my diseases' (Psalm 103: 3).

4 The New Testament gospel writer reports that Jesus, knowing the thoughts of his enemies, asked them concerning a paralysed man prostrated by illness 'Which is easier: to say "Your sins are forgiven", or to say "Get up and walk"? (Matthew 9: 5).

5 Forgiveness restores relationships in every direction (in the family, the church, the community). It restores the soul and releases healing in the body.

The Classic Parable on Forgiveness

1 In answer to a question from Peter about how many times he should forgive someone, Jesus told a parable (Matthew 18: 23-35) in which he compared the kingdom of heaven to a king who decided to bring his *accounts* up to date.

2 In the process one of his *debtors* was brought in who *owed* the king a vast amount of *money*, which he *could not pay*. So the king ordered that this servant, his wife and his children, all be sold to *repay the debt* (18: 25).

3 The man *begged* the king to be patient and he would *pay back* everything (18: 26).

4 The king had pity on him, *cancelled* the *debt* and *released* him (18: 27).

5 The released servant straight away went off and found a fellow-servant who owed him a small sum of money and roughly demanded his *money back* (18: 28).

6 The fellow-servant fell to his knees and *begged* 'Be patient with me, and *I will pay you back*' (18: 29).

7 But his creditor *would not wait* and had the man jailed until he should have paid back the debt.

8 Other servants, seeing what had happened, were very distressed and went and reported everything to their master (18: 31).

9 The king called in the servant he had forgiven and said 'You wicked servant, I cancelled *all* that *debt* of yours because you begged me to. Shouldn't you have had mercy on your fellow-servant just as I had on you?' (18: 32,33).

10 In anger, the king turned him over to the jailors until every penny was paid up.

11 Unforgiveness resulted in the two men being brought into bondage (jail).

12 Jesus concluded: 'This is how my heavenly *Father will treat each* of you unless you forgive your brother from your heart' (18: 35).

The word translated 'jailors' in most versions of the Bible should in fact be 'tormentors', but without some background knowledge of the times this would be difficult to understand. People who had treasure or money would bury it to keep it safe. No one would know where it was buried and the owner could easily deny that he had any at all. The 'tormentors' were employed to 'help' jog the owner's memory and to force him to go and dig up what was buried. The parable sounds horrific, but it is a fact that countless individuals who have justified their unforgiving attitudes or suppressed their resentment against those who have hurt them, are today being 'tormented' by guilt, tension, anxiety, depression, bitterness, inner-conflict and fear, perhaps resulting in physical sickness. These 'tormentors' are being used by God to provoke us into digging up the debt of forgiveness we owe to our fellow beings. Jesus said 'This is how my heavenly Father will treat each of you unless you forgive your brother from the heart.' Seen in this light, the lesson is plain.

Jesus and forgiveness

1 Jesus showed that forgiveness was *costly*. It runs counter to all our society's ideas of justice, which demand payment in full for all the wrongs we have suffered. But Jesus forgives *at his own cost* and demands no repayment from us. He has repaid all our debt to God and cancelled the account (Colossians 2: 14).

2 Jesus showed us that forgiveness should be *unconditional*. From the cross he prayed, 'Father, forgive them, for they do not know what they are doing' (Luke 23: 34).

3 Jesus taught that forgiveness had to be *unlimited*. 'Peter ... asked, "Lord, how many times shall I forgive my brother when he sins against me? Up to seven times?" Jesus answered, "I tell you, not seven times, but seventy-seven times"' (Matthew 18: 22).

4 Jesus taught that forgiveness on our part was *obligatory*. He taught the disciples to pray: 'Forgive us our debts, as we also have forgiven our debtors' (Matthew 6: 12). He enlarged upon this afterwards saying: 'If you forgive men when they sin against you, your heavenly Father will also forgive you. But if you do not forgive men their sins, your Father will not forgive your sins' (Matthew 6: 14–15).

Receiving forgiveness

There are basically three reasons why people do not receive the forgiveness of God.

1 *People do not understand* how forgiveness is possible. They do not know that God is merciful. They are ignorant of the purpose of the death of Christ on the cross of Calvary.

2 *People will not humble themselves* to accept this forgiveness which is freely offered. In his pride, man wants to do something to earn it.

3 *People will not release forgiveness* to others. 'If you do not forgive men their sins, your heavenly Father will not forgive your sins' (Matthew 6: 15). People need to learn to forgive immediately and continually until they know they have forgiven finally.

Releasing forgiveness

To others

We have all suffered hurts – inner hurts from those we loved, respected or trusted. Often these go way back into our past. It is humbling to cancel the debt we feel these people owe us, but that is what forgiveness is all about. We need deliberately to release forgiveness to those who have hurt us and ask God to forgive them also. Then we need to ask God's forgiveness for holding resentment against those who have hurt us.

To ourselves

Resulting from real sin, poor choices and foolish decisions in the past, many of us are weighed down with a sense of guilt. We know that Christ has died to forgive us our sins, but still we are not free because we will not forgive ourselves, even though we may have experienced Christ's forgiveness long ago.

Completing the process

Pray for God's blessing on those we have forgiven and upon ourselves.

Illustration from life

I recollect a case of a woman who was almost paralysed through arthritis. In the process of ministry to her it was revealed that she had been sexually violated in her childhood by her father who had latterly become a 'vegetable' lying in a geriatric ward. Once the woman came to the place where she could forgive her father for what he had done to her she began to experience physical healing in her body. Soon after she discovered from the hospital staff that her father had begun to show some marked improvement himself without even knowing at that stage that his daughter had forgiven him. The case demonstrates something of the nature of the bondage into which we bring ourselves and others by unforgiveness.

24

HEALING OF THE SPIRIT

Introduction

A brief explanation of this type of healing is offered to help towards a definition. Some biblical examples are used to illustrate how the human spirit is spoiled and the process of restoration initiated. Some pertinent points will be made to present a perspective on this kind of healing. Healing of the spirit affects all other areas of an individual's life and personality, though not every particular malaise is attributable to particular sin in the individual being afflicted (John 9: 2-3).

Definition

Healing of the spirit is the renewal and restoration of a person's spiritual life – his/her relationship with God. Sickness of the spirit is caused by the individual's own sin. The first and most profound kind of healing comes through Christ in response to genuine repentance. His salvation, when it is received, results in the healing of the spirit; and the on-going experience of his forgiveness keeps him spiritually healthy.

Biblical examples

The case of Adam and Eve   (Genesis 3: 1-24)

1 They were created *spiritually healthy*, walking with God in the cool of the day.

2 They were tempted through their senses of sight, taste and pride and *sinned* through disobedience (3: 7–8).

3 Their sin brought a sense of *shame* and exposure. The immediate response was to *cover it up* (3: 7).

4 The ensuing guilt resulted in sickening of the spirit and caused the couple to *hide* from God (3: 8).

5 Their *emotions* were affected; they confessed to having *fear* (3. 10).

6 The Lord gently *confronted* them in their sin (3: 11).

7 This led to *blame shifting* which in turn affected relationships (3.12).

8 Their *physical* being was affected. *Pain, sweated labour* and eventual *death* would fall to their lot (3: 17–19).

9 Their environment changed because they were banished from the garden (the presence of the Lord), and they had henceforth to live in a sin-cursed world (3: 17,23).

10 God had mercy on them and forgave them their sin through the shedding of blood (3.21). With this forgiveness came a healing of the spirit although certain privileges and prerogatives had to be forfeited.

The case of Esau   (Genesis 25: 29–34; 27: 34–36,41; 33: 1–15; and Hebrews 12: 15–17)

1 The manner of the birth of the twin brothers Esau and Jacob was prophetic of their later struggles (25: 25,26).

2 Esau's fleshly *appetite* was his particular temptation.

3 By despising his birthright which he sold to Jacob, Esau *sinned* (25: 32–34).

4 Esau *bound himself* by an oath (25: 33).

5 Esau became characterised as a *godless* person (Hebrews 12: 16).

6 Esau then held a *grudge* against Jacob, having fixed these incidents in his memory through a spirit of unforgiveness. (27: 41)

7 This led to real *anger* and a commitment to *murder* (27: 41, 46).

8 The thought of murder was the way Esau chose to handle his *self-pity*, thus revealing the effect it had on his emotions (27: 42).

9 When Jacob escaped Esau's wrath by fleeing, Esau retaliated by *rebelling* against his father (the authority figure) thus causing further disruptions to relationships (28: 8,9).

10 It is not clear how God softened Esau's heart (perhaps through Jacob's prayers and his peace offerings to Esau, 32: 22–32; 33: 1–11) but when they eventually met Esau had apparently *forgiven* Jacob and accepted him.

The case of Saul (1 Samuel 15: 1–35; 16: 14; 18: 5–29; 31: 1–13)

1 Saul was God's man, but his sickness began when he disobeyed God by his failure to annihilate the Amalekites. (15: 9)

2 God sent the seer Samuel to confront him about this sin (15: 10–14).

3 Saul attempted to hide his sin by *lying*, 'I have carried out the Lord's instructions' (15: 13) and then by *blame-shifting*. He claimed 'The soldiers brought them from the Amalekites' (15: 15) and then he pretended *spirituality* 'The soldiers took . . . the best . . . in order to sacrifice them to the Lord' (15: 21)

4 God's judgment, 'The Lord has rejected you as king' (15: 26), brought a measure of *repentance*: 'I have sinned' (15: 30) and, although he was *forgiven* for that incident, he seemed to sustain permanent resentment in his spiritual life.

5 The Holy Spirit was grieved and an *evil spirit* began to afflict him (16: 14). This was the cause of Saul's *mental illness* (a type of neurosis).

6 Although he liked David very much (16: 21) *jealousy* rose up within him because of David's success in the Lord (18: 8, 9). He became insecure and *afraid* (18: 15) and this affected his emotional life.

7 This led to *anger* which in turn repeatedly opened the door to the *demonic presence*. This resulted in the attempted murder of David (the throwing of the spear on two occasions, 18: 10, 11; 19: 9,10). Relationships were thus affected through his sickness.

8 After all this, instead of genuinely seeking God's mercy, he tried to get rid of his 'problem' by sending David

away, deceiving and harassing David through marriage
proposals, and eventually *plotting* to kill David. (18:
13; 18: 24–19: 1).

9 Saul proceeded to hunt David for this purpose. This
period was characterised by moments of *remorse* and self-
pity (false repentance) when David spared his life, (1
Samuel 26: 21) and a consultation with a *witch* (1 Samuel 28:
7). Eventually Saul *died* like a fool, taking his own life (1
Samuel 31: 4). His spiritual sickness destroyed him.

The case of David (2 Samuel 11: 1–27; 21: 1–20; Psalm 32: 1–7; Psalm 51: 1–19).

1 Instead of being out fighting with his troops David was
at home being tempted through sexual desire (2 Samuel 11:
2).

2 This resulted in his committing *the sin of adultery* with
Bathsheba (11: 4) followed by her pregnancy which led
David to try to cover up by *blame shifting* (i.e. bringing her
soldier husband home to make it appear the expected baby
was his, 11: 6–13).

3 This sin *affected relationships* and led to *murder* (11: 14–17).

4 His spiritual sickness caused personal *physical discomfort*.
(Psalm 32: 3; 51: 8).

5 *Emotional* and *mental* turmoil followed (Psalms 32: 3; 51:
8; 12).

6 The prophet Nathan was raised up by God to confront
David (12: 1–7).

7 David's response was to *confess* and *repent* (Psalm 32: 5;
Psalm 51: 1–14, 16).

8 This brought God's *forgiveness* (Psalm 32: 5) and *healing*
of the spirit (Psalm 51: 10–12) and emotions (Psalm 51: 8,
12, 14, 15) and body (Psalm 51: 8) and social relationships.
(Psalm 51: 13).

The case of Nebuchadnezzar   (Daniel 4: 19–37)

1 Nebuchadnezzar was warned by God of the danger of
his *pride* causing spiritual sickness twelve months before it
happened (4: 19–27). Daniel advised Nebuchadnezzar to
repent.

2 Nebuchadnezzar ignored the warning and *sinned* again

through pride (4: 30) thus coming into immediate judgment.

3 He became *insane* (4: 31, 32, 36).

4 Being driven from his people caused a rupture in *social relationships* (4: 32).

5 He behaved like an animal and his *body* was affected. He grew long hair and nails (4: 33).

6 God sovereignly forgave him and restored his sanity (4: 34).

7 His *physical* and *mental* health was restored and his social relationships returned to normal. He became king again and he gave glory to God (4: 34-37).

The case of the man sick of the palsy   (Mark 2: 1-12)

1 The man was physically sick; and his friends brought him to Jesus before the public.

2 His friends' *faith* activated the healing process (2: 5).

3 First Jesus forgave him his *sins* with a word of declaration (2: 5).

4 Then Jesus healed him of his palsy. He did this through an authoritative word (2: 11,12).

5 Clearly Jesus perceived the *spiritual sickness* (caused by sin) as *the root of his illness.* The palsy was directly related to it. (2: 9,10).

The case of the impotent man   (John 5: 1-15)

1 He was *physically sick* – an invalid for thirty-eight years.

2 The man had befriended his own illness because he was otherwise friendless (5: 7). His *social relationships* had clearly been affected.

3 The man seemed to be angry with life and people and without hope. (Note this emotional effect)

4 Jesus had to confront him with the *real issue*: did he want to get well? (5: 6)

5 Jesus healed him with a *word of faith* (5, 8).

6 Jesus later showed the real *cause* behind the physical condition: in this man's case it was the sin which he was committing which made him *spiritually sick*:'See, you are well again. Stop sinning or something worse may happen to you' (5: 14).

The case of the sinful woman   (Luke 7: 36–50)

1 She was *spiritually sick* through the practice of sin (prostitution) and she realised it.

2 She came publicly to Jesus and without a word initiated a process of repentance and healing (7: 37).

3 Through her weeping, *emotional* healing was released (7: 38).

4 The pouring out of her precious ointment over Jesus symbolised that she was giving her all to Jesus for *cleansing* and *acceptance* (7: 37–38).

6 Her tender devotion and *broken spirit* were public acts of faith in Jesus and his mercy. This resulted in her *forgiveness* (7: 38; 47–50).

7 This forgiveness released her from the *social* stigma attached to her, and would enable her to enjoy healthy relationships once again.

A perspective on healing of the spirit

1 At *salvation* a man's spirit is made alive by God's Spirit (1 Corinthians 6: 17). Man is spiritually born again (John 3: 5). He becomes a new creature in Christ (2 Corinthians 5: 17). This is fundamental to all *spiritual healing*.

2 Neglect of our relationship with God and his people (worship, prayer, Bible study, fellowship, etc.) and lack of repentance over wilful or unconfessed sin and certain bondages can cause a believer to become *spiritually sick* again.

3 Since sickness of the spirit affects so many other areas of a person's life it is often the cause of mental (sometimes demonic), emotional, physical and social problems.

4 a) Such basic sickness is dealt with through a confrontation or admission of the sin (maybe through reading God's word, which acts as a mirror (James 1: 22–23), or a sermon or testimony or through a gentle counsellor, etc.)

   b) A prayer of confession.

   c) An appropriate act of repentance. (The restitution of stolen property, etc.).

   d) A declaration of forgiveness (such as Jesus gave

Matthew 9: 2) on the basis of Matthew 18: 18 and John 20: 23.

    e) The receiving of God's forgiveness.

  5 Such healing of the spirit initiates a healing of related maladies at their various levels.

25

HEALING OF THE BODY

Introduction

The subject concerning us here is the healing of physical illnesses caused by organic/chemical factors within the body.

A definition

We are dealing with sicknesses or diseases caused by physical factors within the body and not specifically related to spiritual causes. It is therefore a physical illness caused by an organic or functional disorder. The healing of the body manifests itself through an abatement of the symptoms or a cure.

Illustration

For example, cystic fibrosis is caused by a genetic disorder of the liver glands. This affects the functions of the lungs and the digestive system. It is the most common genetic disease in Britain giving rise to a poor life expectancy. Here then is a clear case of an illness caused by a purely organic disorder. When the cause of illness is most probably physical rather than spiritual, praying for healing often seems more difficult (Mark 2: 9).

An Old Testament example: *Naaman, the leper* (2 Kings 5: 1–15).

He was a leper which is a clear example of a disease emanating from an organic disorder. The Old Testament does not say that his leprosy was the result of sin or 'past hurts'. He was a fine man in every way; a mighty man of valour, '... through him the Lord had given victory to Aram'.

Naaman sought healing from Elisha of whom he had heard (verse 3). Prior to his healing he needed to learn faith and obedience:

1 He could not trust in money or prestige (verse 5b).

2 He could not earn his healing (verse 11).

3 He had to reach a point of obedience and humility (verse 14).

4 He was healed physically (verse 14).

5 He was affected spiritually (verse 17).

A New Testament example: Blind Bartimaeus (Matthew 20: 29–34, Mark 10: 46–52, Luke 18: 35–43).

What Bartimaeus did:

1 He recognised the authority of Christ: 'Jesus, Son of David' is a messianic title (Mark 10: 47).

2 He was determined and shameless: 'He shouted all the more' (10: 48).

3 He understood the will and character of God as merciful: 'Have mercy on me' (10: 47).

4 He had faith: A blind man would not normally throw away his cloak. He would place it carefully where he could 'feel' for it to pick it up again (cf. 10: 50).

What Jesus did:

1 He stopped and called him (10: 49).

2. He was very specific. 'What do you want me to do for you?' (10: 51).

3 He spoke healing to him. 'Your faith has healed you' (10: 52).

The result, according to Mark, was that Bartimaeus received his sight immediately.

Other New Testament cases for reference are the Centurion's servant (Matthew 8: 5–13), the woman with the issue of blood (Mark 5: 21–34), and the deaf and dumb man (Mark 7: 31–37).

Guidelines for ministering healing to the physically unwell.

1 Invite the Holy Spirit and encourage the person being prayed for to welcome him.

2 Watch for the manifestations of the Spirit upon the person's body and bless what God is doing.

3 Listen to God to find out the root cause. Lay hands on affected area (if it is 'personal' let them lay their own hands there). Don't rush this!

4 Listen to God for any specific instructions or words of knowledge which would contribute to the release of healing (cf. Blind man, John 9: 1–7).

5 Find out where the faith lies (cf. Jesus healing the paralytic, Mark 2: 1–5; Paul healing the paralytic, Acts 14: 9).

6 Ask the afflicted person to pray if necessary.

7 Quieten him/her if he/she is emotional.

8 Break the power of unbelief, doubt, fear, etc. in the name of Christ if it appears to hinder the ministry.

9 Speak to the condition and tell it to 'go' or 'be healed' etc. Jesus said we should speak to mountains – the latter is a Jewish metaphor for difficulty, Matthew 17: 20–21; Jesus *rebuked* the fever in Peter's mother-in-law (Luke 4: 39).

10 Ask him/her how he feels. Remember we are looking for some abatement of the symptoms. Bless God for any sign of this and go on waiting if time permits.

11 When those ministering sense that the Holy Spirit is no longer working in power, bring the ministry to a close. Explain that that is as far as they can go now and encourage the sick person to come back for more prayer if it has been a help.

Some conclusions

1 Physical healing is physically experienced – we should never say to a person 'You are healed' if there is no sign of it. People know they are healed when they get better.

2 Sometimes healing is progressive. 'They will get well/ recover' (Mark 16: 18) seems to imply that a process could be involved. Certainly this seems to be the experience of

Francis McNutt (cf: *Power to Heal*, Ave Maria Press 1977 pp. 47–55).

3 If symptoms recur after prayer, there will be need to tackle the real cause which *could* be spiritual, emotional, demonic etc.

4 The devil will attack those who have been prayed for. They must learn to resist. Satan flees when resisted (James 4: 7).

5 Whilst praying, listen to the person – ask questions; listen to God – pray for gifts of revelation.

6 Faith is a vital element. There must be faith in one of three areas:

a) those bringing the afflicted for ministry;

b) the person or persons praying and ministering;

c) the afflicted person being prayed for.

If there is no faith in (c) at the beginning we should be encouraging the afflicted to take some step of faith by the end.

7 Faith may be expressed through various means: by the prayer itself (James 5: 15); by looking straight at the afflicted person (Acts 14: 9); by telling the afflicted person to look straight back (Acts 3: 4); by the laying on of hands (Acts 28: 8); by a spoken word or command (Matthew 8: 13; Acts 13: 11); by other specific acts of faith (Jesus once used spittle) (Mark 7: 33), the disciples sometimes anointed with oil (Mark 6: 13), one woman touched Christ's garment (Mark 5: 27) and Jesus touched (Matthew 8: 15) or took the hands of Simon's wife's mother (Mark 1: 31).

8 The sick person should not be told to give up taking medicine until the patient's physician prescribes otherwise. A healthy lifestyle should be encouraged in diet, exercise, discipline and general bodily care.

Recommended reading:

Morton T Kelsey *Healing and Christianity* Harper & Row 1973
Francis MacNutt *Healing* Ave Maria Press 1974
Francis MacNutt *The Power to Heal* Ave Maria Press 1977
Trevor Martin *Kingdom Healing* Marshalls 1981
Jim Glennon *Your Healing is within You* Hodder & Stoughton 1978

HEALING THE OPPRESSED

Introduction

Some mental or psychic and physical illness is the result of demonic activity. The Greek word *daimonizomai* is best translated 'demonised'. There are degrees of demonisation from afflicting demons to controlling demons. Many healings mentioned in the New Testament were linked with deliverance from demons.

Definition

Sickness caused by a demonic influence may have all or some of the symptoms of any spiritual, emotional or physical disease. Healing in such cases must include the expulsion or deliverance from whatever demonic influences may be causing the disease.

Jesus cast out demons

As Jesus preached the kingdom he healed the sick and *also cast out demons.*

1 Two demon-possessed men, Matthew 8: 28–34.
2. Legion, Mark 5: 1–20.
3 The epileptic boy, Matthew 17: 14–21; Mark 9: 14–29; Luke 9: 37–45.
4 A man in the synagogue, Mark 1: 21–28; Luke 4: 31–37.
5 The Canaanite woman's daughter, Matthew 15: 22–28; Mark 7: 24–30.

6 Many of the demon-possessed, Matthew 8: 16; Mark 1: 32-34; 3: 10-12; Luke 4: 41; 6: 18.

Some Lessons from Christ's Ministry

1 Jesus did not seek out the demonised. He dealt only with those brought to him or to his attention.
2 He never argued with demons.
3 He sometimes 'bound' a demon before casting it out.
4 He commanded demons never to return.
5 He addressed the demons directly.
6 He once cast out demons from a distance.
7 He delivered demonised children.
8 He ministered to the demonised in synagogues, the open air and in their homes.
9 He asked questions to help diagnose the problem before beginning his deliverance ministry.
10 He showed that demons had to obey his orders.
11 His deliverance ministry illustrates that multiple demonisation is possible.
12 Jesus did not allow the disciples to work on their own for ministering deliverance, but in pairs.

Healing and deliverance from demons

Christ's ministry indicated clearly that healing and deliverance from demons were sometimes linked. (Matthew 12: 22; Luke 13: 12; Matthew 9: 32,33; Matthew 17: 14-20; Mark 9: 14-29: Luke 9: 38-43; Luke 8: 35.)

Jesus commissioned his disciples

1 Jesus commissioned the twelve to preach the kingdom, heal the sick and cast out demons.
2 He commissioned the seventy-two to preach the kingdom and heal the sick. They reported back to Jesus, rejoicing that even the demons were subject to them in his name (Luke 10: 17).

3 Jesus told his disciples to make other disciples and teach them *to do everything* he had taught them (Matthew 28: 20). This commission, amplified at the end of Mark's gospel (Mark 16: 17), clearly included *the casting out of demons*.

4 The disciples developed this ministry (Acts 8: 7 and 16: 16–18).

Degrees of demonisation

The Greek word *daimonizomai* does not indicate degrees of demonisation. This will become manifest by the nature of the afflicted person's problem in the process of ministry or be discerned through the relevant gifts of the Spirit, i.e. discernment or words of knowledge. It is almost impossible by the nature of the subject to categorise spirits, since so much depends on the gift of discernment. Some are clearly more powerful than others, but it may be helpful to define according to the area/origin of the spirit's influences on the body, mind or personality of the sufferer.

'Fiery darts'

Some afflictions seem to be 'temporary' and 'external', even though causing an internal illness. Such afflictions may be 'lifted' or cast off in the name of Jesus.

Footholds

These may be provided for the enemy by anger, nursed grievance, deliberate sin, involvement with false cults or the occult (this latter even through such innocent (!) games as glass-tipping, ouija-boards, fortune-telling and horoscopes, etc.) All such need to be renounced and repented of : 'do not give the devil a foothold' (Ephesians 4: 27).

Strongholds

These result from a long-standing rebellion, feud or some deep trauma (in the conscious memory or suppressed). Where repentance is called for it should be made and forgiveness received (see steps in forgiveness related to inner healing pp. 220–21). Often there is a primary need for inner healing, which begins when forgiveness is released to those who have been perceived as causing the hurts. Inner healing alone may expel the spirit by closing a stronghold against the enemy.

Bondages

Some long-term oppressions are caused by such things as covetousness, idolatry, spells, curses, involuntary bonding with the past through the blood-lines or present family relationships, an overbearing parent or any other unhealthy relationships ('soul-ties'). Such bondage may produce a pattern of compulsive behaviour. The bond can be broken in the name of Jesus (Matthew 18: 18; John 20: 23).

Possession

Such a degree of demonisation is not common, but could be one of the preceding in an acute form. The condition is generally caused by a deliberate contract with the devil, either by the sufferer him/herself or by an ancestor. The whole personality is affected when the spirit 'seizes' the sufferer periodically. The sufferer him/herself may admit to a root cause, such as blood sacrifice to the devil or selling his/her soul to Satan, or the Lord may reveal the occult cause through one of the gifts of the Spirit. The spirit(s) should be bound in the name of Jesus and the case reported to the church leadership to deal with as, when, if and however it is deemed right.

Discerning the presence of demons

1 Diagnosis by physicians and psychiatrists:

a) *Personality changes* including changes in intelligence, moral character, demeanour and appearance.

b) *Physical changes:* preternatural strength; epileptic convulsions; foaming; catatonic symptoms; falling (often forward rather than backwards); clouding of consciousness; anaesthesia to pain; changed voices.

c) *Mental changes:* uncontrollable glossolalia; understanding unknown languages; preternatural knowledge; psychic and occult powers, e.g. clairvoyance, telepathy and prediction.

d) *Spiritual changes:* reaction to and fear of Christ, sometimes causing blasphemy; adverse reactions to prayer.

These above diagnostic indications of acute demonic attack have been collated by the Rev. John Richards from eight different authorities (see *But Deliver Us from Evil* Darton, Longman and Todd 1974 p. 156) and slightly adapted from our own experience in this area.

2 Public knowledge. There are extreme cases of people possessed by spirits which make them violent and who are, therefore, generally 'diagnosed' by the local community. Legion was a case in point (Mark 5).

3 Natural discernment: If a demon manifests itself, both those who witness it and the afflicted person know it, or the afflicted person becomes aware of a definite pattern of compulsive behaviour (bondage) which may be symptomatic, such as addiction, sexual perversion of some kind, self-destructive thoughts, etc.

4 'Discerning of spirits': through this gift the kind of spirit at work is revealed (1 Corinthians 12: 10).

In one meeting Smith Wigglesworth ministered to two people who seemed to everyone but Wigglesworth to have identical problems: both were deaf and dumb. Wigglesworth put his fingers into the first person's deaf ears and said 'Be opened in the name of Jesus.' He then placed his hand on the person's lips and said 'Tongue be loosed.' The man was healed. He dealt with the second problem in a different manner. He looked the man straight in the eye and said 'Thou deaf and dumb spirit, come out of him in the name of the Lord Jesus.' The person was wonderfully delivered and received his hearing back.

5 'Word of knowledge': through this gift the spiritual cause behind the affliction is revealed.

6 When the Holy Spirit is invoked over an oppressed person there is frequently a manifest 'power encounter' – shaking, contortions of some kind, eyes rolling upward, localised pain.

7 Sometimes the speech is unusual in its pitch and strange in its content. Sometimes there is a manifestation of a false 'tongue' which is not of God – it is almost uncontrollable in its speaking or its singing. Sometimes there is clearly another voice speaking through the person being ministered to, usually vocalising such things as a boast of its power, a claim to long-time ownership, a plea to be left alone, a threat to expose something in the life of one of those ministering or a challenge to his authority. Sometimes the other voice utters a stream of filthy language and blasphemy.

8 General spiritual sensitivity and experience by which those ministering detect the presence of demonic influences. The pattern of symptoms becomes recognisable: covering emotional, mental, speech and sexual problems, addictions, physical infirmities and religious error, etc.

9 It would be quite wrong to suggest to the afflicted person that the cause of a problem was due to an evil spirit without other corroboration and some manifestation of its presence. Many people seeking help have been greatly frightened by such a suggestion and have retreated from a fellowship which has real help to offer, feeling terrified, condemned or rejected.

10 It is far too easy and damaging to jump to such a simplistic solution. There needs to be clear confirmation: either by evidence of a spirit's 'control' in the sick person's history or through the gifts of the Spirit.

11 Sometimes a sufferer is convinced he/she has an evil spirit but the counsellor is not certain. In such a case it may be right in the name of Jesus to command any dark spirit to manifest itself – which it will do, producing such symptoms as in 6 above.

12 Beware of assuming that all shaking, bodily contortions, hysterical screaming or sudden physical pain etc., is demonic. Many people have deep reserves of suppressed emotion which may become manifest when they are being surfaced to the conscious mind by the Holy Spirit for healing. (see chapter 27)

Dangers in this ministry

1 'If all life is seen as a battle with demons in such a way that Satan and his hosts get blamed for bad health, bad thoughts and bad behaviour without reference to physical, psychological and relational factors in the situation, a very unhealthy demonic counter-part or super super-naturalism is being developed' (J I Packer *Keep in Step with the Spirit* IVP 1984 p. 196).

2 This ministry should never be engaged in without authority from the leadership of the church.

3 It would be unwise to engage in this ministry alone, but in exceptional circumstances there may be no other option.

4 Do not be distracted by exhibitionist or miming spirits, nor be deceived by lying, boasting, mocking, threatening or bargaining spirits. These should be ignored or silenced. 'Be quiet!' said Jesus sternly. 'Come out of him!' (Mark 1: 25).

5 The exercise of forceful physical restraint may easily provoke a physical reaction. Lack of a proper relationship with the Lord on the part of those ministering may also produce this response (Acts 19: 16).

6 There is always a danger of those ministering operating on the basis of a technique, when only the operation of God's Spirit will be effective.

7 The suggestion from an afflicted person that the cause of his/her problem is a demon is not sufficient grounds in itself for initiating a deliverance ministry. *Some* mental and physical illnesses are caused by 'reinforced' feelings, hurts, sins and events from the past. Among these illnesses some require a combination of inner-healing and deliverance from demonic influences, whilst others are the result of a chemical imbalance, etc.

8 Beware of those Christians who are persistently avoiding taking responsibility for their own lives and seek deliverance from demons as an escape. Such people waste precious ministry time. Sooner or later they have to make decisions for themselves if they are to be healed.

Preparation for those ministering

1 A right relationship with the Lord is paramount (John 15: 4).

2 Prayer. 'The Lord's prayer' is especially relevant.

3 Fasting. This may not always be necessary, but there are some kinds of spiritual affliction for which it is helpful (Mark 9: 29).

4 Scriptures which recount Jesus's victory on the cross, the defeat of Satan, and the authority which Christ gives to his disciples should be meditated upon (Mark 16: 15–20; Luke 11: 21, 22; Romans 8; 1 Corinthians 2: 14; 2 Corinthians 10: 3–5; Colossians 2: 15; Revelation 18, etc.).

5 All known sin must be confessed and cleansed (1 John 1: 7,9).

6 The whole armour of God should be put on (Ephesians 6: 10–18).

Ministering deliverance

1 It is always best to minister in groups to encourage each other; to allow some to minister whilst others pray or sing praises and still others listen to God.

2 It is possible to minister quietly but firmly at all times.

3 It is helpful to sit in a circle with the leader of the group facing the afflicted person.

4 It is better to minister in a private place – preferably in some room in the church building, where non-interruption may be ensured; better not late at night.

5 In the course of this ministry some dark secret or sin may come to light. Those ministering must avoid any appearance of shock or disgust if such is mentioned.

6 The afflicted person needs to feel secure in the love and confidentiality of the group.

7 A prayer may be offered for protection through the blood of Christ over all who are present and the members of their families just where they are.

8. It may help for someone in the group to lay one hand lovingly on the person's shoulder to give him/her a sense of assurance. The dignity of the person being ministered to should be preserved, though this may not always be possible.

9 The ministry may begin with a brief dialogue covering the following areas:

a) Personal occult involvement (cf. questionnaire at end of this chapter).

    b) Family history – especially of those who died immediately prior to the onset of the symptoms (cf. questions at the end of the chapter).

    c) Any false religion, cult involvement or masonic links.

    d) Any sexual liaison with another demonised person or one with occult involvement.

    e) General case history.

10 The afflicted person will need to repent and renounce all work of the occult and of the flesh (Galatians 5: 14–21 and Colossians 3: 5–10). If these are not dealt with, they can become demonic strongholds – areas of resistance to the Holy Spirit's ministry of deliverance.

11 One of the group will call down the Holy Spirit upon the one seeking help. The afflicted person will be encouraged to invite the Holy Spirit to come into his/her life, welcome him, and thank God for his coming.

12 Sometimes by the infusion of the Holy Spirit (a power-encounter may be manifest), demons are driven out by the same operation.

13 It is possible to exercise a degree of deliverance ministry without any mention of demons at all. The writer has sometimes simply addressed the 'darkness' in a person and commanded it to leave. The affliction may be commanded to go or its power broken in Christ's name. It is important to remember this when any mention of demonic activity would be counter-productive.

14 The afflicted person should co-operate and share the nature of the demon's activity as far as he/she can recognise it, where it is and what it does. The ministry group will need to keep their eyes open – even in prayer – to see what God is doing to the person or may be saying to the others in the group.

15 When ministering, we may address the afflicted person or the evil spirit and it is necessary to specify to whom we are speaking.

16 The voice should be clear and commanding, but to speak too loudly or excitedly is undesirable and is often counter-productive.

17 In addressing the evil spirit, it is good to look straight into the afflicted person's eyes, (Matthew 6: 22) though sometimes the eyes will roll upwards, hiding the pupils.

18 The spirit may speak aloud through the afflicted's own voice or within the afflicted's own mind, especially to maintain 'a lie', such as 'I don't have to go', 'Don't believe him', etc. The writer has heard a demon clearly say he was not a demon!

19 When the spirit speaks, the afflicted person's own mind is often somehow 'blanked' out.

20 It is important to sense God's leading before beginning any deliverance ministry. To minister to someone who is unwilling to continue in obedience to Christ is to risk the last state being worse than the first (Luke 11: 26b).

21 Demons may try every delaying device or tactic, pretending they will not come out right up to the last minute – but they have to yield to Christ's name, the sword of the Spirit which is the word of God, and prayer.

22 In the case of a spirit manifestly resisting the command to come out in the name of Jesus, it may be better to stop the proceedings and ask the Lord to reveal what foothold the enemy still has in the afflicted person's life.

23 Spirits get weary and very fearful (this sometimes manifests itself in the afflicted person).

24 Experience in this ministry will help in discerning when the spirit has left the afflicted person. This could be manifest in a variety of ways. When Jesus delivered the deaf and dumb boy, 'The spirit *shrieked, convulsed* him *violently* and came out. The boy *looked* so much *like a corpse* that many said, "He's dead"' (Mark 9: 26). But the act of deliverance may simply produce an immediate sense of peace.

25 In ordering an evil spirit to leave, it is wise, for some people's peace of mind (though not essential), to command the spirit to go to the place God has prepared for it.

26 The afflicted person should put his own will to his deliverance and should him/herself verbally renounce the spirit, telling it to go. 'Submit yourselves, then, to God. Resist the devil, and he will flee from you' (James 4: 7).

27 Experience would indicate that there are sometimes more than one spirit to cast out. (Mark 5: 9,10; Luke 8: 2).

28 Forgiveness and repentance are normally a prerequisite, but not necessarily so.

Counterattacks on those ministering

It is important to be alert to the enemy's tactics. He hates any penetration of his kingdom.

1 He may attempt to make us boast of the fact that God is using us in this ministry. When the seventy-two disciples returned from their first mission saying 'Lord, even the demons submit to us in your name', Jesus warned them 'Do not rejoice that the spirits submit to you, but rejoice that your names are written in heaven.'

2 On the other hand he may try to convince us that we have 'bungled' it and failed our Lord.

3 Frequently, those who have been ministering (especially women) sense a feeling of oppression following this deliverance ministry. It is vital to learn to resist the devil (James 4: 7).

Conclusion

1 If any attempt is made to write up what has happened (which is always useful) it should be done in such a way as to disguise the treated person's real identity.

2 Once a person has been 'delivered', he/she should be encouraged to seek and receive a greater fullness of the Holy Spirit to fill any void left by the spirits expelled (Matthew 12: 43–45).

3 The person delivered must be warned of the dangers of falling into similar sin again.

4 When a person has been 'delivered', it is important that he/she should be integrated into a homegroup or a caring cell. Some other follow-up ministry may also be necessary.

5 All *objects* which have contributed to, or were associated with, the demonic affliction – books, jewellery, symbols, cards, etc., are best destroyed (Acts 19: 19).

6 Some who have experienced genuine deliverance have subsequently suffered a brief period of disconcerting turmoil, causing confusion about the effectiveness of the ministry received – a kind of 'post-op depression', including feelings of condemnation and rejection and fears that nothing has changed at all. Alarmingly, some problems

reassert themselves more intensely than ever. This will normally pass after a few days when the person has regained his spiritual, psychological and emotional equilibrium. During this time the person will need someone to minister the truth of God's word to him/her; to talk and pray with him/her.

7 If any further deliverance ministry is required, it is important that the afflicted person *returns to those who previously ministered*, unless the church leadership feels one of the other staff should take it over.

8 Some who have experienced genuine deliverance may be open to any suggestion from those ministering and will respond psychologically, emotionally and physically to the merest hint of residual demonic activity. Such need to be discouraged from being ministered to further and taught of their security through the blood of Christ (1 Peter 1: 2) and how to put on the whole armour of God (Ephesians 6: 10–18).

9 Some who have experienced genuine deliverance and are very open to God easily begin to blame demons for every sinful response in their own fallen nature. Such need to be taught the biblical truths about fallen man's old nature and his new nature in Christ and be led to understand that sanctification (holiness) is a process of daily dying to self and rising to Christ (Luke 9: 23; 1 Corinthians 15: 31).

10 We should not assume the role of demon-seekers for every spiritual problem. The devil would love to preoccupy our ministry time with this and it is very counterproductive for the one receiving ministry.

11 If it is clear that there is a case of demon control which needs exorcism, the spirit should be bound in the name of Jesus and the case referred to the leadership of the church.

12 It is essential to give God the glory for every victory won.

Postscript on the occult

Wherever there is demonic oppression or possession there is usually some history of involvement with the occult which must be repented of and renounced. It may be necessary to explain what an abomination the occult is to God and show how it affects the personality before leading the oppressed person through the prayer of renunciation in the appendix to this section.

Definition of the occult

The occult is a satanic counterfeit of God's true supernatural power and manifests itself in three areas – *miracles, communication* and *knowledge of the future.*

Scriptures which teach about the occult

Exodus 22: 18; Leviticus 19: 26; Deuteronomy 18: 10–22; Deuteronomy 32: 17; 2 Kings 21: 6; 1 Chronicles 10: 13; Psalm 106: 36,37; Isaiah 8: 11–22; Acts 16: 16–18; Acts 19: 19; 1 Corinthians 8: 4; 10: 20; Revelation 16: 12–21; 18: 23; 21: 8; 22: 15.

Why the occult is forbidden

1 It places a person under the control of a power which is not God's – a power which is hostile to the Lord (1 Corinthians 10: 19–21.)

2 The lust for knowledge which is forbidden to mankind was the cause of man's fall – it is an attempt to by-pass God's specifically stated boundaries (Genesis 3: 3–5).

3 The desire to dominate and control is opposed to God's will (Exodus 3: 7–9; Isaiah 47: 12–15; Micah 6: 8).

4 It creates a dangerous and destructive personality (Mark 3: 27; Mark 5: 1–20).

5 It is rank disobedience to God; this is rebellion and arrogance (1 Samuel 15: 23).

Recommended reading:
John Richards *But Deliver us from Evil* Darton, Longman & Todd 1974
Michael Green *I Believe in Satan's Downfall* Hodder & Stoughton 1981
Michael Harper *Spiritual Warfare* Hodder & Stoughton

APPENDIX A:

A suggested form of prayer of renunciation and ministry for release from the occult

Person being ministered to:

I thank you, Lord God, for your life as man on this earth; for your death on the cross for my sins; for your triumph over evil by the resurrection from the dead and your ascension into glory. I thank you for your intercession for me now as my High Priest, and the hope of your coming again to establish your reign for ever as my King. Amen.

I CONFESS:

I have disobeyed you, Lord; I need your help and grace to repent and ask you now to cleanse me in body, soul and spirit through the blood of Jesus Christ. Amen.

I have sought supernatural experience apart from you. Please forgive me, Lord.

I renounce all witchcraft and magic, both black and white.

I renounce ouija-boards and all other occult games.

I renounce all necromancy, seances and spiritualist mediums, all E.S.P., second sight, mind-reading, levitation, body-lifting or hypnosis for evil purposes.

I renounce all fortune-telling, palm-reading, tea-leaf reading, crystal ball glazing, tarot and other card laying.

I renounce all astrology and interest in horoscopes.

I renounce all table-tipping, psychometry and automatic writing, numerology and metaphysics of the occult.

I renounce astral projection and other demonic arts.

I renounce everything psychic and occult.

I renounce all literature I have ever read which encourages such practices and promise to destroy all such books in my possession.

I renounce every cult that denies the power of Christ's shed blood.

I renounce every philosophy that denies the divinity of Christ.

I renounce the heresy of the reincarnation and participation in Yoga meditation.

I renounce any spirit that binds or torments me.

Person ministering:

In the name of Jesus I break any curse placed on you from occult sources. I break all psychic heredity and any demonic hold upon your family line due to any disobedience of your ancestors. I break any bonds of physical and mental illness and all demonic subjection to your mother, father, grandparents, great grandparents or any other human beings.

APPENDIX B:

*A form of questionnaire used in healing the oppressed for
information-gathering*

When an appointment is requested for this ministry, the
oppressed person may be given a form such as this to
complete and return before the appointment is due, if
possible.

NAME .... PHONE (day) ....(eve.) ....

ADDRESS ....

OCCUPATION ....

HOW LONG A CHRISTIAN ....
WHEN BAPTISED .... CONFIRMED ....

IN WHICH CHURCH ....

DENOMINATION .... PLACE ....

REASON FOR APPOINTMENT (Nature of problem) ....

RECURRING PROBLEM ....

REFERRED BY ....

PRIOR COUNSELLING ....

HOW LONG ....

MEDICATION ....

HOSPITALISATION (How many times) ....

NUTRITION RELATED PROBLEMS ....

SINGLE ....MARRIED ....DIVORCED ....

HOW MANY CHILDREN.........   ABORTIONS ....

DESCRIBE SIGNIFICANT RELATIONSHIPS ....

....

....

....

....

HAVE YOU EVER EXPERIENCED THE DEATH OF A CLOSE
FAMILY MEMBER OR LOVED ONE? ....

WHO? ....

ANY PERSONAL OCCULT INVOLVEMENT ....

ANY FAMILY OCCULT INVOLVEMENT ....

ANY SEXUAL RELATIONSHIP WITH A PERSON INVOLVED
IN THE OCCULT ....

DESCRIBE BRIEFLY YOUR RELATIONSHIP WITH YOUR
FATHER ....

....

DESCRIBE BRIEFLY YOUR RELATIONSHIP WITH YOUR
MOTHER ....

....

DESCRIBE BRIEFLY YOUR RELATIONSHIP WITH YOUR
BROTHERS AND SISTERS ....

....

DESCRIBE ANY LONG-TERM HURTS ....

....

DESCRIBE ANY EXPERIENCES OF REJECTION ....

....

27

INNER HEALING

General comments

Inner healing is distinct from physical healing and/or deliverance, though it may not always be disassociated from either. The normal and natural processes of physical healing are frequently impeded by deep inner hurts from the past. Sometimes deliverance from a demon may only result when the associated inner hurt has been dealt with first.

Definition

'Inner healing' or 'healing of the memories' is the healing of the inner man and covers areas commonly referred to as *mind*, *will* and *heart*, but includes other areas related to the emotions, psyche, soul or spirit.

Psychological focus

1 Any secular view of how a personality is formed and influenced, which is not inconsistent with the biblical doctrine of man, may be used to help in this healing ministry.

2 After experimentation with the human brain, Wilder Penfield, one-time neuro-surgeon at McGill University, Montreal, Canada, drew up some conclusions:

  a) The brain records every experience a person has.

b) The brain also records the feelings accompanying these experiences.

c) Through the process of remembering, a person can be conscious of the present whilst reliving a past experience.

d) The past experiences recorded still exist even though a person is not consciously aware of them. Some of these can be recalled at any time, whilst others are buried deeper (suppressed) in the sub-conscious mind and may be made available through dreams or external promptings.

e) These past experiences influence not only the present, but also the future – shaping, guiding and often limiting.

Christian counsellors' focus

1 Individual Christians have problems that sometimes remain untouched by confession, repentance and conversion, the renewal of the Holy Spirit, deliverance, Bible study, prayer and sacraments.

2 Hurts and traumas surrounded by feelings hidden in the recesses of the subconscious *currently affect the individual Christian's present life.*

3 The purpose of inner healing is to minister to those hurtful memories in such a way that they are no longer remembered with any feelings of pain and have no negative effect in the present or future of the individual. The objectives are twofold: to extend the lordship and healing power of Christ into an individual's past life – even to pre-conversion experience, and to sever whatever bondage past experiences may produce.

Spiritual focus

Jesus died for our sicknesses, our sorrows and our sins (Isaiah 53: 4,5) and came to bind up the broken-hearted and set the captives free (Isaiah 61: 1). He is the same yesterday, today and for ever (Hebrews 13: 8).

1 He can heal old wounds that still affect our present lives.

2 He can show us how to drain the poison of bitterness out of past hurts.

3 He can fill all of these areas in us with his love.

4 Such healing is not necessarily instantaneous and may come progressively, requiring several sessions.

5 This kind of healing calls for openness to the Holy Spirit and a deliberate renunciation of sinful attitudes, such as resentment and jealousy. Those who are perceived as having caused the hurts must also be genuinely forgiven.

6 'Inner healing' is often fundamental to physical healing (man being a psychosomatic whole).

7 It is often integral to a deliverance ministry also.

Origins of traumatic experience

1 Hurts can be due to living in a sinful world: Life's experiences which were not of one's own choice and were beyond one's control, e.g. incidents of history, accidents of nature, disease and poverty. Such experiences were accompanied by feelings of fear and terror, followed by anxiety.

2 Hurts may have been inflicted by those we love (parents and rival siblings, etc.) These may have been intentional or unintentional, actual or perceived, often arising through *failed instinctive expectations at a time of special vulnerability* even in the womb itself and reinforced by further experiences in life. Such experiences produce a sense of rejection, anger, resentment and rebellion.

3 Alternatively, hurts could be self-inflicted: These are effected by wrong choices or sin. Such experiences are followed by feelings of guilt and failure. These produce a sense of self-condemnation.

Reaction to past traumatic experiences

1 Such experiences, which may have originated in this way, may be *either*: acknowledged and nursed, leading to anti-social behaviour patterns, which are often blatant in childhood *or* confessed and repented of, bringing healing, *or* suppressed, resulting eventually in chronic depression,

phobias, physical illness, neurotic perfectionism, etc.

2 In many cases traumas are a compound of all three origins. These all hinder a man's ability to relate to God, to others and to himself and thereby sabotage a man's attempt to obey the first two commandments.

Those ministering inner healing should:

1 Pray for the leading of the Holy Spirit.

2 Be wise as serpents and harmless as doves (Matthew 10: 16).

3 Practice the art of listening. Most people don't. Listening has been defined as 'not thinking about what you are going to say before the other person has finished speaking'.

4 Beware of interrupting the counselee's expression of feelings; of being judgmental; of showing disgust; of offering 'good advice' or pat answers; of using the Bible too much (Bible bullets); of over curiosity, (Pray: 'Lord make me sensitive without being intrusive'); of unctiousness – solemn holy homilies; patronising or syrupy religious sentiments – of excusing everything the person's own conscience is condemning; of being bound by a system or method in your approach; of imposing your imagination; of going on too long and too late; of the ego trip; of over emphasis on *particular techniques*, (which can easily become an attempt to psychic manipulation; an effort to *produce* an experience).

5 Let the Holy Spirit do the directing. If you don't know what to do or say, do or say nothing. Just wait on God.

6 Learn to listen not simply to what people are saying, but to the feelings beneath their words. It may be helpful to ask, 'How did you feel about that?' or draw the story out with the comment 'That must have really hurt!' etc.

7 Watch a person's body language – tone of voice, eyes, facial expression, a drooped shoulder, etc., to gauge how his words match up to his feelings.

Ministering inner healing

1 Explain the approach to the person requiring healing.

2 Invite the Holy Spirit to indicate particular areas of need (by words of knowledge, etc.).

3 It is vital to *take time* over this.

4 When past hurts are highlighted, invite the Lord to minister healing to those areas specifically.

5 It may help if the counselee repeats the prayers for him/herself.

6 Encourage the counselee to respond actively by deciding to reject evil and emotional bondage.

7 Encourage the counselee to release forgiveness to those who have caused the hurt and to ask forgiveness from God for holding resentment, etc. Forgiveness is an essential element in both receiving and giving this inner healing (see separate heading on this).

8 It is not sufficient to minister to the emotions alone. The mind needs renewing (Romans 12: 2). This comes through the Holy Spirit and the word of God.

9 It is God alone in his mercy who heals. Indicate to the sufferer that he/she has the power through Christ to maintain new freedom, even though there may be times of struggle.

10 Encourage the person to be faithful in prayer, in regular worship, Holy Communion and to be part of a supportive Christian fellowship.

Dangers in this ministry

Inner healing has been beset by distinct problems.

Problem of superficiality

Michael Scanlon calls this the 'pray and leave it all to God' approach. Sometimes healing does indeed come through a sovereign work by God. Often, however, healing is ineffectual because the afflicted person has not been helped to deal with *real* problems in his/her life, which may be:

1 The underlying causes of anxiety and depression.

2 The possible presence of sin which calls for repentance.

3 The possibility of hardness of heart due to resentment, bitterness or refusal to forgive.

4 The possibility that a person who has carried a deep

trauma over a period of years has been 'giving place to the devil'. The person may be in need of some form of deliverance, which will be dependent upon his repentance and renunciation.

Problem of passivity

The healing power is blocked where an afflicted person is allowed to remain passive during the period of ministry: not taking authority over his life when necessary; not repenting for sinful behaviour, and not making the necessary decision to accept God's healing.

Problem of emotional dependence

It is all too easy for those of us ministering to foster emotional dependence upon the counselee. This is why it is always best, if possible, to minister in a team of two or more, with one of the same sex as the sufferer included. Anyone who discovers a desire to bind a needy person to him/herself should avoid ministering in this way until he/she has dealt with that problem in him/herself. Christ does not bind – he sets us free (John 8: 36).

Limitation of emotion alone

There is a theory that to bring the sufferer to the place where he/she can ventilate feelings and relive past experiences is to initiate the healing process. It may be emotionally cleansing to recall the pain and loneliness of earlier years, but merely to relive these experiences is not to receive inner healing.

Limitations of truth alone

The search for the root cause of the problem must never be an end in itself.

1 There must be a sincere release of forgiveness to those who have caused the hurts.

2 There must be repentance for resentment and acceptance of forgiveness from the Lord.

3 There must be an openness to receive the healing love of Jesus through the Holy Spirit.

4 There must be a commitment to seek the Lord's answer for right living in the kingdom of God.

Problem of opposite sex ministry

Although counselees often respond well to someone of the opposite sex, it cannot be stressed too strongly that wherever this is the case there should be more than one counsellor, one preferably of the same sex as the counselee. The reason is obvious, but it is tragic that what often begins as a sincere desire to bring healing can end in a scandal.

Concluding comments

Inner healing essentially involves a deeper release of the Spirit 'within us'. This work of the Holy Spirit is ongoing. We thank God for any past experiences, but are told to go on being filled with the Holy Spirit (Ephesians 5: 18).

There are often areas in our lives that are 'walled-off' from the Holy Spirit, of which we may not be fully aware at the time of conversion or at subsequent spiritual commitments and other Holy Spirit experiences. These areas are not fully under the lordship of Jesus Christ. Once we become aware of a 'walled-off' area, there should be a decision to open this to God; to forgive where necessary; to repent of resentment where appropriate; and to pray for the Holy Spirit to exercise his lordship in that, as in every area of life.

Recommended Reading: John and Paula Sandford *The Transformation of the Inner man* Bridge Publishing Inc. 1982.
Frank Lake *Tight Corners in Pastoral Counselling* Darton, Longman & Todd 1981
Reginald East *Heal the Sick* Hodder & Stoughton 1977

APPENDIX C:

A suggested form for a prayer of forgiveness, to be used when ministering inner healing

Our Father, forgive us our sins for we also forgive everyone who sins against us (Luke 11: 4).

Heavenly Father, I choose as an act of will to forgive ....

I forgive .... for (list offences specifically) ....

I release ....

Heavenly Father, I ask you to forgive ....for all these things as well and that you do not hold things against him/her on my account. I ask you to release him/her.

Heavenly Father, I ask you to forgive *me* for holding unforgiveness, bitterness, resentment, etc., in my heart toward .... I receive your forgiveness now and your cleansing of my heart from all unrighteousness.

Heavenly Father, forgive me for holding resentment *towards you* for allowing these hurts to happen to me.

Heavenly Father, if I have any *more negative feelings* stored up within me towards .... I ask you to cleanse them from me now. I open myself to replace these negative emotions with the fruit of your Spirit (love, joy, peace, patience, etc.)

Heavenly Father, I ask that you *now heal the wounded places in my soul.* Heal every memory of those offences so that I can look back on them realistically, accepting that they were hurtful, but also trusting that you, Lord, have redeemed the hurt. Enable me to use this experience to help others with whom I come into contact.

Now, Holy heavenly Father, I ask that you bless ....
with your abundant mercy.

Prosper .... in every way, body, soul and spirit, in
the name of Jesus Christ.

It is profitable to continue to ask God to bless and prosper
this person until all negative feelings toward him/her are
healed. And each time you begin to feel anything towards
him/her use this as an opportunity to bless and intercede
for him/her.

N.B. The counsellor him/herself will sometimes need to
speak (declare) God's forgiveness through Christ to the
repentant counselee. (cf. Matthew 18: 18, John 20: 23).

28

MINISTERING HEALING TO THE DYING AND THEIR FAMILIES

Introduction

We all have to die, but the antecedent suffering may sometimes be very difficult to bear. However, even in dying there can be healing, in the sense of understanding the nature of death and Christ's victory for us over it. We also have a ministry to help the dying through the whole experience.

We believe that according to God's creative will no one should die from sickness or accident, but in fact people do and this must be attributed to God's permissive will. It is important to explain this so that people do not sense unnecessary rejection or alienation from God when illness appears to be terminal. There is also the aspect of caring for the bereaved. First we offer a definition of healing the dying and then the whole issue of death will be dealt with. Then we discuss the process involved in dying and grieving.

A definition

Ministering healing to the dying means helping the terminally sick to come to terms with approaching death and to cope with the mental and spiritual processes involved. Ministering to their bereaved families means helping them to recognise the processes of bereavement and supporting them in their grief.

Our objective

The first step towards healing the dying is a proper

understanding of death itself. Then our objective is to help people through the experience of death, both the one dying and those who are being bereaved.

The issue of death

1 The Bible teaches that death comes to everyone and the event is a divinely appointed time in life (Ecclesiastes 3: 2; Hebrews 9: 27).

2 When God created man it was not his purpose for man to die, but death came upon man through sin; and so Satan gained the power of death (1 Corinthians 15: 26: Romans 5: 12; Hebrews 2: 14). Death is man's last enemy (1 Corinthians 15: 26).

Reconciling death with God's will

1 In the story of Job we see that Satan (who is little mentioned in the Old Testament) has the power to kill, but this power has limitations decreed to it by God. 'He is in your hands: but you must spare his life' (Job 2: 6) (N.B. These trials suffered by Job were not because of any sin of his own. The Bible specifically states that 'in all this Job did not sin' Job 2: 10).

2 By his coming, Jesus declared war on Satan and invaded his domain of death (Hebrews 2: 14,15). Satan's power is ultimately destroyed through the cross, but presently only curbed (Greek, *deo* 'to bind') (Matthew 12: 29).

3 At Christ's second coming there will be a general resurrection and death will be swallowed up in victory (1 Corinthians 15: 54–57).

Summary

1 There is a time appointed for us to die.

2 Satan still destroys people prematurely today. (His attacks are mainly directed towards the church. Some recent examples being: Martin Luther King in the USA,

Archbishop Janani Luwum in Uganda, Archbishop Romero in El Salvador, Fr. Popieluszka in Poland).

3 Some people die before their time because of judgment (e.g. Ananias and Sapphira – Acts 5: 1–10; cf. 1 Corinthians 11: 29–32).

4 Some through prayer, faith and obedience can appropriate Christ's victory and the Father's protection from premature death (Mark 16: 18; Luke 10: 19; and Acts 28: 5 where Paul shook off the viper which was fastened to his hand into the fire and suffered no ill effects.)

Stages in dying

Some similar stages of experience occur in both the dying person and the grieving family but there is no hard and fast order for these. It is helpful to be aware of them so as to enable those dying to express their feelings by listening without judgment. This has a healing influence on both the dying person and on the family. (See *On Death and Dying* by Elizabeth Kubler-Ross, New York, MacMillan, 1970). Obviously for those with a real faith in Christ these stages are not always applicable because they are going to be with the Lord. For unbelievers who are dying the real healing lies in coming to faith in Christ. Those dying usually pass through the following stages:

1 *Shock and numbness:* the realisation that one is dying frequently produces a state of shock and a number of the emotions.

2 *Denial and isolation:* at this stage the person will find himself, saying 'No, I'm not going to die. They are mistaken.' He desires to be isolated so that he will not be reminded continually that others seem to be enjoying 'immortality'.

3 *Anger:* the dying person will respond 'Why me? Why not someone else?' He feels that he is being cheated out of all that life could have offered him. The grieving family will often respond by saying, 'It's not fair. Why take someone who still has so much to give?'

4 *Bargaining:* the dying person begins to bargain, offering anything he has in exchange for 'time'.

5 *Depression:* faced with death, a person begins to experience a sense of hopelessness. He becomes dejected at the realisation of many missed opportunities in life – in business, with his family and friends.

6 *Acceptance:* finally, the dying man comes to accept what is happening to him. This does not mean that death will follow immediately. Neither does it mean he will not continue to vacillate between the preceding stages.

Stages in grieving

For those left behind after a loved-one has passed on, life must continue. Adjustment has to take place. Our objective is to help those grieving to mourn without guilt, to listen to their hurts and to pray with them for God's healing. Faith in Christ (his life, death and resurrection) and fellowship with his people enhances the healing process.

1 *Shock and numbness.* When a person dies, either expectedly or unexpectedly, those who remain are left in shock and experience a sense of emotional numbness.

2 *Fact and fantasy become blurred.* Those mourning still expect the deceased to reappear at any moment. Little things suddenly remind them of their loved one.

3 *Unexpected emotion.* Because people, especially the English, tend to restrain their emotions, these often break through at a later stage. There should be no shame attached to this. It is normal to weep. Jesus showed us how (John 11: 35).

4 *Association.* The most difficult times that a bereaved person experiences are special days like anniversaries, birthdays and Christmas, etc. At these times grieving people need extra care. Association will constantly trigger off the sense of loss.

5 *Acceptance.* At this point the difference between fact and fancy has become real. This does not mean that the emotions will no longer be triggered off, nor the associations recur. It simply means that the person grieving has accepted reality.

6 *Facing the future.* A person who has shared his/her life with someone else can never forget it. However, he/she can, with help, begin to adjust to life in the absence of the

loved one. It is important to remember that each person is different. Sensitivity, compassion and listening will help to heal the other's bereavement.

Summary

1 We must be aware of the true nature of the problem and realise that there is a proper time for everyone to die.

2 We must be listening to God in our prayers for the dying.

3 When it is clearly the person's time to die we should release him/her to God.

4 By prayerful listening to God we can help the dying person prepare for death as much as possible. Reading from the psalms (especially Psalm 23) is often greatly appreciated.

5 Grieving is an important part in the adjusting a bereaved person has to make. Those ministering should be sensitive and compassionate.

29

RAISING THE DEAD

The resuscitation of the dead is by far the most difficult area for the Western mind to cope with. There is no rational framework for this to happen although it has happened and still does. The purpose here is to review the resuscitations in scripture, as well as some that have occurred in the history of the Church. This does not include the resurrection of Christ, which is the only one of its kind and the first fruits of ours. A few remarks about our perspective on healing the dead will conclude the section.

Towards a definition

Resuscitation is the divine miracle of restoring life to a deceased person. It is the raising of the dead back to a temporal life in the body, as opposed to the resurrection of the dead at the end of the age. It is a visible act of God's power which clearly shows his ability to invade Satan's stronghold and overpower him in his own domain of death.

Old Testament cases

The widow of Zarephath's son   (1 Kings 17: 17–24)

1 The illness and consequent *death* of the son (17: 17) resulted in the widow's *anger* against the prophet (17: 18).

2 She interpreted the death *as punishment* for her sin, and so she came under a false sense of *guilt* (17: 18).

3 Elijah was evidently moved by compassion and anger,

because he took the dead boy upstairs and *boldly challenged* God (17: 20).

4 He performed an *act of faith* (stretching, covering the boy three times, 17: 21).

5 He *prayed* for life to return (17: 21).

6 God *answered* Elijah's prayer because of his mercy (17: 22). The boy came back to life.

7 *Relationships, emotional harmony* and a *healthy respect for God* (and his servant) were restored (17: 23,24).

The Shunammite woman's son (2 Kings 4: 18–37)

1 The boy, given to the mother as a miracle of God, suddenly *died* (4: 18–20).

2 The mother lay the dead boy in the prophet's room and went to look for him. She obviously had *faith* for a resuscitation of the boy. (4: 22–25).

3 Her answer to Gehazi, 'Everything is all right', showed veiled anger/impatience (4: 25,28). She was obviously very *distressed* (4: 27).

4 Notice that Elisha was *listening for God* and explained openly that he did not hear anything (4: 27).

5 Elisha sent Gehazi on ahead to *lay his staff* on the boy's head. Nothing appeared to happen (4: 29,31).

6 The mother's *persistence* with Elisha demonstrated her faith (4: 30).

7 Elisha shut the mother and Gehazi out and first *prayed* to God (*privacy* to hear God and exercise faith, 4: 33).

8 He then lay (crouched) on the boy's body as an *act of faith*. When the body became warm, Elisha paced the floor (still waiting on God!) and lay again on the body. The boy then *came to life* (4: 34,35).

9 Relationships and emotional harmony were restored (4: 36,37).

Elisha's bones (2 Kings 13: 14–21)

1 Elisha *died* of an illness (13: 14), and was buried (13: 20).

2 Later another burial was in process when invading Moabites appeared. It was decided to let down the corpse of the dead man into Elisha's tomb. When his body touched Elisha's bones the dead man revived and stood upon his feet (13: 21).

3 In some way *healing power* was released through *contact* with Elisha's bones. This has happened elsewhere in the history of the Church. The preserving of relics is a respected practice, but they must, of course, never be worshipped.

4 The overall purpose of these resuscitations was to *inspire faith* in God in the hearts of the Israelites.

New Testament cases

Jairus' daughter   (Mark 5: 21-24, 35-43)

1 Jairus' *faith* caused him to seek out Jesus to heal his daughter who was near death (5: 21-24).

2 The bad news of the daughter's death brought *unbelief* into the crowd; but before it affected the father, Jesus quickly responded, *'Don't be afraid; just believe'* (5: 35,36). Jesus had it all under control; because after this commitment to heal the daughter, he had to spend time healing the woman with the haemorrhage on the way (5: 24-34).

3 Jesus needed the *right atmosphere* to raise the dead – no cynicism nor excess emotionalism, but a small group that could exercise faith (he took in only Peter, James, John, and the parents, but put out the mourners, 5: 37-40).

4 Jesus made a *positive statement of conviction* that the child would live again, even in the face of mockery (5: 39,40). By doing this he seemed to rebuke the *spirit of death*.

5 Jesus *took the dead girl by the hand* and then *commanded* her to get up (5: 41).

6 Immediately she came to life, rose up and walked around. Notice Jesus's concern for her privacy and complete restoration (5: 42,43).

Widow of Nain's son   (Luke 7: 11-17)

1 This was a *sudden* and *public* happening.

2 Jesus was motivated by *compassion* for the widowed mother (7: 13). He first *comforted* her saying 'Don't cry'.

3 Jesus stopped the procession, *touched the coffin* and *commanded* the young man to 'get up' (7: 14).

4 *Immediately* 'the dead man *sat up* and began to talk'! 'Then Jesus gave him back to his mother' (7: 15).

5 This had spiritual, emotional, and relational effects in the immediate family and in the community (7: 16,17).

The raising of Lazarus (John 11: 1–57)

1 A message from the sisters of Lazarus reached Jesus, saying their brother was ill. It was a plea for help (11: 3).

2 Jesus had a *conviction* (word of knowlege) that ultimately this sickness would not be death, but rather a revelation of 'for God's glory' (11: 4). Notice how calm and controlled his *faith* is.

3 Jesus *knew* God was in control: although he loved Mary and Martha, he stayed where he was for two extra days (11: 5,6). He was not *acting* on external pressures, but he *waited* on His Father.

4 Once Lazarus had died, Jesus went up to Bethany. Jesus had *a word of wisdom* about his death (11: 11–15).

5 The *purpose* in raising Lazarus was to glorify God, inspire faith in the disciples and others, and to help Mary and Martha (11: 4,15,33).

6 The fact that Lazarus had been dead for four days means that he was *really dead* – the spirit had left his body, the body was decomposing (11: 39).

7 Jesus first spent time comforting Mary and Martha by giving them *hope* and *faith* in Him (God, see 11: 21–40). He *wept* with them (11: 35).

8 Notice the tragic *environment of unbelief*, but Jesus was not affected by it because he had a gift of faith (assurance from the Father, 11: 33–40). Martha had *faltering faith* (11: 22,27,39).

9 Jesus did not pray for Lazarus' resurrection, but *expressed gratitude* to the Father for the intimacy they enjoyed (11: 41,42).

10 He made preparation (by rolling the stone away and prayer), and then he *commanded* in a loud voice, 'Lazarus, come out! (11: 43).

11 The *miracle* happened, and then Jesus concerned himself with the *total restoration* of his friend ('Take off the grave clothes', 11: 44).

12 This resuscitation *resulted* in spiritual renewal. It also caused persecution as well! (11: 45–48).

'Many holy people' (Matthew 27: 52–53)

They came out of their tombs after Jesus' resurrection and
appeared in the holy city.

Peter raises Dorcas (Acts 9: 36–42)

1 This woman died of a certain illness and was laid in an
upper room (9: 37).

2 The *faith* of the believers was quickened by news of
Peter's proximity, and they sent for him (9: 38).

3 Peter came in response to their faith, but later *prayed*
for direction (9: 40).

4 He put all the mourners out of the room to *ensure a
positive atmosphere* (9: 40).

5 After *prayer*, he *commanded* the dead woman to 'get up' (p.
40).

6 She opened her eyes, Peter *helped her up* and presented
her alive (9: 41).

7 This affected the whole region in spiritual revival (9:
42).

Paul raises Eutychus (Acts 20: 7–12)

1 This death was caused by an *accident* (20: 7–9); Eutychus
fell to his death whilst sleeping during Paul's long teaching.

2 Paul *immediately* went down and *embraced* the young man
(act of faith!), and then reported, 'Don't be alarmed! He's
alive!' (20: 10).

3 So Eutychus came to life and the people were greatly
comforted (20: 12).

Historical example (Augustine AD 354–430)

Two weeks before Easter in Augustine's church in Hippo,
North Africa, in 424, a brother and sister came to Hippo
both suffering from convulsive seizures. They gave a sad
account of parental rejection and came each day to pray at
the shrine for healing. On Easter morning before the
service, the young man was in the crowded church, praying
as he held on to the screen around the reliquary (a box

which held the bones which were venerated as the relics of St Stephen the Martyr). Augustine was still in the vestibule prior to entering the body of the Church when the young man fell down as dead. People near were filled with fear. But the next moment he got up and stood staring back at them, perfectly normal and cured. Three days later the same thing happened to the sister, while Augustine was preaching about St Stephen the Martyr (Morton Kelsey: *Healing and Christianity*, pp. 185–186).

Modern day examples

1 Trevor Martin in *Kingdom Healing* (Marshall's, 1981) relates helpfully and in honest detail an unforgettable experience which ended in apparent failure. He had 'felt led' to go and raise the body of a beautiful fourteen-year-old Christian girl who had died of cancer and whose remains were resting in a hospital mortuary. Although he sensed amazing power pulsating through him, his attempts were frustrated and he saw no resuscitation.

2 Albert Hibbert tells of the remarkable ministry of the Bradford plumber, Smith Wigglesworth (1860–1947) in a book entitled *The Secret of his Power* (Harrison House Inc., Oklahoma, 1982). Hibbert reported fourteen occasions when the dead were raised during Wigglesworth's ministry. Sometimes he would pray; but at other times he would just speak the word.

On one occasion he called at the home in which the family was mourning the loss of a five year old boy. Wigglesworth stood looking at the corpse in the coffin with tears running down his cheeks. Wigglesworth requested the father to leave him alone in the room. He locked the door behind the father, lifted the corpse from the coffin and stood it up in the corner. Wigglesworth rebuked death in the name of the Lord Jesus and commanded it to surrender its victim. An amazing miracle occurred when the child returned to life.

On another occasion he was used to resuscitate a corpse. The man was raised however still suffering from the disease which killed him. Wigglesworth told the family that unless they repented and put matters right within their home, the man would die again. The family repented. Wigglesworth prayed for them and the Lord healed the man, who lived for thirty years more (pp. 44–46).

3 We are indebted to Eileen Vincent of 'Outpouring Ministries' (Hemel Hempstead) for an account of a conversation with a medical doctor, James Van Zyl, who frequently holds evangelistic healing missions at the invitation of churches in South Africa. Van Zyl told her about a number of resuscitations in which he had been involved.

One instance was during a visit to the Apostolic Faith Mission Church in Secunda, an industrial area. Among those coming forward to receive Christ following the gospel preaching, was a man with severe asthma. As he was walking to the front, he suddenly collapsed to the floor. Dr Van Zyl examined him and found that he was dead. Immediately he called the spirit of death out of him. The deceased man shook, seemed to revive and then expired again. Once more the doctor called the spirit of death out of him, commanding it to leave the man. Once more the man shook and revived a little, but expired. This happened four times. Eventually the man revived completely. He got up, was healed and walked away.

On another occasion, at a place called Warmbaths, an elderly woman died as Dr Van Zyl was preaching. She had been simply sitting in her seat. Disturbed by the sudden commotion with everyone turning, staring and talking, Van Zyl went over and verified that she was in fact dead. He proceeded to command the spirit of death to come out of her, whereupon the old lady shook herself, stood up and was perfectly well. Eileen Vincent's comment was that God raised the woman, not because the elderly should not die, but as a 'sign' to unbelievers and to provoke faith.

4 Captain R. E. Wilbourne in his leaflet *Life after Life* (Church Army Insight Paper, New Series, No. 2, October, 1982, tells how as a young Church Army student thirty years ago he fell ill with pneumonia and pleurisy and was rushed to Crumpsall Hospital in Manchester and placed on the danger list. It was before the days of miracle drugs. His relatives were called and came in time to see him before he died. He was certified by the doctors as dead. His body was

wheeled off on a trolley to the mortuary. He described his experience of 'life' in heaven which followed. Whilst there he heard a voice which grew louder and louder, repeating 'O God, don't let him die! O God, don't let him die! He has work to do for you.' He then felt as if he was falling through space and came back down to the slab in the mortuary at the hospital. Whereupon he sat up and asked the attendant where he was – much to the latter's horror! The next thing he knew was that he was back in the hospital ward, where he had a long haul back to health.

He had been dead for three hours. He learnt later that his landlady Daisy Green, had knelt by his bedside and prayed, 'O God, don't let him die.'

5 Kurt Koch in his book *The Revival in Indonesia* (published by Evangelization Publishers in Germany, 1972) reports the case of a nine-year-old boy, who collapsed and died at the beginning of a meeting. It was not until five hours later that evangelist Saul came to see the dead boy. As he stood beside him he began to pray. It was then that the Lord said to him, 'Blow into the boy's mouth and nose and put your hand on his forehead.' Saul obeyed and after fifteen minutes there was some movement, but it was some time before he became fully conscious. Taking the boy with him to the front, Saul held him up before the congregation and gave praise to God. As a result of the miracle, many people turned to the Lord. (p. 129)

A twenty-five-old illiterate girl named Anna became a highly gifted servant of God. She was used to evangelise and to heal both the blind and the deaf. 'On other occasions she has even prayed for those who have died, although only if the Lord directly commanded her to do so. She never took the responsibility of the decision upon herself. Once she was led to a two-year-old child who had died. After she had prayed for him he was raised up like Jairus' daughter . . .' (p. 138).

Another illiterate lady whom God used was Mother Sharon, who was instrumental in bringing a child, dead for six hours, back to life. After the scriptures were read, mother Sharon prayed with the dead child and when she had finished, its life returned. (p. 141)

Another instance which was also confirmed concerned a

child dead two days already. Ants were crawling about over its eyes and body. The parents, however, instead of burying the child on the first day, as is the custom in the tropics, called in Mother Sharon. Two days later she arrived. After a time of prayer, the child was restored to life. (p. 141)

A pastor told Kurt Koch of two other people on a neighbouring island who, after they had died, had been carried out of the hospital in which they had been patients. After prayer they had both come back to life (p. 142).

6 Ron Skele, in his book *Plundering Hell* (Marshalls 1984 p. 173) tells, the remarkable life story of Reinhard Bonnke and includes an account of Brother Alexander in Zaire, a man of rudimentary education, who was conducting a meeting, when the corpse of a young woman was carried in. Her fiancé challenged him defiantly, 'You say God raises people from the dead. Here is a test for you.' The woman had already been dead for four days and the stench in the small, stuffy room was almost unbearable. Alexander called the little congregation together and they lifted their hands and began to praise God and rejoice for about twenty minutes. 'Suddenly Alexander felt someone tugging at his jacket and when he opened his eyes he saw that the corpse was missing. He looked around and saw the "dead" woman standing among those who were praying, eyes closed, hands up, praising God. When the rest of the congregation saw her, they bolted out of the door with Brother Alexander in hot pursuit. The miracle shook the whole area and people turned to God in large numbers.' Reinhard Bonnke commented that missionaries with all their training and sophistication had failed to achieve in a hundred years what was now being accomplished by an indigenous man who preached a simple gospel message and who believed that Jesus is alive today to perform the same miracles he did on the shores of Galilee (p. 173).

7 Jean Darnell relates in *Heaven Here I Come* (Marshalls 1982) the story of her mother's death and resuscitation. The registered nurse told her that Jesus had taken her mother home to be with him. Jean wrote: 'I dropped to my knees sobbing. The nurse started to pull the sheet over mother's face ... "Jesus", I cried, "Don't take my mother from me. Bring her back. Bring my mother back to me.' I

was in a corner with my face to the floor. The pastor called round and the nurse whispered "She is dead".' The pastor was astounded because Jean's mother had only been telling him that very morning how she was going to be with the Lord that same day and was discussing funeral arrangements with him. Jean Darnall continues the story. 'Daddy had depended so much upon mother. How would I cope? I was fifteen years old. What would happen after I graduated from high school? "O please Jesus, bring my mother back to me..."' In spite of discouragement from the pastor, she prayed all the more. '"Bring my mother back to me" I cried out. My words echoed in the strange silence that followed. Dad's voice broke that silence. "Look at her eyes". Her eyelids were fluttering – then they closed. Her lips were moving – no sound – only movement. She slowly turned her head. She opened her eyes and looked at me. "Why did you bring me back?" At this stage the doctor arrived and diagnosed a major heart attack. "I must warn you she may not last the night," he said. But she gradually recovered. For several days mother was reluctant to talk or eat. Mostly she slept. Slowly she regained her strength and responded to what was going on around her.' When her mother was able to walk, Jean asked her what had happened. Her mother described her experience in heaven, but told her: 'Your voice was clear, insistent. I heard you cry, "Oh Jesus bring my mother back to me." Jesus looked at me and said, "Grace, I will have to take you back."'

8 Paul Yonggi Cho was speaking at a meeting when he received a call from his wife 'Come home, your son is dying.' (This was his second son, Samuel, now a schoolboy. His mother had discovered to her surprise, through a dream about Hannah, that he had been conceived. She was told it was a boy and was to be Samuel – a most unusual name in Korea.) Samuel was one of eight schoolboys who had already died after eating deep-fried silkworms sold by a street vendor. The country farmer who brought the catch to town used packaging previously used for insecticide. The boy's last message as he lay in his father's bed was 'Tell Daddy to pray for me – but I'm pretty sure I'm going to heaven tonight.' Cho arrived home to find his wife frantic. He began to cry out 'No, Samuel! You cannot go away.' Then, kicking off his shoes, he crawled to the middle of the

bed beside the lifeless body and prayed, 'Father, I will not let my boy go!' He found it hard to pray and his words sounded hollow. He did two things. He closed his eyes and focused on the healthy robust picture of the son he remembered Samuel to have been – a well-rounded boy, leader of the pack – a sportsman skilled in the traditional art of self defence. He also began to ask God's forgiveness for every wrong that came to mind – not in generalities, but exact sins . . . the times he had wronged his wife in word or deed, his ingratitude for his children, etc. This went on for an hour or two.

When he opened his eyes again, Samuel, his son, still appeared lifeless – impossible to rouse or communicate with. He began to plead with God for Samuel's life and then he praised God till past midnight. The focus of his imagination was not on the lifeless body beside him, but on the tall, vigorous and jovial Samuel he wanted to see again.

Then he got off the bed and, facing the boy, he thundered 'Samuel!', clapping his hands in a loud jolting manner. 'Samuel! In the name of Jesus Christ of Nazareth, rise up and walk!'

The boy sprang to his feet, whilst Cho almost fell backward in fear. Samuel crumpled and fell half-way across the bed, vomiting. He gestured with his hand, 'Say hello to Jesus, Papa.' He repeated it, 'Say hello to Jesus. He's right there.' The boy pointed. His father bowed toward the place indicated and said softly, 'Hello, Jesus.' 'Didn't you see us coming down the hall-way? Didn't you see us, Papa? Jesus carried me in his arms. He was carrying me to a *beautiful* place – brighter than anything I've ever seen – the most beautiful music my ears have ever heard. I couldn't recognise the tune, but we kept getting closer and closer to it. Then Jesus said to me, "We have to go back." "No", I said. "Yes, we have to go back. Your father won't let you go." And he was bringing me back to the bedroom. Didn't you see us coming down the hall? You were calling me and you commanded me to get up. That's when Jesus let go of me. There He is – Oh, He's not there. He must have gone back, I guess.'

(Nell L. Kennedy *Dream Your Way to Success* Logos International 1980)

9 Professor Peter Wagner tells the story of Sarah Cadenhead and her son, John Eric:

'Sarah Cadenhead, who attends our church, was out in the back yard of her home just before Thanksgiving, 1982, when she noticed her 12-month old son, John Eric, had disappeared. She found him face down in the swimming pool. He had stopped breathing and had turned blue. She called the paramedics, who declared him legally dead, but a police officer, who had also stopped by, volunteered to take him to Huntington Hospital (Pasadena) in the patrol car. It just so happened that the two pediatricians, Richard Johnson and William Sears, who took the case, are also members of our church. My wife, Doris, became very much interested in the event, so she later talked to the pediatricians, received permission from Sarah Cadenhead to examine the medical records, and wrote the story for *Christian Life* magazine.

As it turned out, John Eric had been without vital signs for a minimum of 40 minutes, probably more. Medication did restore some heart motion, but it was so artificial that the doctor wrote on the medical instructions, 'Do not resuscitate.'

A call had gone in to the Los Angeles Christian television channel, T.B.N., and special prayer went up. Late that night, Sarah went back to the hospital in obedience to the voice of the Lord, took the cold body, and began to rub it with hospital lotion. After several hours, warmth began to come into the body, and soon John Eric opened his eyes and pulled the glasses off the nurse! The neurologists predicted 100% brain damage, but in a week he was out of the hospital and soon he was perfectly normal in every way. The medical personnel in the hospital named him 'Baby Lazarus.' *The Pasadena Star News* featured the story on the front page, under the headline: MIRACLE. Sarah and John Eric attended my Sunday School class for a time, so we got to know them well.'

10 In the same article, published in 'First Fruits', September/October, 1985, Peter Wagner reports cases in Brazil and Argentina:

'When I was in Brazil in 1983, I heard three reports of dead people being raised, all by very credible Christian workers. One, a Nazarine pastor, had been raised from the dead himself. When he was two years old, he died at 3.00 one afternoon. During the wake ... (as) neighbours and relatives were mourning, the parents were in another room praying, 'God, if you let us have our boy, we will dedicate him to be a pastor.' At 11.00 that night, he rolled over, knocked the flowers off the table, and got up alive.

I visited Argentina in 1985 and met a sister named Lydia who had died when the car in which she was riding crashed into a lake and she was trapped under the water for a half hour. She clearly describes the experience of her spirit being out of her body, then returning. According to my friend, Omar Cabrera, who was driving the car, angels must have pulled her out of the car because there was no natural explanation of how she could get out of the car and onto the bank. Others might interpret it differently, but the parties involved believe they witnessed a miracle.'

A perspective

1 Death is man's enemy and causes innumerable and varied disruptions.

2 There is a fundamental difference between resuscitation (being revived but still mortal) and resurrection (being raised a spiritual body like Christ's after the resurrection, which is immortal).

3 Reviving the dead (resuscitation) is a powerful and visible sign of the power of God.

4 God chooses sovereignly when and for what reason a person is brought back to life. He may communicate this to believing and listening Christians through a prophecy, a word of knowledge, a gift of faith, or 'working of miracles'.

5 Important elements in this ministry would seem to be:

    a) Prayer and waiting on God for specific direction.

    b) Repentance by the living.

    c) A 'word' from the Lord.

(Notice that this point (c) covers all of the following, because once God has spoken, the rest follows).

    d) The presence of faith (a calm control and conviction).

    e) A removal of excess emotion, unbelief, etc.

f) A rebuking of the spirit of death.

g) Some act of faith.

h) A commanding of the dead man to live in the name of Jesus (based on Christ's authority over death).

6 The effects of raising the dead are impossible to calculate, but they would certainly stir people out of complacency, awaken faith, and bring glory to God.

7 The healing of the dead is not common; but its occurrence will increase in frequency till the return of the Lord.

30

MINISTERING TO THOSE
IN HOSPITAL

Introduction

1 Our oldest hospitals have Christian roots, being founded by the Church to bring the love of Christ and healing to the suffering.

2 Now that most have become 'secularised', we still recognise a great debt which society owes to the wonderful skill, dedication and care which our hospital staffs give to the suffering. We respect them for their work's sake.

3 Neither secular society nor modern science, however, can actually bring healing to the patient. ("I dressed him: God healed him" – Ambrose Pare). Our doctors may prescribe, our surgeons may operate, our nurses may care very lovingly, but God brings the healing. Sometimes this is overlooked and God speaks to the inhabitants of the secular world by demonstrations of his power to remind them of who he is, and that he alone is the healer.

Approach

1 As God's servant we remind ourselves that we are entering another man's domain when we enter a hospital ward. The hospital staff are entitled to our respect (Romans 13: 1–7).

2 It will rarely be possible to function in the same way in hospital as in the church.

3 The methodology in the various categories of healings (already mentioned) is still applicable, though we must

never be governed by systems and technique – only the Holy Spirit and the word of God.

Preparation

We need spiritually to 'put on the uniform' and recollect the authority we have in Christ Jesus. 'Put on the armour of light and the Lord Jesus Christ' (Romans 13: 12,14).

Recollect who Jesus is and what he has done

1 He is the mighty God – able to heal (Isaiah 9: 6).

2 He is the compassionate God – willing to heal (cf. the leper – Mark 1: 41).

3 He gave his life to make us whole: 'He himself bore our sins in his body on the tree, so that we might die to sins and live for righteousness; by his wounds you have been healed' 1 Peter 2: 24.

4 He has conquered evil and is now over every authority and power – every knee must bow to his name – Ephesians 1: 20–23; Philippians 2: 6–11.

Recollect who we are in Christ

1 We are God's children and servants (1 John 3: 1).

2 We are righteous in Christ (2 Corinthians 5: 21).

3 We sit with Christ in heavenly places (Ephesians 2: 4–6).

4 We are God's co-workers (2 Corinthians 6: 1).

5 We will be given gifts to discern what the Father wants us, his children, to do.

Remind ourselves of our authority and mission to heal

1 Just as Jesus has been sent, so are we (John 20: 21).

2 We have actually been commissioned to heal (Matthew 10: 7–8; 28: 18–20).

3 We have been empowered to heal if we know the anointing of the Holy Spirit (Acts 1: 8; 10: 38).

Remind ourselves of our human weakness

1 We can do nothing by ourselves (John 15: 5).

2 We empty our minds of preconceptions and presumptions (Psalm 19: 13).

3 We ask God to reveal what he wants us to do (John 5: 19).

4 We invite the Holy Spirit to minister (Luke 11: 13; Matthew 18: 19) and honour and bless what he does.

Create the right environment

1 We try to discern the 'atmosphere' when we enter the room.

2 If necessary, we may ask people to leave (Acts 9: 40).

3 If possible, we invite others to join us (Mark 5: 40).

4 We rebuke oppressive spirits affecting the atmosphere (death, depression, unbelief, etc.).

5 We do not concentrate on the condition, but on what God is doing or saying.

Respond accordingly

1 We seek to discover the problem and discern the cause.

2 We show love – we may take the person's hand (cf. Mark 1: 31; Mark 5: 41).

3 We read some appropriate scriptures and/or pray. (It does not matter if the person should appear to be unconscious. It is remarkable how the word of God and prayer 'get through'.)

4 We do what God is saying and apply the appropriate methodology for the category of healing needed. (We are not going to minister deliverance if we discern that simple repentance and confession are all that is necessary.)

31

MINISTERING TO CHILDREN

Introduction

This is an area of ministry about which there seems to be little material available and our own experience is limited. As the churches become increasingly involved in ministering to children, there will be more lessons to share. There have been many cases of disturbed children where the real ministry required has been to the parents.

Biblical examples of ministry to children

There are six accounts of ministry to children in the Bible. Two are from the Old Testament (both result in resuscitation from the dead) one concerning the ministry of Elijah to the son the poor widow of Zarephath and the other of Elisha to the son of the rich Shunammite woman. Four are from the New Testament (also resulting in two resuscitations from the dead) – being on record as part of the ministry of Christ himself. One was a twelve-year-old girl, who was resuscitated, whose father had a prominent position in the synagogue. Another was a boy who suffered from epilepsy and had a deaf and dumb spirit. Thirdly there was the case of a Gentile girl who had a demon who was 'cured', possibly without being in the physical presence of Christ. Finally there was the case of the royal official's son from Capernaum, who was certainly healed of his fever by Jesus at a distance.

Old Testament examples

Elijah the Tishbite, ministered to a poor widow in Zarephath and miraculously provided meal and oil for her and her household (1 Kings 17: 10–16).

1 The widow's son became severely sick and died (v. 17).

2 She called Elijah, thinking that judgement might be upon her for some past sin (v. 18).

3 Elijah took the corpse to his room and laid it on his own bed (v. 19).

4 Elijah cried to the Lord for his 'landlady' (v. 20).

5 He stretched himself upon the child three times and prayed that the child's soul might come back to him (v. 21).

6 The Lord heard him and the soul of the child came into him and he revived (v. 22).

7 Elijah took the child and gave him to his mother, saying 'Look your son is alive!' (v. 23).

8 The woman replied, 'Now I know that you are a man of God and that the word of the Lord from your mouth is the truth' (v. 24).

Elisha ministered to a rich and influential Shunammite woman who had provided occasional accommodation for him. (2 Kings: 4; 8–37). She was barren and her husband was old, but Elisha prophesied she would have the son which was born to her (verse 15,16).

1 When the child had grown he went out one morning with his father to harvest but apparently suffered severe sunstroke (verse 19).

2 He was taken home to his mother, who took him on her knees till noon, when he died (verse 20).

3 She went with a servant to look for Elisha, whom she found at Mount Carmel (verse 25).

4 He sent his servant Gehazi to meet her. 'Is your child all right?' asked Gehazi. 'Everything is all right', she replied(!) (verse 26). She clearly did not want to delay by going into explanations.

5 When she came to Elisha she fell down and clung to his feet. Gehazi tried to thrust her away (verse 27).

6 Elisha said, 'Leave her alone. She is in bitter distress, but the Lord has hidden it from me and has not told me why' (verse 27).

7 Once Elisha learned it was to do with her son, he sent Gehazi ahead of him, taking Elisha's staff, with instructions to lay it on the face of the child (verse 29), which he did (verse 31).

8 But the boy neither spoke nor heard. Gehazi reported back to Elisha, 'The child has not awakened' (verse 31).

9 When Elisha reached the house the dead child was laid upon his bed, so he went in and shut the door. He was there alone with the corpse of the child (verse 33).

10 Elisha prayed to the Lord (verse 33).

11 He lay upon (crouched upon) the child, put his mouth to the child's mouth, his eyes to the child's eyes, and his hands on the child's hands (verse 34).

12 As Elisha stretched himself upon the child and embraced him, the child's flesh became warm (verse 34).

13 Then he left the room and walked to and from in the house before returning once more to the boy (verse 35).

14 Again he stretched himself (or crouched) upon the child's body. The child sneezed seven times and opened his eyes (verse 35).

15 Elisha summoned his servant and told him to call the Shunammite woman (verse 36).

16 When she came, he said 'Take your son' (verse 36).

17 She came and fell at his feet, bowing herself to the ground; then took up her son and went out (verse 37).

New Testament examples

Jairus' only daughter: a twelve-year-old, who was dying (Matthew 9: 18; Mark 5: 22,23; Luke 8: 41,42).

Jairus, a ruler of the synagogue, asked Jesus to come to his daughter. Jesus got up and went with him, but was interrupted en route by the woman with a haemorrhage, who was healed. Meanwhile a message was sent to say that Jesus should no longer be bothered as the child was dead, but Jesus replied, 'Don't be afraid; just believe, and she will be healed' (Luke 8: 50). Reaching the house, he said that the child was not dead and was mocked for it. The crowd were put out at his request and Jesus went in. He took the girl by the hand, called out, 'My child, get up!' and her spirit returned. She got up immediately and he directed that she should be given something to eat (Luke 8: 55). Her parents were amazed! (Luke 8: 56).

The Syrophoenician woman's daughter: A girl who was demonised
(left at home!) (Matthew 15: 22; Mark 7: 25,26).

This gentile mother pleaded with Jesus, but he did not
answer at first. Later he commended the mother for her
great *faith*. He assured her that her request was answered
and the girl was healed immediately.

A boy who had epileptic symptoms (Matthew 17: 15; Mark 9:
17,18; Luke 9: 38,39). This epileptic boy, who had suffered
much, was also deaf and dumb. The father brought him to
the disciples, who could not do anything. Jesus rebuked the
deaf and dumb spirit. He commanded it to come out and
never enter him again. The spirit shrieked, convulsing the
boy violently, and threw him on the ground. The boy
appeared corpse-like (Many said 'He's dead'). Jesus took him
by the hand and lifted him to his feet.

The royal official's son (John 4: 43–54).

This official came and begged Jesus to come and heal his
son. Jesus chided him 'Unless you people see miraculous
signs and wonders, you will never believe', but the father
was not put off and urged him to come before his child died.
Jesus replied simply 'You may go. Your son will live'. The
official took Jesus at his word and departed. Whilst on the
way home, the servants met him and told him his son was
well. Checking the time of his recovery, the father found
that it was exactly the same hour in the previous day that
Jesus had said 'Your son will live'. The official and all his
household believed.

Background teaching about children

1 Jesus said of little *children* 'the kingdom of God belongs
to such as these' (Mark 10: 14).

2 Jesus warned most seriously against anyone causing
children who believed in him to *stumble* (Matthew 18: 6).

3 Jesus warned against despising or scorning 'little ones'
for 'I tell you, *their angels* in heaven always see the face of my
Father in heaven' (Matthew 18: 10).

4 The Son of Man came to save that which was lost. He says it is *not his Father's will* 'that any of these *little ones* should be *lost* (Matthew 18: 14).

Summary

1 Children, through their innocence, have a 'special' relationship in God's kingdom.

2 Little ones have angels who are protecting them and looking to God the Father to do whatever he bids concerning their welfare.

3 It is not the Father's will that any little ones be lost or perish.

4 This should encourage us to minister to children with every confidence.

5 Let those who minister take a leaf out of the angels' book and seek to be always in the presence of God the Father and looking to him to show us what he wants to be done.

Places and ways to minister

1 Some children want to be prayed for in church. They see adults being prayed for and so it is perfectly natural for them to ask for the same kind of help. In which case we pray as the child will have seen us praying for adults.

2 For some home is the place for ministry because that is where they are sick. If the child is very sick, then the prayer will be at the bedside. This may be when the child is awake or asleep.

3 If the child is awake in bed, it is good to be as informal and disarming as possible. It is also good to have at least one parent, or someone else close to the child, present.

a) Express sympathy for the child being in bed.

b) Ask what the problem is. (Sometimes the child can not say but a skilled minister can often learn a lot by making the child draw some pictures of home etc.)

c) Possibly read a healing story about Jesus from the gospels.

d) Suggest a short silence when we can all confess our sins and get right with God. Make a declaration of forgiveness in the name of Jesus.

e) Ask the child what Jesus should be requested to do.

f) Then ask Jesus to do it specifically.

4 If the child is asleep, it is good to gather with a parent or someone else close to the child. Obviously it is best to minister quietly. Maybe lay a hand lightly on top of the bed clothes over the body or perhaps on the head, hand, arm or shoulder. Pray silently for a while. Some will find it helpful to pray quietly at this time in tongues. Then speak firmly and directly to the condition in the name of Jesus. Rebuke a fever. Break the power of any affliction.

5 If the child is up and about, it is important that we engage in quiet conversation in such a way that the child is disarmed. We then proceed generally along the same lines we use ministering to a child who is awake in bed. We keep the ministry informal. We do not mind childish interruptions. We want the child to know why we are praying, but we should avoid creating any alarm about the child's illness.

6 Sometimes a child will be in need of deliverance. Again we keep the ministry low key and pray as for healing the oppressed.

7 When the child is hospitalised, we proceed as for ministering to any hospitalised person, bearing in mind whatever is relevant from the above. Much will depend upon the privacy available. It would be very unwise to create a situation which would leave a child vulnerable to ridicule.

If the parents have requested a prayer for the healing of their child, we take olive oil and simply anoint in the name of Jesus, after having read the passage in James 5 about elders being called, sins being confessed and the afflicted being anointed. We allow time for heart searching before anointing.

We keep the ministry *brief* and leave after having assured the child or parents that if desired we will be happy to come again. We often encourage *the parents* to continue ministering in the name of Jesus until the child is better. They can minister as we have just modelled for them or they can stretch their hands briefly over the bed or put them on the afflicted part of the body as the child sleeps each night.

8 Sometimes the right course may be to minister healing in the presence of relatives, but with the child absent.

9 When praying for sick children always picture them as happy and well.

Finally, we include a modern-day example sent to us after a visit we made to Europe recently, which goes to prove that whilst other people's experiences help, in the end we shall and must be guided in each case by the Holy Spirit.

We would like to tell you something the Lord did to our family. Our daughter 9 years of age, was adopted by us at the age of 2. The memory of her mother, who left her, has been difficult to her, though she does not want to speak of it. But she has been a problem to my wife, as she has not been able, as it seems, to accept my wife, as her mother. The girl has been insecure and often violent. After the meetings, I came home. The situation was then very tense. I took the girl in my arms and told her that she could now take the hand of Jesus, who would never forsake her, and with her little hand firmly in His steady hand, say good-bye to her own mother. The girl fell immediately in a deep sleep. The situation with her has been radically changed ever since. There is a new atmosphere at home, a new relationship and a new girl, thank God.

32

KEEPING OUR HEALING AND DELIVERANCE

Proposition 1: *It is possible to lose one's healing!*

Jesus healed a man who had been an invalid for thirty-eight years (John 5: 8,9). He said, 'See, you are well again. Stop sinning or something worse may happen to you.' In this case – but by no means always (John 9: 3) – the man's infirmity had come through some particular sin. To return to that sin was to open up the door for the infirmity to return in a worse form.

One of the first healing miracles of which we ever had firsthand knowledge concerned a young man in Chile whose hearing was wonderfully restored following the visit of a Puerto Rican evangelist. When he prayed for the deaf who had all come to a platform rigged up in the Valparaíso football stadium this young man suddenly leapt up shouting 'I can hear. I can hear.' The evangelist called him to the microphone and began to cross examine him. He had lost the hearing in his left ear and two surgical operations had not improved it. Now the evangelist was blocking the boy's right ear and testing the left one so recently healed. It was perfect. 'Who did that?' cried the evangelist. 'Jesus' roared back the crowd. It was certainly impressive and even more so when I discovered that he was one of our own young men who gave his testimony in an Anglican Church the following Sunday.

About a year later I was talking to him and happened to ask after his hearing. 'It's funny you should ask that now', he said. 'It's just gone again!' 'What are you going to do about it?' I asked. 'I shall go to see the doctor' he said. 'I think that if I were you,' I said, 'I would first give myself to prayer and fasting and ask the Lord to show me if there was any reason why I had lost my hearing.' But he was clearly not keen on the idea. Strangely enough, I heard later that the minister of his own church had talked to him about it when they were travelling on a bus together and had given him the same advice. The young man was so angry that he left his seat and got off the bus three stops before his home! One cannot say that the loss of his hearing was definitely due to some sin, but it was a possibility and the fact that he was unwilling to seek the Lord about it added to one's concern.

Proposition 2: *It is possible to lose one's deliverance!*

Jesus gave the illustration (in Luke 11: 24) of an evil spirit coming out of a man and then going through arid places seeking rest and finding none. It says to itself 'I will return to the house I left.' When it goes back it finds the house swept clean and put in order. Then it goes out and takes seven other spirits more wicked than itself and they go in and live there, so that the final condition of that man is worse than the first.

In the case of a man healed of his infirmity, Jesus warned him to stop sinning 'or something worse may happen'. In the case of deliverance from an evil spirit, Jesus warned that reform was not enough and that in such a case the final condition would be worse than the first.

1 It is important to keep on *being filled with the Holy Spirit.* The filling of the Holy Spirit is not necessarily a second blessing. It may be a third, fourth or fifth blessing. Every Christian should go on being filled with the Holy Spirit (Ephesians 5: 18).

2 It is important to *repent* continuously.

We note the case of a married couple who received ministry in the Vineyard Fellowship in Orange County, California. She was a physician and was healed of a physical ailment. The husband was filled with the Holy Spirit at the same meeting: When they went home everyone was remarking on the wonderful change in her husband and the wife began to feel so jealous of him that her healing left her.

She phoned her pastor in great anguish. He discerned the root of the problem and told her to repent of this jealousy, which she did. Her healing returned immediately.

3 It is important to *keep on forgiving*.

Jesus taught his disciples to pray 'Forgive us our sins as we also forgive everyone who sins against us.' We cannot retain all the benefits of God's forgiveness if we are not constantly forgiving others.

We were ministering in Toronto, Canada, and a lady knelt at the communion rails to ask God's forgiveness for herself now that she said she had forgiven her family. With tears in her eyes she asked 'Do you think God will understand that although I forgive them I never want to see them again?' Even as she said it she knew that was not forgiveness. Forgiveness heals relationships between man and man, and man with God. The health of our relationships is often reflected in the health of our individual being.

4 It is important to *resist the devil*.

The devil will often try to come back in the same way he came before. I myself was healed from internal spasms which had plagued me for about fifteen years. These started during my time as a missionary in Chile and the only relief I could get was through a very hot bath – frequently in the middle of the night. Soon after we began regular ministry at the communion rails at St Andrew's, Chorleywood, I went forward in response to a 'word of knowledge'. I was healed, praise God. I used to have one of these turns almost weekly, but about a dozen times since then I have sensed the threat of a spasm and once since then I have had a turn bad enough to need a hot bath, and that was when I failed to do what I knew I had to do – rebuke it deliberately in the name of Jesus and then relax. Each time I have done that the sensation has gradually subsided. 'Resist the devil, and he will flee from you. Come near to God and he will come near to you', 'Do not give the devil a foothold' (James 4: 7,8; 1 Peter 5: 8,9; Ephesians 4: 27).

Whether giving ministry in God's name or receiving ministry, we need to put on the whole armour of God, which protects his servants both in the offensive or on the defensive (Ephesians 6: 10–18). (See chapter 22 on the equipment we need.)

33

WORSHIP – WHERE IT ALL BEGINS

Christian worship

'Christian worship is the most momentous, the most urgent, the most glorious action that can take place in human life' (Karl Barth). In our traditional churches worship, however, has often become lifeless and boring. Ask the young people or the visitor! In fact, ask yourself! In his 'Church Growth' lectures to clergy around Britain, Dr Eddie Gibbs frequently asked 'If you did not *have* to go to your church, would you go next Sunday?' The wry smiles on many faces told their own story.

The importance of worship

Worship (individual and corporate) is the primary obligation of all God's people. God says 'I am the Lord your God ... you shall have no other gods before me' (Exodus 20: 2,3). Man was made to worship. God is jealous for this worship. He says 'I, the Lord your God, am a jealous God' (Exodus 20: 5). He does not permit us to worship any other gods. 'You shall not bow down to them or worship them' (Exodus 20: 5). Idolatry is seen as spiritual adultery – unfaithfulness.

The first question in the *Westminster Catechism* runs: 'What is the chief end of man?' and the simple but sublime answer is: 'Man's chief end is to glorify God and to enjoy him for ever.' If we can never remember anything else from the catechism, we should remember that.

Definition of worship

'Worship is the dramatic celebration of God in his supreme worth in such a manner that his 'worthiness' becomes the norm and inspiration of human living' (Ralph P. Martin).

'Worship is the submission of all our nature to God. It is the quickening of the conscience by His holiness; the nourishment of the mind with His truth; the purifying of the imagination by His beauty; the opening of the heart to His love; the surrender of will to His purpose – and all this gathered up in adoration, the most selfless emotion of which our nature is capable and therefore the chief remedy for that self-centredness which is original sin and the source of all actual sin' (William Temple).

Meaning of the words

There are two principal Hebrew words used for worship in the Old Testament. One of them, *hishtachawah* means literally 'a bowing down' – a prostration before God. This is the nearest to the Greek word *proskunein* (John 4: 24), which is by far the most commonly used word for worship in the New Testament, and conveys the idea of 'coming towards to kiss'. There should be a real sense of adoration and tenderness in worship.

The other Hebrew word is *abodah*, meaning service. The Greek equivalent in the New Testament is *latreia*. This service is the offering to God of ourselves as tokens of his worth and honour.

The word 'worship', which is used in the translation of all these words, has come into modern English from the old English 'weorthscipe'. This became 'worshipe' and finally 'worship' – *giving worth to someone.*

Old Testament worship

In the Old Testament a strong sense of God's holiness and awesomeness was elemental in worship. Both the detailed instruction for ritual sacrifice and the liturgy of the psalms

taught the worshipper the priority of repentance, thanksgiving, praise and prayer. There was also provision for
festivity, celebration and spontaneity.

New Testament worship

The worship of God in the New Testament clearly reveals
some carry-over from traditional Jewish worship. The
perennial feasts and Temple ritual both contributed. The
Lord's supper was instituted in the setting of the Passover
celebration. Both Jesus and the disciples continued to
worship on the Temple premises. So did the early
Christians, who were accustomed to meet together in
Solomon's Colonnade (Acts 5: 12). Then there was the
synagogue where the first Christians continued to worship
weekly for as long as they were permitted by the local
Jewish elders. This worship included the main elements of
praise, prayer and instruction, which were also incorporated in the New Testament patterns.

Christian worship was born out of the fusion of the
Jewish Temple worship, the annual Festal celebrations, the
synagogue, the upper room and Pentecost. But beside the
ritual and formality, an element of spontaneity continued
in the post-Pentecost church (1 Corinthians 14: 26,27 and
Ephesians 5: 19,20). This was necessary if the gifts of the
Spirit were not to be quenched.

In spite of the many details of their worship, however,
there is no full and objective description of an early
Christian service of worship. Possibly the clearest example
is in the account of Paul's visit to Troas (Acts 20: 7–12).

Key-words for Christian worship
Jesus provides two: 'spirit and truth' (John 4: 24). Paul adds
two more: 'decency and order' (1 Corinthians 14: 40 and
Colossians 2: 5).

Spirit and truth

It is possible to be unbalanced by too much Spirit and too
little truth. In South America we found many Pentecostal

churches majoring wonderfully on the Spirit, but, because of insufficient knowledge of the truth (God's word), they were (frequently) 'way out' doctrinally.

It is also possible to be unbalanced by too much emphasis on truth and very little experience of the Spirit. In many evangelical churches we have found Christians full of the truth; whose stress is rightly on the Bible, the word of God, but they are lacking the freedom of the Spirit. The same goes for 'catholic' churches, where the truth is seen enshrined in the liturgy and ritual and there is normally no freedom for the Spirit of God to operate outside the restrictions of the letter. Paul says 'The letter kills, but the Spirit gives life' (2 Corinthians 3: 6).

Our Lord Jesus Christ poured out the Holy Spirit upon us so that we might have within us again the power to comprehend him and his love (Ephesians 3: 18). The Spirit, like water, must flow to meet us where we are; however, while the union of the Holy Spirit with our spirit may be full and real, without the ingredient of truth, such experiences of the heart may be easily distorted. We could believe that the embrace of his love and compassion in the midst of our suffering is confirmation that a wrong way in us is not only right, but God's will for us. When our spirits meet his, our understanding must also match God's or we will have started a relationship which cannot be sustained.

That is why Jesus said 'In spirit and in truth' (John 4: 24). 'Spirit to spirit without truth causes a relationship to flow like a bankless river in the desert – soon gone!' On the other hand, 'truth alone is only mind to mind – and barren! Neither without the other can produce or sustain fellowship. Both spirit and truth together spark and enhance in crescendo to blessedness.' (J and P Sandford *The Transformation of the Inner Man* Bridge Publications 1982 p. 209).

Decency and order

The context of Paul's words 'decency' and 'order' shows that they apply to the conduct of meetings where the gifts of the Spirit are being exercised.

'Decency' or 'what is fitting' is a relative term and varies from one culture to another. (In some it is fitting to belch after a good meal!) With regard to the use of gifts, it may be fitting in some cultures to use the gifts in an emotional way, but others would find this very off-putting. The gifts may be exercised in a very low-key unemotional way and be all the more effective for that – especially in an English culture.

'Order' also refers not to the precise and detailed instruction which may be read in the 'Order for Common Prayer', but in the orderly way the gifts are handled in the church. This implies no straitjacket. For example, if there are 'tongues', the order is that there should be no more than two or three before there is an interpretation – preferably an interpretation should follow *each* tongue (1 Corinthians 14: 28).

There is the order of death – a cemetery where all that is required is for an occasional whitewash of the tombstones and a clipping of the surrounding grass. There is also the order of life, a nursery where those responsible are constantly bringing the place to order. That is the kind of order Paul speaks of – teasing order out of the untidiness of forms of worship where *'everything is done'*.

Means for expressing worship in the Bible

Vocal expression:

1 Singing as with one voice (2 Chronicles 5: 13).

2 Singing antiphonally (Exodus 15: 21; Numbers 10: 35; 21: 17; 1 Samuel 18: 7: Nehemiah 12: 24,31).

3 Praying with the Spirit (1 Corinthians 14: 15) and praying with the mind (1 Corinthians 14: 15).

4 Singing with the Spirit (1 Corinthians 14: 15; Ephesians 5: 19) and singing with the mind (1 Corinthians 14: 15).

5 Shouting (Psalm 47: 1).

6 Silence (Psalm 46: 10).

7 Weeping (1 Samuel 1: 10).

Physical expression

1 Clapping (Psalm 47: 1), dancing and leaping (2 Samuel

6: 16), kneeling (Psalm 95: 6), beating the breast (Luke 18: 13).

2 Bowing down (Psalm 95: 6), prostrating (Ezekiel 1: 28b), raising hands (Psalm 63: 4 and Psalm 134: 2), standing (Psalm 134: 1, RSV).

Instrumental expression

1 Harps, lyres and cymbals (1 Chronicles 25: 1).

2 Cymbals, harps, lyres, 120 trumpets and other instruments (2 Chronicles 5: 12).

3 Trumpet, harp, lyres, tambourine, stringed instruments, flute, cymbals (Psalm 150).

4 The musical instruments King David had made – and trumpets (2 Chronicles 7: 6).

Liturgical expression

1 Psalms.

2 Words such as Amen (Romans 1: 25), Hallelujah (Revelations 19: 1,3,4,6), Hosanna (Matthew 21: 9).

3 Songs such as Marana tha (1 Corinthians 16: 22).

    a) Gloria in Excelsis (Luke 2: 14),

    b) The Magnificat (Luke 1: 46–55),

    c) The Benedictus (Luke 1: 68–79),

    d) The Nunc Dimitis (Luke 2: 29–32),

    e) Other New Testament songs, see Ephesians 5: 14; Philippians 2: 6–11; Colossians 1: 15–20; 1 Timothy 3: 16; Hebrews 1: 3; Revelations 7: 12; 19: 1–8.

Sacramental expression:

1 The Lord's supper (1 Corinthians 11: 17–34).

Symbolic expression: Incense (Revelations 8: 3,4).

2 Golden lampstands (Revelation 2: 1).

3 White robes (Revelation 3: 4).

Summary:

'True worship must always be directed towards the living God. It is not a performance in order to display the talents of priests, preachers, musicians, singers, dancers or anyone else' (David Watson). The focus must be God.

Abandonment and sacrifice in worship

When Michal criticised her husband, King David, for his undignified dancing, he replied 'It was before the Lord, who chose me ... I will celebrate before the Lord. I will become even more undignified than this, and I will be humiliated in my own eyes' (2 Samuel 6: 21,22). The essential attitude is one of *abandoned self-giving* to God. Christ commended the same in Mary when she *wasted* precious ointment in anointing him (John 12: 7,8).

Crescendo in worship

The Old Testament seems to indicate a 'gradual' in worship. There were psalms of invitation to worship, of ascent – going up to the city of God, entering the Temple gates, coming in to the courts of the Lord and delighting in the very presence of God, seeking his face.

There needs to be a sense of movement forwards and upwards. At some point in time, the worship should reach a climax. This may come at the end and be followed by silence or the manifestation of the gifts. Or it may come in the middle and the worship will fall away gently, gradually melting into silence or the manifestation of the gifts of the Spirit, which are often released to the body at such a time. (Though, of course, we can never make rules for God's Spirit.)

Context for ministering in the gifts

1 Worship provides the setting for the pouring out of the Spirit. The Holy Spirit was first given when the first disciples were all together in one place – doubtless worshipping God (Acts 2: 1).

2 Worship provides the ideal climate for the operations of the gifts of the Spirit. These, if permitted, become manifested 'when you come together' (1 Corinthians 11: 18,20,33,34) for 'the Lord's Supper' (1 Corinthians 11: 17–34) with 'a hymn, or a word of instruction, a revelation, a tongue or an interpretation' (1 Corinthians 14: 26).

Conclusion

Recently I talked to a pastor of a growing church in Honolulu and his wife. This small free church group had been struggling on one of the islands. The wife (a quiet person) felt so oppressed at the Sunday service that she withdrew from the church for a while. Outside she prayed desperately – 'What is wrong, Lord?' She could hardly believe what she sensed the Lord telling her to do. Although she begged to be excused, God seemed to be insisting, so she answered; 'Well, Lord if my husband asks me to say anything when I return (which she knew was most unlikely), I will do it.'

As she re-entered the building her husband glanced in her direction. 'Have you anything for us from the Lord?' he asked. Her heart sank, but she knew what she had to do. Nodding that she had, she went to the centre of the church, and with a hurried apology, she spat on the floor and cried 'That's what God thinks of our worship!' In that instant the Spirit of God fell on the congregation in a most extra-ordinary way – people slumped to the floor and wept in repentance. From that surge of new life the church was swept forward.

No one should try to repeat that, of course, but we would all do well to ask 'What does God really think of *our* worship?' Does it please him? Does it touch his heart?

Recommended reading:
Ralph P. Martin *Worship in the Early Church* Eerdmans 1983
Michael Marshall *Renewal in Worship* Marshalls 1982
Graham Kendrick *Worship* Kingsway Publications 1984
Andrew Maries *One Heart, One Voice* Hodder & Stoughton 1986

34

OPERATING WITHIN A LITURGICAL STRUCTURE

Definition of Liturgy

'A liturgy is the form of service or regular ritual of a Church' (*Chambers Dictionary*). From the Greek word *leitourgia*, which originally meant a public duty of any kind.

Defence of Liturgy

1 Liturgy is *scriptural*, e.g. Amen, Hallelujah, Hosanna, Maranatha, Gloria in Excelsis, Ter Sanctus, Magnificat, Benedictus, Nunc Dimittis, the Lord's Prayer, the confession 'Jesus is Lord', etc., are expressions of worship found in the New Testament.

2 Liturgy is *traditional*. New Testament worship inevitably retained some elements carried over from Jewish worship, e.g. the setting of the Lord's supper. The Old Testament psalms, of course, were part of the Jewish liturgy. Liturgy has also retained many choice expressions of worship from down the ages.

3 Liturgy is *educational:* its constant use is mentally formative, and when it enshrines orthodox teaching it is beneficially instructive.

4 Liturgy *ensures that the essentials* of worship are not overlooked – repentance, confession, absolution, praise, prayer, creeds, etc., are all regularly included.

5 Liturgy is *a legitimate mode* of expression in worship when made alive by the Spirit. Ballerina Pavlova, when asked why she danced, replied 'If I could tell you, I would not

dance.' Liturgy brings in a dimension to worship which extempore worship cannot do – but the same is true for extempore worship, which should not be excluded either.

6 Liturgy is *almost inevitable*. This could be observed to be emerging in the Chilean Pentecostal Church as pastors would make a habit of calling on their congregations to give God the glory. Invariably all the people would stand in response and shout three times:– 'Gloria sea a Dios' (Glory be to God).

7 Liturgy is *a commonly accepted understanding* and a means of expression. Like good manners in a social context, it facilitates communication and keeps relationships flowing smoothly.

Danger of Liturgy

When all is said and done, Paul's observation is relevant: 'The letter kills, but the Spirit gives life' (2 Corinthians 3: 6). To keep worship alive, liturgy must never be allowed to stagnate – it must flow. It must not become stifling, but be constantly adjusting to the wind of the Spirit.

Evolution in Liturgy

Church services

Without going back as far as the first Prayer Book of 1549, following the Reformation, or the Act of Uniformity which authorised the *Book of Common Prayer* in 1662, we can detect a constant evolution in the history of our liturgical expression and practice. In spite of the Revival, which John Wesley wished for the Church of England, the turn of the nineteenth century marked a 'low' in Church of England church attendance.

But wherever a congregation gathered and whenever a clergyman was available to minister, Sunday worship would normally begin at 10 a.m. with Morning Prayer, followed by the Litany, Antecommunion and a sermon sometimes lasting an hour. There was frequently no Evening Prayer on a Sunday in many churches.

Celebrations of Holy Communion were rare – usually Christmas, Easter, Whitsun (and perhaps Michaelmas – Harvest time). In the parish of Barrington, Cambridge, during the lengthy non-resident incumbency of the Rev. R. W. Finch at the end of the eighteenth century there were no celebrations of Holy Communion for twenty-five years!

The Rev. (later Bishop) Daniel Wilson, an evangelical leader at Islington in the early 1800s, was the first to have 8 a.m. Holy Communion (to attract the poorer classes who could not afford a rented pew at 10 a.m.). In the 1840s, the Rev. J. C. Miller, an evangelical incumbent of St Martin's, Birmingham, was apparently the first to separate the three morning services. Even Morning Prayer included the Lord's prayer twice, etc. Miller also introduced afternoon and evening celebrations of Holy Communion (1852).

The Oxford movement (1833–45), which followed J. Keble's 'Assize Sermon' in 1833, was a renewal movement which attempted to bring back the High Church ideals of the seventeenth century. This was followed by the introduction of Catholic ceremonial: new teaching, new rites, prayers for the dead and to the saints, new forms of dress, liturgical colours, the position of the priest at Holy Communion, incense-burning, breast-beating, crossings, bowings, genuflections, new church furniture (bells, candles, tabernacles, statues of the Madonna and the saints), daily celebrations, wafers in place of bread, the reserved sacrament, the confessional, etc.

All this stirred up considerable opposition. The saintly Bishop Edward King of Lincoln was summoned to an ecclesiastical court in a test case presided over by Archbishop Benson in 1890 for seven ritualist offences. Benson decided in King's favour. The latter has since undergone a form of Anglican 'canonisation' and is remembered by the Church of England annually on March 8th!

Choral services

Most eighteenth-century congregations heard little music, but if there was any it was usually provided by a small local band with some singers who followed the Tate and Brady version of the metric psalms (known as the 'singing psalms'). The singers and band were normally installed in the west gallery above and out of sight of the congregation. They played and sang the psalms, and in the more ambitious churches even sang an anthem, at which time the congregation would turn around in the pews – hence the expression 'to turn and face the music'.

The Methodists had showed the Established Church that congregations enjoyed singing hymns in worship. The small evangelical element in the Established Church soon followed suit, but generally it was decades before the rest of the Church of England showed any willingness to learn from a non-conformist insight. By the 1850s choral services were being introduced. Chancels (which had previously provided a hiding place for cleaning materials) were now fitted with choir stalls, where the young, being trained to sing, could sit under the eagle eye of the vicar. Organs and harmoniums were installed to replace the local band. Psalms were chanted (using the new *Cathedral Psalter*) and new hymns introduced (many borrowed from the Methodists). Singing was becoming a fresh dimension in worship. The first *Hymns Ancient and Modern* was published in 1861.

Implementing the changes was not easy and there was often bitter opposition from displaced musicians and singers. T. T. Carter described the removal of the gallery and the break-up of the choir at Clewer as a 'terrible grievance'.

Other innovations

A continued evolution in parish worship was reflected in a flow of:

1 *New Services:* Harvest Festivals (introduced by the Rev. R. S. Hawker of Morwenstow in 1843), Remembrance Services (1919), Family Services, Pet Services, Pram Services, Inter-Faith Services, etc., etc.

2 *New Sites:* the nineteenth century saw a move to take services to the people. This was deeply suspected to begin with. In 1818 the people of Redcar met in a *schoolroom*. The Archbishop of York refused to consecrate the room, but applauded the experiment. The Bishop of London deplored the growing practice in the 1830s, but later accepted that it

would help to build up new 'lower class' congregations! In 1853 Lord Shaftesbury succeeded in changing the law by which previously public meetings of over twenty people (except in a church building) were prohibited. John Burgon wrote in his *Church Handbook* of 1864 'The quasi-irregularities of *cottage lectures* and *fancy services* in the schoolroom we altogether deprecate and dislike.'

By the mid 1870s the evangelicals had begun holding services regularly in theatres, railway stations, factories, tents and in the open air. William Haslam held meetings in the barns of Norfolk farmers, well beyond the boundaries of his own parish of Buckenham. Doubtless all these evangelicals had been influenced and inspired by the North American revivalists Moody and Sankey who had first visited England in 1867 for large and popular off-church-site meetings.

When the evangelical leader J. C. Ryle became the first Bishop of Liverpool (1880), he gave priority to the building of mission halls. The cathedral was not begun until 1904 by Ryle's successor. Some of the informality ('fancy services') of the worship conducted off consecrated premises was creeping back into the worship in the churches themselves.

Liturgical movement

From the beginning of the twentieth century there have been serious moves for liturgical change. 1928 saw the revision of a new Prayer Book (rejected by Parliament, though approved by the Convocations and the Church Assembly). Some influence came over from the Roman Catholic Church and may be traced to the Conference of Malines (1909) which has contributed to the rediscovery of the corporate nature of the Church. There has been some restoration to the laity of active participation in worship, replacing the solo role of the priest.

This evolutionary process has continued and resulted in:

1 *New series.* Since 1965 we have had Series I, II and III and, in 1980, the Alternative Service Book.

2 *New emphasis* – Parish Communion is now the main Sunday worship in many churches.

3 *New hymns.* A recent check on a survey published in 1900 showing the then hundred best loved hymns reveals

that only a handful are still being sung by British congregations today. New hymn books are still coming off the press.

4 *New designs in church building.*

5 *New blessings* have been introduced (one by Archbishop William Temple).

6 *New Bible translations* have been authorised for public worship – recently the New International Version.

7 *New prayers.* During the last twenty years Canon Frank Colquhoun (among others) has produced three thick volumes of prayers for all occasions.

8 *New forms of expression.* Dance, drama and films have become an acceptable element in worship.

9 *New ministries.* Many laymen and women preach occasionally with no licence at all and most Bishops will licence laymen and women to minister both the bread and the cup at Holy Communion. These may also take the 'reserved' sacrament to the sick and shut-ins. In some parts of the Anglican Church women are ordained priests, following the unilateral action of the Bishop of Hong Kong. New forms of leadership have also emerged in fellowship groups in homes.

10 *New hang-ups.* Some clergy no longer have their own children baptised and many will not wear the statutory dress for conducting worship etc.

11 *New things.* God does new things. 'See, I am doing a new thing! Now it springs up; do you not perceive it?' (Isaiah 43: 19). New things will always be happening where the Holy Spirit blows and will have to be incorporated and expressed in new worship forms.

Introducing change today

Is it legally possible?

In considering the legality for introducing variations into the services of the Church, we include some helpful guidelines from the pen of the Venerable Michael Perry, Archdeacon of Durham, in his *Handbook of Parish Worship* (Mowbrays 1977).

1 Any minister has discretion to make or use variations

in their services, provided that they are not of substantial importance, that they are reverent and seemly, and that they do not depart from the doctrine of the Church of England in any essential matter. In case of doubt or question, the matter should be referred to the bishop of the diocese for his guidance and advice (p. 2).

2 Where neither the *Book of Common Prayer* nor General Synod has provided a form of service, forms may be approved for use by the Convocations of Canterbury or York, the Archbishop, or the Ordinary (who in most cases is the diocesan bishop). Again, they must be reverent, seemly and doctrinally sound and individual ministers are at liberty to make minor amendments at their own discretion (p. 2).

3 On occasions for which no provision has been made by the Synod or other provincial or diocesan authority, the minister is at liberty to use services of his own devising. The same rules about reverence, seemliness and sound doctrine continue to apply (p. 2).

4 Where no other authorized provision has been made ... the minister may compile his own services. Under this heading come Sunday School worship, family services, missions or evangelistic events, healing services, or services for the work of any particular group or organisation which has asked for the use of the Church (p. 4).

Is it doctrinally acceptable?

In the Church of England the final test must always be the written word of God.

1 Article 20 states clearly that it is not lawful for the Church to ordain anything that is contrary to God's word written, neither may it so expound one place of scripture that it be repugnant to another.

2 The Church of England has never been uniform (in spite of the Act of Uniformity, 1662). It has always boasted of its comprehensiveness. This comprehensiveness has not been limitless, of course. It has amounted to agreement over fundamentals, but liberty over secondary issues.

3 We would regard God's sovereignty and belief in the trinity, the incarnation, the atonement through the cross, the resurrection, the ascension, Christ's reigning in glory

and intercession on our behalf, the second coming, man's free will, man's fall and the possibility of man's justification by faith, the authority of the word of God, etc. as fundamental.

4 There are many who are tolerated within the Church of England – even given high authority – who are not faithful to these fundamentals, which for us are essential to orthodox Christian faith.

5 We have seen nothing which is in our proposed practice incongruous with the scriptures. We would regard the practice of the ministry of healing, etc., as spelt out in this book as a secondary issue. We would certainly find it strange for authority from above to oppose our practice, though not be surprised at local congregations feeling disturbed, as would be the case with any change.

Radical change through prophetic action

When Archbishop Fisher and Bishop Hall met in 1945, almost a year after the latter had taken unilateral action over the ordination of Deaconess Li Tim Oi as the first woman priest of the Anglican Communion (in Hong Kong 1944), they found themselves in an *impasse.* The Archbishop believed in change coming from within the Church through the due processes of discussion and legislation, while Bishop Hall held to the belief that *change occurred through necessity and prophetic action* which legislators would after-wards endorse or reject. Bishop Hall had no grand theological justification to offer for his actions; he had taken the decision not in order to advance the cause of women but *to advance the cause of the kingdom of God* under acute war-time conditions (cf. Ted Harrison *Much Beloved Daughter: The Story of Florence Li* Darton Longman and Todd 1985). That 'scandalous' action took place forty years ago; today there are some 600 ordained women in the Anglican Church worldwide.

Is it traditionally tolerable?

It was never the intention that the Church of England should be bound by tradition, though, understandably and inevitably, tradition will quickly become integral to the life of any church.

2 'It is not necessary that traditions and ceremonies be in all places one, and utterly like for at all times they have been divers and may be changed according to the diversities of countries, times, mens' manners, so that nothing be ordained against God's Word' (Article 34 in the *Book of Common Prayer*, 1662).

3 'Every particular or national Church hath authority to ordain, change and abolish ceremonies or rites of the Church ordained only by man's authority so that all things be done to edifying' (Article 34).

Conclusion

The liturgy and history of the last 300 years reveals that change in liturgical practices has frequently been initiated at the level of the local minister or to meet local needs. When there is sufficient ground swell then the demand for order results in official readjustments, provided always that the changes are demonstrably orthodox.

We believe that not only is it very desirable, but it is lawful, scriptural and fully compatible with the Church's understanding of tradition to introduce the simple practical suggestions outlined below into the liturgical structure of the Church. Such change would greatly enrich the life of the Church. Change has always been resisted. It will come as no surprise to find that change invariably provokes opposition.

Incorporating a healing ministry

We offer some simple practical suggestions for incorporating 'open' worship and a 'power' ministry within a liturgical structure.

New hymns may be learnt and practised as the congregation gathers for a service. We deliberately avoid calling them choruses as we sincerely believe many of them are nearer to the hymns found in the New Testament than are those of either Isaac Watts or Charles Wesley.

New hymns for 'open worship' can be readily introduced (gradually increasing their number) after the (second) lesson, or the prayers or sermon. Time may be allowed expressly for members of the congregation to exercise the gifts of the Spirit. This should be limited to members of the congregation. (The lunatic fringe from other charismatic churches will quickly appear if they think that in your church they can get away with what their own churches will not tolerate.) Insist that the gifts are used un-emotionally. Silence will also play its part.

Similarly, time may be allowed for open worship in the ASB Holy Communion service. If the extra time taken causes real problems, people can be made to feel that there are places in the services where it's OK to leave. Words of knowledge may be asked for from the congregation at the end of the service (or read out, having been taken down at a pre-service prayer meeting).

Prayer ministry may be offered for all who require it, including those responding to words of knowledge, immediately following the blessing. Some churches offer this ministry at the communion rails (often the person prayed for will be kneeling, but maybe standing). Some have the ministry in the (side) pews and others in an adjoining room or side-chapel.

35

ORGANISING THE HEALING MINISTRY

The practices outlined here have been developed primarily in the church of St Andrew's Chorleywood

Purpose of Ministry

1 To bring salvation, wholeness, healing, deliverance and peace to broken people, relationships and situations – between God and man – between man and man – and in the personality of the individual.

2 To invoke the Holy Spirit, offer prayer, laying-on of hands, brief counsel, encouragement and ministry to all who have a need.

3 To respond to words of knowledge.

Order

1 One of the clergy, the deaconess or a lay reader should be present to oversee this ministry.

2 We do not operate with set teams, but small groups of two or three people will normally assemble each time to minister to each person coming forward for prayer, with at least one experienced person leading, who will seek to include the others – to any of whom may be given special anointings for the ministry in hand.

3 Where possible, *one* of the same sex being prayed for should be in the group. (Look around for someone if no one has immediately come forward and ask him/her to join.)

4 Where a particular situation develops requiring more, or specialised, experience, then this may be called in. Those ministering must learn to recognise when they have reached their limit and be willing to stop and seek advice.

5 No one (except one of the clergy, a deaconess or a lay-reader) may step in or 'take over' unless so requested by the person in charge.

Who may Minister?

1 Those who have been invited and/or approved by the vicar to minister at the rail after each main service. The congregation and those coming forward for prayer must have confidence in those who are ministering – outsiders may *not* minister in the church building without the vicar's authority. The vicar may authorise people sent by their own church leaders to learn how to minister.

2 The vicar will always be glad to hear of people wanting to be involved in the healing ministry. Newcomers can always talk to the vicar about being involved. Home group leaders are encouraged to tell the vicar of people they think are ready to be involved. The diffident, the cautious, and the humble need to be encouraged to take part.

3 No one should be involved in this ministry who is not able to take correction from the vicar.

4 When starting to minister at the rails, newcomers and young people are encouraged to come forward and be linked with the more experienced.

5 Uncontrolled emotionalism in ministry is out of order. It may be more appropriate for 'emotionally charged' people (through personal crisis or personality) to simply give prayer support to those ministering, rather than to be directly involved in ministry themselves. However discernment needs to be exercised here; sometimes 'words of knowledge' are given by someone feeling compelled to 'act out' the area of hurt.

Preparation

1 Preparation for the 'after-service ministry' is available

in the prayer time before each service.

2 No one should feel that he/she cannot come forward to minister because he/she cannot come to the 'preparation time', but its value is stressed and accepted by all.

3 'Words of knowledge' are sought and received during the time of preparation, as they can be within the service itself. Time is deliberately spent in listening to what the Lord is saying.

4 In the name of Jesus, God the Father is asked for these words of knowledge, through the Holy Spirit. This frees those ministering from any fear that the 'enemy' will take over in an area which is basically so subjective.

5 When a word is received during the actual service and no appropriate time seems available to share it, whether a word of knowledge or prophecy, then a note can be sent up, either to the vicar or the person leading the service. These can be read out before the blessing with others received in the preparation time.

Those coming for ministry

We need to be sensitive to those coming for ministry and it is helpful to ascertain if they are:

1 Christian? ('Do you know Jesus?') If so, what stage in their spiritual pilgrimage have they reached?

2 Part of the fellowship or not – or are they new?

3 Ready to receive? Are there any known barriers?

4 Some have already prepared – e.g. to commit themselves to the Lord or to ask for specific prayer for healing, whereas others have come up on the impulse and need to clarify their need. This is the time to ask for a 'word of wisdom'.

5 Sometimes people are quite clear about what their problem/need is, but the presenting problem is not always the one for which the Lord has brought them to the front. There may well be a deeper need of which they are unaware.

6 Loved ones or friends may be inclined to hold their afflicted relative or friend in an embrace of some kind as they kneel at the rails. This should be gently discouraged.

These 'supporters' should release the person ministered to and direct their own compassion into silent prayer.

Phases of Ministry

1 Keep the dialogue with the individual to a minimum. Ask what the person wants Jesus to do. Don't let it develop into a life history. Jesus asked pertinent questions. The interviewer must maintain the initiative.

2 Seek to discern the faith level of the afflicted person and encourage the interviewee to articulate his belief that Christ can heal.

3 Invite the Holy Spirit to come down in the name of Jesus. Encourage the individual to welcome him. Relax and wait for the Holy Spirit to minister – keep your eyes open to see what God is doing; bless and honour what the Lord is doing.

4 Take plenty of time to seek or wait for further words of wisdom or knowledge to be given to yourself or other members of the group. Introduce these when given by indicatory prayers or suggestion – but not too directional. The person prayed for may be asked what he/she is feeling.

5 Hands 'on' or 'off' is not a major issue. It is good for one person to place his hands on the sick person – the others can identify by putting a hand on the shoulder of the person ministering. Be led in the situation, but don't overburden physically with too many hands! Be sensitive if praying for one of the opposite sex in a delicate area. The afflicted person can put his/her own hand on the afflicted area and then the person ministering can place his/her hand on his/her arm.

6 Encourage the individual to be 'open' to the Holy Spirit, receiving Him thankfully, to be relaxed and not striving in prayer whilst receiving – not even speaking 'in tongues'.

7 Let the Holy Spirit do any convicting needed – those being ministered to must not be left under condemnation, feeling too unworthy of God's mercy or lacking in faith to receive it. Nor should it be suggested that a person should go and 'claim' his healing. Most of the New Testament healings are miraculous/spontaneous, but there is clear

evidence to show the efficacy of prayer in spiritual healing over a longer period (soaking prayer) in the current literature reporting the work of many of those engaged in the healing ministry where it is being blessed by God (e.g. Francis MacNutt).

8 The work of the Holy Spirit is ongoing and may not immediately be obvious. Take time even if nothing apparently is happening. The person should be encouraged to come forward again if he feels the ministry has been partially beneficial.

9 Be ready, if necessary, to speak to the condition 'In the name of Jesus I command you to be healed ... to be made whole ... (the swelling) to go ... to receive your sight.' It is good to emulate the words of Jesus himself, whenever this is appropriate in the healing ministry.

10 Sometimes a person being prayed for may appear to faint or to fall asleep under the power of the Holy Spirit. In this case it is best to lay the person out flat on the floor and simply bless what God is doing. We believe there is 'inner healing' going on at this time.

11 If the person 'resting in the Spirit' in this way is a woman; it may be seemly to have a small blanket available for a covering if she has fallen in an undignified position. The blanket can be placed over her without disturbing her.

12 There are times when people have been taken home apparently in a 'drunken' condition. It is best for them to be put to bed. They will be perfectly all right when they awaken (see chapter on 'Falling under the power of God').

13 Frequently there are manifestations of a 'power encounter'. See chapters on 'Healing the oppressed' and 'Inner healing'.

14 Encourage the afflicted person to take a step of faith if he/she is *compos mentis*, i.e. if it is an arm he cannot bend – see if he can bend it now.

Follow up

1 The person ministered to should not be told he is healed (he will know if he is) or to leave off taking his medicines (only a doctor is qualified to do that). Of course

the Holy Spirit may tell the person himself to do this, but that is entirely between the healed person and the Lord.

2 Where a 'follow up' is proposed directly as a result of the ministry within the church, then it should be noted on a 'follow up' sheet and passed to the vicar or one of the staff. Some church members may already be being supported by a counselling ministry approved by the vicar.

3 Have someone present from the previous team where possible for those who come for 'soaking prayer'. Recognise that it is the same Spirit who is meeting the person and don't be pre-occupied with the need to go over the previous sessions. It is reasonable to ask in what way the Lord helped last time.

4 Those ministering should be discouraged from giving their own names, addresses, or phone numbers to the persons ministered to.

5 There is no case for anyone developing their own independent follow-up ministry. Some who become involved in the healing ministry may tend, without realising it, to bind people to themselves in this ministry, whereas Christ wants to set us free.

Difficulties

1 There will be some who don't want to come up to the rails for prayer. There is a place for 'prayer in the pews' from friends. Others will want help in private – perhaps later in the week.

2 If anyone ministering is in any doubt, he should ask for help, and not be afraid to discuss.

3 'Deliverance' from some 'bondage' or 'afflicting spirit' may be called for as a result of ministry at the rail (see chapter on 'Healing the oppressed').

4 'Exorcism' is for people who are 'possessed' and requires special preparation and should *not* be part of our after-service ministry. The spirit should be bound in Christ's name and the case referred to the vicar.

5 Where anointing with oil is considered necessary, it is normally ministered by one of the ordained staff. This is usually ministered at the request of the sick person for his

anointing at home. 'Is any one of you sick? *He* should call the elders of the church to pray over him and anoint him with oil' (James 5: 14). But clearly anointing with oil was not restricted to 'elders' in the Bible (Mark 6: 13) and it may be used more generally in the healing ministry.

6 The devil may well try to reproduce the symptom (of the sickness or the guilt) again later. Encourage the person to rebuke the affliction himself in the name of Jesus, should this happen.

Testimony

1 There is a time to encourage a testimony – 'Go home . . . and tell' (Mark 5: 19).

2 The first direction following healing may be 'show yourself to the doctor' (cf. Luke 17: 14). On the other hand, the Lord may want the person to 'Go and tell no man' and not to rush ahead to tell others (cf. Mark 5: 43).

3 When someone has 'committed his life to the Lord', he should be encouraged to testify to this fact (Matthew 10: 32,33).

4 Our experience is that few people healed share their blessing widely, but the good news does circulate amongst those nearest to them.

5 In all cases of blessing it is important to give thanks and the glory to God.

APPENDIX 1

REFERENCES TO HEALING AND DISEASE IN THE OLD TESTAMENT

GENESIS

12: 17
17: 13
18: 10,14
19: 11
20: 17,18
29: 32
38: 9-10
43: 28
50: 20

EXODUS

1: 12
3: 7
4: 11,24-26
9: 1-10
11: 4-7
12: 17,29,30
15: 26
16: 20-24
23: 25
32: 35

LEVITICUS

13: 2
14: 2

LEVITICUS

15: 2
16: 29,30
19: 14
21: 28
22: 4
26: 16-25

NUMBERS

5: 1-3
11: 11, 33
12: 1-15
14: 33
16: 41-50
21: 6-9
29: 17

DEUTERONOMY

7: 15
8: 16
24: 8
26: 7
28: 22-35,60
29: 22
32: 39

JOSHUA

22: 17

JUDGES

13: 5,24

RUTH

1: 21

1 SAMUEL

1: 19-20
3: 18
5: 6
6: 1-12
16: 14-23
18: 10
19: 10
25: 38

2 SAMUEL

5: 6
12: 15
20: 9
24: 10, 15

1 KINGS

8: 35
11: 39
13: 4–6
17: 17–23

2 KINGS

1: 2
2: 22
4: 8–37
5: 1–14, 27
6: 18, 33
8: 8
13: 21
15: 5
20: 1–11

2 CHRONICLES

6: 26, 27
13: 20
16: 20
16: 12
20: 9
21: 15
26: 19
32: 24
33: 12

NEHEMIAH

9: 21

JOB

1: 21
2: 6–10
5: 17
7: 20
10: 15
13: 15
30: 30

JOB

34: 31

PSALMS

6: 2
18: 6
21: 4
22: 15
25: 18
27: 4–5
32: 3–5
34: 19
35: 13
38: 7
39: 9
41: 4
42: 11
43: 5
44: 2
46: 5
50: 15
53: 4
55: 16–19
56: 3
66: 11
67: 2
71: 14
78: 34,50
90: 7
103: 1–4
105: 1
106: 42
107: 17, 20
116: 3–9
119: 50,67
135: 8

ECCLESIASTES

6: 2

SONG OF SOLOMON

2: 5

ISAIAH

1: 5
3: 17
6: 10
9: 1
10: 12
25: 4
30: 20
32: 4
33: 19, 24
35: 5,6
38: 1–8, 12, 21
43: 7,22
43: 2
48: 10
49: 13
53: 5
57: 18
58: 6–8
61: 2
64: 5

JEREMIAH

6: 14
8: 11,15,22
14: 19
16: 19
17: 14
29: 17
30: 12, 17
31: 13, 18
33: 6
39: 17
42: 16
50: 4

LAMENTATIONS

1: 5,12
2: 13
3: 39

EZEKIEL

6: 13
20: 38
34: 4,16
47: 12

DANIEL

4: 32, 34

HOSEA

5: 13,15
6: 1
7: 5

HOSEA

9: 14
11: 3
14: 4

JOEL

2: 32

MICAH

7: 9

NAHUM

1: 7,12
3: 19

HABAKKUK

3: 5

ZEPHANIAH

3: 12

ZECHARIAH

12: 4

MALACHI

4: 2

APPENDIX 2

THE HEALING MINISTRY OF JESUS

Description	Matthew	Mark	Luke	John
Lameness, Palsy, Paralysis				
Centurion's servant	8: 5		7:1	
Man with palsy	9: 2	2: 3	5: 18	
Man with withered hand	12: 10	3: 1	6: 6	
Woman bound by Satan			13: 10–16	
The lame	21: 14			
Leprosy				
Leper	8: 2	1: 40	5:12	
Ten lepers			17: 12	
Fever				
Peter's mother-in-law	8: 14	1: 30	4: 38	
Nobleman's son				4: 47
Blindness				
Man born blind				9: 1
Blind Bartimaeus	20: 30	10: 46	18: 35	
Blind man		8: 22		
Two blind men	9: 27			
The blind	21: 14			
Deaf				
Deaf and dumb man		7: 32		

Description	Matthew	Mark	Luke	John
Dropsy				
Man with dropsy			14: 2	
Restored physically				
Malchus' ear			22: 50	
Demonic				
Gadarene demoniac	8:28	5: 2	8: 27	
Syrophoenician's daughter	15: 22	7: 25,26		
Child with evil spirit	17: 15	9: 17	9: 38,39	
Man with unclean spirit		1: 23	4: 33	
Mary Magdalene and others			8: 2	
Dumb demoniac	9: 32			
Multitudes	4: 24			
Multitudes	8: 16			
Blind and dumb demoniacs	12: 22		11: 14	
Many demons		1: 32,39		
Multitudes	3: 10;	6: 13		
Multitudes			4: 41	
Multitudes			6: 18	
Multitudes			7: 21	
Raised from the dead				
Jairus' daughter	9: 18	5: 22,23	8: 41	
Lazarus				11: 1
Widow's son			7: 12	
Dealt with sin				
Man with palsy	9: 2	2: 3	5: 18	
Impotent man				5:15
Healed on Sabbath				
Man with unclean spirit		1: 23	4: 35	
Man with withered hand	12: 9	3: 1	6: 6	

Description	Matthew	Mark	Luke	John
Woman bound by Satan			13: 11	
Man with dropsy			14: 2	
Impotent man				5: 5
Man born blind				9: 1

Flow of blood

Woman with issue of blood	9: 20	5:25	8: 43	

Multitudes

A few sick people	13: 58	6:5		
Multitudes	14: 35	6: 55		
Multitudes	4: 24		6: 17–19	
Multitudes	9: 35			
Multitudes	14: 14		9: 11	6: 2
Great multitudes	15: 30			
Great multitudes	19: 2			
Multitudes			5: 15	
Various persons			13: 32	
Multitudes	11: 4,5		7: 21	

All kinds of disease

	4: 23	6: 5	9: 11	
	9: 35			
	11: 5	6: 55		
	14: 14			
	14: 35			
	19: 2			

Similar wording

Demon possessed added	8: 16	1: 32	4: 41	
		3: 11	6: 18	
			8: 2	

These and other categories

	4: 24		7: 21	
	15: 30			
	21: 14			

APPENDIX 3
THE HEALING MINISTRY OF OTHERS

Description	Matthew	Mark	Luke	John	Acts
The Twelve sent	10: 1–14	3: 13–19	9: 1–6		
The Seventy Two sent			10: 1–24		
Disciples attempt to cast out demons	17: 14–21	9: 14–29	9: 37–45		
Power to bind, loose and forgive	18: 18			20: 23	
Great commission	28: 16–20	16: 14–20	24: 44–53		1: 1–11
Signs and wonders at Apostles' hands					2: 42–47
Peter heals lame beggar					3: 1–4,22
Prayer for boldness and healing signs					4: 23–31
Signs and wonders at Apostle's hands					5: 12–16
Ministry of Stephen					6: 8–15
Ministry of Philip					8: 4–13
Ananias and Saul					9: 10–19
Peter heals Aeneas (Lydda)					9: 32–35
Peter raises Dorcas (Joppa)					9: 36–43
Magician struck blind by Paul					13: 4–12
Paul and Barnabas in Iconium					14: 1–7
Lame man at Lystra					14: 8–18
Paul raised at Lystra					14: 19–20

Description	Matthew	Mark	Luke	John	Acts
Slave girl at Philippi					16: 16–40
Paul at Ephesus					19: 8–20
Eutychus raised from the Dead					20: 7–12
Paul recalls Ananias					22: 12–21
Paul on Malta					28: 1–10
Galatians 3: 5					
Hebrews 2: 4					
James 5: 13–18					

Thanks are due to the following for permission to quote from their works:

Rosemary Atlee	William's Story	Marshalls
John White	The Cost of Commitment	I.V.P.
T.C. Hammond	In Understanding be Men	I.V.P.
James I. Packer	Keep in Step with the Spirit	I.V.P.
R.A. Torrey	What the Bible Teaches	Marshalls
T. Martin	Kingdom Healing	Marshalls
R. Bonnke	Plundering Hell	Marshalls
I. Andrews	God can do it for you	Marshalls
J. Darnell	Heaven Here I Come	Lakeland
K. Koch	God Among the Indians	Haussler
K. Koch	The Revival in Indonesia	Evangelisation Publishers
Paul Y. Cho	Prayer Key to Revival	Word Inc. Waco Texas
F.L. Cross	The Oxford Dictionary of the Christian Church	O.U.P.
D. & J. Huggett	It Hurts to Heal	Kingsway Publications
Michael Green	To Corinth with Love	Hodder & Stoughton
Jackie Pullinger	Chasing the Dragon	Hodder & Stoughton
Donald Bridges & David Phypers	More Than Tongues Can Tell	Hodder & Stoughton
John & Paula Sandford	The Transformation of the Inner Man	Bridge Publishing
John & Paula Sandford	The Elijah Task	Bridge Publishing

| Peter Wagner | Look Out, the Pentecostals are Coming | Creation House, Illinois |
| Peter Wagner | First Fruits | Vineyard Ministries International, September/October 1985 |

Extracts from letters to the author by Eileen Vincent and Christopher Cocksworth.

Extracts from Renewal edited by Edward England, citing Edward England, Rosemary Attlee and John Gunstone.

Extracts from the Book of Common Prayer of 1662 which is Crown Copyright in the United Kingdom, are reproduced by permission of Eyre & Spottiswoode (Publishers) Ltd., Her Majesty's Printers, London.